CRIPPING GIRLHOOD

Corporealities: Discourses of Disability
Series editors: David T. Mitchell and Sharon L. Snyder

Recent Titles

Cripping Girlhood
   by Anastasia Todd

Down Syndrome Culture: Life Writing, Documentary, and Fiction Film in Iberian and Latin American Contexts
   by Benjamin Fraser

Blind in Early Modern Japan: Disability, Medicine, and Identity
   by Wei Yu Wayne Tan

Cheap Talk: Disability and the Politics of Communication
   by Joshua St. Pierre

Diaphanous Bodies: Ability, Disability, and Modernist Irish Literature
   by Jeremy Colangelo

Embodied Archive: Disability in Post-Revolutionary Mexican Cultural Production
   by Susan Antebi

Beholding Disability in Renaissance England
   by Allison P. Hobgood

A History of Disability, New Edition
   by Henri-Jacques Stiker

Vitality Politics: Health, Debility, and the Limits of Black Emancipation
   by Stephen Knadler

Blindness Through the Looking Glass: The Performance of Blindness, Gender, and the Sensory Body
   by Gili Hammer

HandiLand: The Crippest Place on Earth
   by Elizabeth A. Wheeler

The Matter of Disability: Materiality, Biopolitics, Crip Affect
   by David T. Mitchell, Susan Antebi, and Sharon L. Snyder, editors

Monstrous Kinds: Body, Space, and Narrative in Renaissance Representations of Disability
   by Elizabeth B. Bearden

Autistic Disturbances: Theorizing Autism Poetics from the DSM to Robinson Crusoe
   by Julia Miele Rodas

Foucault and Feminist Philosophy of Disability
   by Shelley L. Tremain

Academic Ableism: Disability and Higher Education
   by Jay Timothy Dolmage

Negotiating Disability: Disclosure and Higher Education
   by Stephanie L. Kerschbaum, Laura T. Eisenman, and James M. Jones, editors

Portraits of Violence: War and the Aesthetics of Disfigurement
   by Suzannah Biernoff

A complete list of titles in the series can be found at www.press.umich.edu

CRIPPING GIRLHOOD

ANASTASIA TODD

University of Michigan Press
Ann Arbor

Copyright © 2024 by Anastasia Todd
Some rights reserved

This work is licensed under a Creative Commons Attribution-NonCommercial 4.0 International License. *Note to users*: A Creative Commons license is only valid when it is applied by the person or entity that holds rights to the licensed work. Works may contain components (e.g., photographs, illustrations, or quotations) to which the rightsholder in the work cannot apply the license. It is ultimately your responsibility to independently evaluate the copyright status of any work or component part of a work you use, in light of your intended use. To view a copy of this license, visit http://creativecommons.org/licenses/by-nc/4.0/

For questions or permissions, please contact um.press.perms@umich.edu

Published in the United States of America by the
University of Michigan Press
Manufactured in the United States of America
Printed on acid-free paper
First published May 2024

A CIP catalog record for this book is available from the British Library.

Library of Congress Cataloging-in-Publication Data

Names: Todd, Anastasia, author.
Title: Cripping girlhood / Anastasia Todd.
Other titles: Crippling girlhood
Description: Ann Arbor : University of Michigan Press, [2024] | Series: Corporealities: discourses of disability | "Crip, slang for cripple, is a term in the process of being reclaimed by disabled people." | Includes bibliographical references and index.
Identifiers: LCCN 2023056370 (print) | LCCN 2023056371 (ebook) | ISBN 9780472076741 (hardcover) | ISBN 9780472056743 (paperback) | ISBN 9780472904426 (ebook other)
Subjects: LCSH: Young women with disabilities—United States—History—21st century. | Youth with disabilities--United States—History—21st century. | Children with disabilities—United States—History—21st century. | Girls—United States—Social conditions—21st century. | People with disabilities in mass media—History—21st century. | Girls in mass media—History—21st century. | BISAC: SOCIAL SCIENCE / People with Disabilities | SOCIAL SCIENCE / Media Studies
Classification: LCC HV1569.3.W65 T63 2024 (print) | LCC HV1569.3.W65 (ebook) | DDC 305.9/08083420973—dc23/eng/20240131
LC record available at https://lccn.loc.gov/2023056370
LC ebook record available at https://lccn.loc.gov/2023056371

DOI: https://doi.org/10.3998/mpub.12769443

The University of Michigan Press's open access publishing program is made possible thanks to additional funding from the University of Michigan Office of the Provost and the generous support of contributing libraries.

Cover credit: Ashley Bravin, *Cripping Girlhood* (2023). Gouache on paper, 8.5 × 11 inches.

Contents

List of Illustrations — vii

Acknowledgments — ix

Introduction: Cripping Post-ADA Disabled Girlhood — 1

1. The Futurity of Disabled Girlhood — 34
2. From Disabled Girlhood 2.0 to the "Crip-fluencer" — 65
3. Domesticating Disability: Crip Girls and Their Dogs — 103
4. The Crip Afterlife of Jerika Bolen — 139

Coda: Cripping Disability Visibility in Fascist Times — 169

Notes — 175

Bibliography — 185

Index — 209

Digital materials related to this title can be found on the Fulcrum platform via the following citable URL: https://doi.org/10.3998/mpub.12769443

Illustrations

Figure 1. Delaney using a gait trainer (*Miss You Can Do It* 2013)   46
Figure 2. Alina in Ukrainian orphanage (*Miss You Can Do It* 2013)   50
Figure 3. Charisse Living with Cerebral Palsy YouTube Channel   70
Figure 4. Rikki Poynter YouTube Channel   71
Figure 5. Rikki Poynter in her YouTube video, *Learning Sign Language as a Deaf Adult* (2016)   77
Figure 6. Charisse in her YouTube video, *Walking & running with Cerebral Palsy* (2010)   78
Figure 7. Charisse in her YouTube video, *Charisse's Story—My Life Journey with Cerebral Palsy* (2012)   82
Figure 8. Rikki Poynter in her YouTube video, *Shit Hearing People Say (Things You Don't Say to Deaf & Hard of Hearing)* (2014)   86
Figure 9. An LGBT No More CRAPtions t-shirt from Rikki Poynter's merch store   96
Figure 10. Charisse in her YouTube video, *10 Years of Becoming Beautifully Different—Bullied Then Becoming an Inspiration* (2020)   99
Figure 11. The service dog George, Bella, and her parents at the AKC Humane Fund Awards for Canine Excellence from *George (Great Dane)-2015 AKC Humane Fund Awards for Canine Excellence* (2016)   119
Figure 12. Claire and Rosie, her service dog, in her TikTok video, "She's my yellow . . ." (2021)   126
Figure 13. Rosie's tail being dyed in TikTok video, "Why Rosie's tail is Dyed! . . ." (2021)   130

Figure 14. Lexy and Lady, her service dog, in her TikTok video, "Pretty sure she's a lesbian also . . ." (2021)   131

Figure 15. Lexy and Lady in her TikTok video, "#greenscreen #greenscreenvideo yes I know . . ." (2021)   135

Figure 16. Lady, Lexy's service dog, in her TikTok video, "we had to put my other . . ." (2021)   137

Figure 17. "J's Last Dance," Jen Bolen's GoFundMe campaign   157

Acknowledgments

As many can attest, this book has been a long time coming. It's hard to describe the feeling of knowing that this project will finally be out in the world. I first started researching and writing about disabled girlhood over 10 years ago when I was at the beginning stages of my PhD program. I confess often to my students that, for me, writing is hard and even painful at times. It doesn't come easy to me. Completing this book was one of the most difficult things I have ever done, and many people and non-human animals helped carry me through the process.

First, I want to thank my department, the department of Gender and Women's Studies at the University of Kentucky for the institutional and personal support. Many thanks to my colleagues: Mel Stein, Srimati Basu, Karen Tice, Charlie Zhang, Frances Henderson, Jenn Hunt, Aria Halliday, Carol Mason, Ellen Riggle, and Elizabeth Williams. A special thanks to Carol for looking at drafts of chapters and giving me the final push needed to send it to Michigan. Thank you to Michelle Del Toro, our department manager, for the infinite institutional wisdom and willingness to always answer my many questions.

As many of you all know too well, writing can be profoundly isolating. I cannot even begin to put into words how thankful I am to everyone who has been in my various writing groups over the years. My Cooperative for the Humanities and Social Sciences writing group—Doug Slaymaker, Liang Luo, and Srimati Basu most specifically—you all were my rock during some of the most challenging months with this manuscript. Not only did you all give me incredible feedback, but you helped me build confidence as a scholar. LTT, my first writing group—Sharon Yam, Elizabeth Williams, and Karrieann Soto Vega—I have found such beautiful community here in Lexington with you all. To my current writing buddies Colleen Barrett and Regina

Hamilton—you all have not only been my hype people, but you have given me what I love most: structure and consistency. A special thanks to my bestie Karrieann for reading so many iterations of the manuscript and for being there when I needed it the most. I hope this one makes you proud.

Many thanks to the people at Arizona State University who were there when this project was in its infancy. To my invaluable superstar of a mentor, Heather Switzer: I would not be where I am today without your care and insight, your confidence in me and my ideas, and your brilliant work. I could not have asked for a better advisor. I want to express my sincere gratitude to Mary Margaret Fonow, my co-advisor who also shepherded me through graduate school. Special thanks to Lisa Anderson and Georganne Scheiner Gillis. To Abby and Rachel, I wouldn't have made it out without you.

This book is a product of being in scholarly community. Thank you to all the feminist disability studies and girlhood studies scholars who have engaged with my work over the years and who have had a profound impact on my thinking and writing, especially, Claudia Mitchell, Ann Smith, Natalie Coulter, Susan Driver, Sarah Hill, Aly Patsavas, and David Mitchell. Special thanks to Nirmala Erevelles and Xuan Thuy Nguyen, the editors of the GHS special issue that pieces of this project first premiered in. Deep gratitude to all my cohort members and Marisa Olson from the 2022 Digital Ideas Summer institute at the University of Michigan. I felt so supported and held in community right as I was finishing the first full draft of this.

Thank you to everyone at University of Michigan Press, especially my editor Sara Jo Cohen, for your insightful feedback, patient responses to my many emails, and confidence in this project. Thank you, Annie, for your work on all the tedious bits. And thank you to the anonymous reviewers. I hope to have done your enthusiastic and productive feedback justice.

To the rest of my Lexington and Madison "framily"—you all have reminded me that life is more than work. Jared, Bizu, Jon, Megs, Dan, Chelsea, Jack, Nari, Crystal, Rubin, Erin, and Sam. A special thanks to Erin, my brilliant FDS friend and colleague, for reading drafts (sometimes unexpectedly), offering crip wisdom, and singing karaoke with me.

I would not have been able to finish this book without my non-human animal best friends and writing buddies—Prudence, Joey, and Jan. You all have taught me the importance of rest and play and have brought me so much joy during some of the darkest moments writing this book.

And finally, thank you to my family. I love you all so much. Mom, Chris, Alex, and Miles—I don't know how you all put up with me. I take so much inspiration from my Mom, who is the most insightful person I know. Cindy,

Lala, Monica, Savannah, Olivia, Gabriel, Will, Robert, Grandpa, John—your confidence in me and support has meant so much to me over the years. To Momo—my best friend and partner. There are no words that could convey my deepest gratitude to you. Not only have your brilliant insights helped shape this book for the better, but you have taught me the importance of trusting myself in spite of myself.

My deepest gratitude to the countless others who have helped move me and this book forward, especially my therapists, psychiatrists, and my students at UK. Lastly, I hope to do justice to all the disabled and crip girls that are part of this project. This project would be nothing without your wisdom, knowledge, humor, and radical politics. Thanks to you too, reader. I hope you enjoy.

Introduction

Cripping Post-ADA Disabled Girlhood

"Disabled girls are American girls, too"
—Melissa Shang (2014)

In 2017 I was riding a bus in Los Angeles that was barreling down Sunset Boulevard when I came across a curious bus bench billboard. The billboard was an image of a young, white girl with Down syndrome. Her light brown hair was braided and pulled back. This drew my attention to her youthful face, painted in its entirety as an American flag. She was holding a paint brush and gazing at herself in the mirror. Is she admiring her work, I wondered? It appeared that she was in the intimate space of her bedroom. I noticed that behind her was a dresser and lamp, and next to her, hanging alongside the mirror were red, white, and blue beads and a bronze sports medal. I wondered what the image was trying to tell me. As I fumbled around in my backpack for my phone to take a picture, I took note of the hashtag hiding unobtrusively in the corner, "#WeAreAmerica." Next to it was the phrase, "Love Has No Labels." I felt ambivalent as I pondered my encounter with the image of the disabled girl that was at once spectacular and mundane.

I begin *Cripping Girlhood* with this scene of encounter because I suggest that it illustrates the workings of a new representational politics of disabled girlhood. In the 2010s, the disabled girl curiously emerges across a range of different sites in the United States' mediascape. No longer represented solely through discourses of risk, pathologization, and vulnerability, and taking drastically different forms than in Jerry Lewis Telethons or in advertising for the March of Dimes, the disabled girls that come to hypervisibly materialize in the recent cultural imaginary are pageant queens, social media influencers, and disability rights activists. Unlike decades previous, these spectacular disabled girls are not only figures to be looked at, but to be listened to.

Cripping Girlhood is interested in what happens and what it means when certain disabled girl subjects gain cultural recognition and visibility as "American girls, too," to use the words of Melissa Shang, who in 2014 created a viral Change.org petition imploring American Girl to create a disabled doll of the year. The book explores the promise and peril of this newfound cultural visibility for select disabled girls. In examining representations and self-representations of disabled girls and girlhoods across the mediascape at the beginning of the twenty-first century, spanning HBO documentaries to TikTok, *Cripping Girlhood* uncovers the variegated ways the figure of the disabled girl is imbued with meaning and mobilized as a spectacular representational symbol. Frequently, the book suggests, the figure of the exceptional disabled girl emerges at this moment in media culture as a resource to work out post-Americans with Disabilities Act (ADA) and neoliberal anxieties about citizenship, labor, the family, healthcare, and the precarity of the bodymind. She often operates in service of US disability exceptionalism as "representational currency" signaling a mythic achievement of tolerance and acceptance of disability, marking the United States as departing from and mastering linear teleologies of progress (McRuer 2018, 44).

The book is equally invested in the stories that disabled girls have to tell about themselves. In examining closely disabled girls' self-representational practices, *Cripping Girlhood* goes beyond a critique of the figure of the exceptional disabled girl, or the privileged disabled girl subject who is granted entrance into the national imaginary, to explore how disabled girls, more than symbolic figures to be used in others' narratives, circulate their own capacious re-envisioning of what it means to be a disabled girl. The book reveals the cultural and political work that disabled girls' self-representational practices perform, from cultivating disability community through generating intimacy online, to affirming the value of care labor and interdependence across the species barrier.

Cripping Girlhood offers a new theorization of disabled girls and girlhoods. The book does so by advancing "cripping girlhood" as a heuristic. The project calls on the radical potential of *crip*, a term reclaimed and used by disability activists, cultural workers, and scholars (Clare 1999; Sandahl 2003; McRuer 2006, 2018; Kafer 2013). Crip has come to signify many things at once: an "in-your-face" and prideful reclamation of disability, a capacious and flexible term encompassing all sorts of non-normative embodiments, and, according to Eli Clare (1999), a "word to help forge a politics" (70). I utilize crip throughout the coming pages as a term that recognizes the political and cultural power of disabled girls and girlhoods, even in the most quotidian of scenes. To *crip* or *cripping*, in the simplest of characterizations, is a practice that interrogates or unsettles assumptions about disability and disabled people, and specifically in the case of this book, assumptions about disabled girls and girlhoods. As a heuristic, I mobilize "cripping girlhood," in two distinct but intimately connected ways. First, I examine how disabled girls *crip* girlhood. In a range of cultural sites that I explore throughout the book, but most centrally on YouTube and TikTok, I show how disabled girls actively upend what we think we know about them and their experience, recasting the meanings ascribed to their bodyminds in their own terms. Second, I mobilize "cripping girlhood" as an analytical practice in which, throughout each chapter, I uncover how ablenationalist logics, racialized and cis-heteronormative discourses of ideal girlhood, and normative affects collide to facilitate the recognition and cultural valuation of certain disabled girl subjects more than others.

Why disabled girls, why now? *Cripping Girlhood* positions itself as a feminist disability studies intervention that remedies the lack of critical, scholarly attention paid to disabled girls and girlhoods. The intersection of disability and girlhood has been considered in fields such as psychology, sociology, nursing, public policy, and education. More often than not, however, in the studies that come out of these fields, the disabled girl is rigidly defined by a medicalized and gender essentialist framework, and her girlhood is understood through discourses of risk and vulnerability.[1] The disabled girl is presented as an object of theory, rather than a subject who theorizes. Within these fields, disabled girls are often understood solely as future disabled women, or disabled women in training. Even in girls' studies and the broader field of gender and women's studies, both fields from which this project is indebted to and is in conversation with, the disabled girl rarely makes an appearance. This is because disability has been understood as a "trump card," according to Deborah Stienstra (2015), or as something that is all-encompassing and that explains all. This understanding of disability as a "trump card" has muted critical explorations of disabled girls' experiences of gender, sexuality, race, and their girlhood, writ large.

Cripping Girlhood contends that studying the disabled girl's complex role in contemporary media culture and the "grudging recognition" she has been granted—or perhaps not so grudging as this book will delve into—is necessary work, as it deepens our understanding of the ever-evolving social and political meaning(s) attached to both disability and girlhood (Mitchell and Snyder 2015, 2). The book stretches feminist disability studies to account more thoroughly for age in its intersectional analyses, and at the same time, it ruptures the unwitting assumption in girls' studies that girlhood is necessarily non-disabled. In its concerted effort to explore disabled girls' self-representational practices, the book is also deeply invested in "how disabled subjectivities are not just characterized by socially imposed restrictions, but, in fact, productively create new forms of embodied knowledge and collective consciousness" (Mitchell and Snyder 2015, 2). As I show throughout the book, disabled girls' cripistemological insight, or knowledge gleaned from the "critical, social, and personal position" of disability and girlhood offers new ways to think about care, community, and intimacy in a mediated world (Johnson and McRuer 2014, 134). The book works in profound solidarity with other scholars of disability and girlhood, all who have sought to illuminate the political and theoretical exigency of studying disabled girlhood, such as Nirmala Erevelles and Kagendo Mutua (2005), Deborah Stienstra (2015), Subini Annamma (2018), Sarah Hill (2017; 2022) and Xuan Thuy Nguyen (2020).

There is a temporal urgency to the critical study of disabled girls and girlhoods precisely because there has been a recent and fervent proliferation of representations and self-representations in media culture. So, in returning to my question, "Why disabled girls? Why now?," the book contends that not only is it about time, but that the time is now. The bus bench billboard that I began this chapter with is one such site that suggests the emergence of the figure of the disabled girl has much to tell us about the contemporary moment. *Cripping Girlhood* uncovers how the exceptional figure of the disabled girl, although produced and circulated in various iterations—as a disabled "future girl," an object of happiness, an online disability educator cum social media influencer, a sentimentalized testament to the rehabilitative properties of the service dog, and as a pedagogue of death—emerges in media culture at this moment to serve as a resource to work through contemporary anxieties about the family, healthcare, labor, US citizenship, and the precarity of the bodymind. These exceptional disabled girls offer lessons to the non-disabled viewer about tolerance, benevolence, and love in neoliberal, post-ADA times. Most often, representations of disabled girls who are exceptionalized, or recuperated as valuable, shore up logics of white supremacy, national exceptionalism, and, paradoxically, able-bodied supremacy. I track how the process of recuperation or exceptionalization is incredibly uneven. The disabled girls who become valuable and visible in media culture become valuable and visible because they ossify existing, normative understandings of disabled girlhood and girls: as potentially productive, as heterosexual, as potentially reproductive, as rehabilitatable, and as empowered and empowering. But, in turning to disabled girls' self-representations, the book contends that disabled girls are actively contesting this process of ossification through charting their own meaning of what it means to be a disabled girl, as well as through imagining and building a world otherwise. It is a world where they grow "sideways" with their service dogs, dwell in stillness, claim cripness in the face of compulsory able-bodiedness/mindedness, and enact their desires, even if it makes adults uncomfortable.

Ultimately, although this is a book about representation, *Cripping Girlhood* is concerned with the material stakes for disabled girls caught up in the shifting politics of disability visibility. As cultural studies scholars remind us, representation matters; it is inherently connected to the "real." *Cripping Girlhood* grapples with the variegated ways disabled girls are represented and represent themselves and unearths how visibility for some disabled girls does not translate into liberation for all disabled girls. The disabled girls who circulate as emblems of post-ADA progress, those who are constructed as productive, happy, and empowered, obscure how discourses of disability and girlhood collude with other systems of oppression and function as regimes of normalization, exclusion, and depoliticization.

The Post-ADA Disabled Girl

I encountered the bus bench billboard on my way to a disability studies conference at UCLA called Disability as Spectacle. The aim of the conference was to explore the shifting terrain and meaning of disability visibility, as the conference organizers, and more recently cultural pundits and disability activists alike, suggest that a disability visibility revolution is currently underway in twenty-first century media culture. News articles abound lauding the proliferation of "authentic" and diverse representations of disability. There are more representations of disability than ever in "traditional" media (e.g., television, film, advertising). As of 2021, according to information, data and market measurement firm, Nielsen (2022), the volume of television and film content inclusive of disability has increased 175% over the past decade, compared to the ten years prior. There has also been an explosion of self-representations, most often taking the form of self-authored narratives of disability on the internet.[2] In the words of disability activist and creator of the blog RampYourVoice! Vilissa Thompson (2019),

Blogging, Vlogging, social media platforms such as Facebook and Twitter, and online forums shatter [. . .] barriers and give us the freedom to be seen, heard, and to tell our truths, call out the -isms and -phobias that we fight against every day, and most importantly, connect with those who "get us."

Cripping Girlhood suggests that disabled girls are at the forefront of the disability visibility revolution. Throughout the coming chapters, I explore how a multiplicity of cultural, political, and technological shifts at the beginning of the twenty-first century, including the proliferation of girls' empowerment narratives, the mainstreaming of disability rights frameworks, and the emergence of Web 2.0 engendered the production and visibility of disabled girls in US media culture. Although this chapter refers to the contemporary disabled girl as the "post-ADA" disabled girl, many of the disabled girls that are the focus of this book ascended into visibility two decades or more after the ADA was first signed into law. A decade prior to my serendipitous encounter with the billboard, the UN adopted the Convention on the Rights and Persons with Disabilities (which the United States has still not ratified as of this writing). Three years after, in 2009, former president Obama established the White House Council for Women and Girls and specifically addressed disabled girls in his statement, effectively signaling a new era of national recognition for disabled girls and women. Two years later, in 2011, the UN declared October 11 the International Day of the Girl Child, and in 2016 Obama once again addressed disabled girls in the proclamation, committed to "forging a future [. . .] where all girls know they can hold any job, run a company, and compete in any field" because "everyone has a role to play and everybody deserves the chance to pursue their dreams."

A wave of disabled girl activism was also starting to build during this time. For example, in 2008, eight-year-old disabled girl Rosa Marcellino captured national attention with her efforts campaigning for the erasure of the stigmatizing term "mentally retarded" from government lexicon, proposing to replace the term with "intellectual disability" (Cyphers 2015). Her "Spread the Word to End the Word" campaign proved successful, and in October of 2010 Obama signed "Rosa's Law." Rosa's law also changed descriptors of IQ-based intelligence in federal statute to "profound, severe, and moderate" from the outdated descriptors "idiot, imbecile, and moron." In 2014, another disabled girl, Melissa Shang, made news headlines when her Change.org petition for a disabled American Girl doll went viral. The petition called for a 2015 disabled American Girl doll of the year who uses a wheelchair, "so that all girls can learn about the difficulty of being born with a disability" (DiBlasio 2014). In the video accompanying her online petition, Melissa says, "Disabled girls are American girls, too. We face challenges and overcome them every day."

Disabled girls were also gaining newfound cultural visibility on the screen and on the runway. As a few examples of many, in 2013, Ali Stroker, a young woman who uses a wheelchair, became a guest on *Glee*, an immensely popular musical comedy-drama television series on Fox. In 2015, eighteen-year-old Madeline Stuart became the first model with Down syndrome to walk the runway. Also in 2015, Sesame Street introduced the character, Julia, a preschool girl with autism. Julia, as part of their campaign "See Amazing in All Children," is the first character to have a disability that, in Sesame Street's words, is not easily recognized.

Despite the shift in political climate as the United States entered and moved through the Trump era (and despite the Trump White House's regressive institutional attitudes toward disability), representations and self-representations of disabled girls and girlhoods have only proliferated. For example, aside from the explosion of self-representations online, in 2020 Jennifer Keelan-Chaffins published *All the Way to the Top: How One Girl's Fight for Americans with Disabilities Changed Everything*, a children's book that documents her activism as an eight-year-old girl with cerebral palsy, and most famously her participation in the Capitol Crawl. American Girl finally named their first doll with a "visible" disability, Joss Kendrick, who uses a hearing aid, as their 2020 doll of the year. And, in 2022 an infant named Isa became the first Gerber Baby with a limb difference. As Simi Linton (1998) might say—a bit cheekily—disabled girls are "everywhere these days" (4).

But why disabled girls, and why now? Girls' studies scholars have shown that the girl strategically appears again and again in US media culture as a conduit for various social, cultural, economic, and national anxieties (Odem 1995; Harris 2004; King 2005; Gonick 2006; Driscoll 2008; Projanksy 2014; Wright 2016). In the words of Claudia Castañeda (2002), the child's incompleteness or "not-yet-ness" is one reason why they are made available as a resource for wider cultural projects (2). Specifically, since the turn of the twenty-first century, the girl has appeared with ubiquity in media culture as a fabulous/scandalous object onto which we gaze (Gill 2007; Harris 2004; McRobbie 2009; Projansky 2014). A century before, adolescence became constructed as a "social space in which to talk about the characteristics of people in modernity" (Lesko 2012, 5). The creation of proper youth proto-citizens was a preoccupation for the United States and United Kingdom, as both nations were undergoing massive cultural, economic, and civic shifts.

Eugenic logics of racial progress informed new interests and developments in youth education and child development, as the state, educators, policymakers, and scientists attempted to mold young people into the ideal gendered embodiment of national progress.

Anita Harris (2004) argues that a similar situation has happened at the turn of the twenty-first century, but instead of young people, or adolescence, this time it is girls and girlhood that have our preoccupation. The turn of the twenty-first century has been described variously in terms of flux, globalization, dislocation, and a peculiar reconfiguration of the state. Scholars use the language of late modernity, late-stage capitalism, and neoliberalism. For the purposes of this text, I am settling on neoliberalism, which can be described as a specific configuration of governance characterized by the application and privileging of free-market logic to the domain of life-itself, the deregulation of corporate and financial sectors, the privatization of land and resources, the defunding of public and social services and supports, and accumulation by dispossession, or the centralization of wealth and power for the few through the government's process of dispossessing the public of collectively held spaces (Duggan 2004; Harvey 2011). Puar (2017) adds that neoliberalism profits off the tension between debility and capacity because neoliberal regimes of biocapital produce bodies as never healthy enough, thus compelling bodyminds to strive toward endless processes of capacitation. Furthermore, under the auspices of neoliberalism, Julie Elman (2014) argues that citizenship is no longer "guaranteed in advance by the nation-state but rather as an endless 'contractual' negotiation that is contingent on perpetual self-surveillance and healthy (read: normative) behavior" (16). She proposes that good citizenship has become tethered to rehabilitation—a cultural logic that evokes understandings of disability as loss and able-bodiedness as wholeness, or as something that one can restore or approximate if one works or desires hard enough. Rehabilitation dovetails with the neoliberal ethos of personal responsibility and together they suggest that people, like markets, are healthiest when self-regulating.

Somewhat paradoxically, the shifting labor conditions under the auspices of neoliberalism in combination with the gains of feminism, have tenuously created new possibilities for certain young women. Specifically, girls have been positioned as the inheritors of the structural and ideological gains of feminism, for example, increased educational and employment opportunities, as well as ideas about "girl power" and "freedom of choice regarding their bodies, work, family, and relationships" (Harris 2004, 7). According to Harris (2004), girls have become "constructed as a vanguard of new subjectivity" (1). She explores the emergence and hypervisibility of what she terms "future girl," a certain kind of ideal girl who is celebrated and upheld as an example of the "desire, determination, and confidence to take charge of [. . .] life, seize chances, and achieve [. . .] goals" (Harris 2004, 1). Future girls are constructed as "highly efficient assemblage[s] of productivity" and as "exemplars of social possibility," (McRobbie 2009, 59). Neoliberalism requires citizen subjects who are self-enterprising, flexible, self-surveilling, can manage risk on an individual level and develop strategies for making the "right" choices in a landscape of uncertainty, which is presented under the guise of freedom (of choice). The future girl embodies the flexible subjectivity of neoliberalism; she is understood as someone who successfully takes advantage of the opportunities granted and is innovative, self-managing, responsible, and productive. The future girl is imagined as best able to cope with the shifting political, economic, and cultural landscape at the turn of the twenty-first century, as well as best positioned to teach others how to successfully construct their own "reflexive biographical project," or how to forge a future through self-reflexively cultivating an identity, or a self-brand as I discuss in chapter 2 (Kelly 2001). She is often touted as a post-feminist achievement, suggesting that equality has been achieved for women and girls, signaling the redundancy of feminism as a political project.

A lot is riding on girls; they have become luminous, or in the Deleuzian sense put under a spotlight, and interpellated into the cultural imaginary as a "metaphor for social mobility and social change" and as one of the stakes on which the national future rests (Ringrose 2007, 472). This newfound interest in or spotlight on girls, however, is not just celebratory, but it is regulatory (Harris 2004). The future girl functions to insidiously orient all girls on a path toward a normative "good life," with all its cis-heteronormative, ableist, and neoliberal trappings. So, not all girls can become future girls, as cultivating a successful life trajectory and future girl subjectivity largely depends on structural forces hidden beneath a veneer of equal opportunity. The girls who are positioned as "failing" or "at-risk" of not being able to cultivate a successful future or move through girlhood smoothly on toward womanhood (defined in terms of normative temporality, e.g., school, work, marriage, reproduction) are often those who are historically marginalized and do not have privilege or structural support—most often, poor girls, queer girls, trans girls, Black girls, brown girls, Indigenous girls, and disabled girls. They are more heavily surveilled, policed, intervened on, and punished. Their failures are understood individually, or as a matter of willfulness, pathology, lack of personal effort, as the result of poor choices, or a "natural" outcome of dysfunctional families or communities. This understanding covers over how systems of oppression circumscribe the life chances and the choices or lack of choices that are made available to girls depending on their social location. The future girl's foil, the "at-risk" girl haunts, and she functions to discipline all girls.

One might deem this conceptualization of future girls at fundamental odds with disabled girls. One might even consider the disabled future girl an ontological impossibility, as disability has historically signaled a future foreclosed, or, in Alison Kafer's (2013) words, a "future no one wants" because it is one that "bears too many traces of the ills of the present to be desirable" (2). Disability, in the dominant, medicalized understanding as abnormal, deficient, and in need of intervention, most often signals a foreclosure of future opportunities, of reproduction, and of productivity. Disabled children and youth, more broadly, are commonly regarded as developmental failures, as unable to grow up or move forward toward a complete future adulthood, defined by autonomy and rationality (Slater 2012; Apgar 2023). Furthermore, because the disabled bodymind challenges heteronormativity and gender norms, disabled girls' "girlness" has historically been called into question (Erevelles and Mutua 2005).

But as the bus bench billboard, and the stories above of Rosa Marcellino, Melissa Shang, and the disabled Gerber Baby Isa attest, a critical mass of disabled girls and girlhoods have visibly emerged in media culture who are imbued with futurity. The disabled girl has transformed into one of the stakes on which the national future rests. In the coming chapters, I explore how similar representations, including disabled pageant contestants, social media influencers, and disabled girls who have gone viral, push back on the understanding of disabled girls as always, already developmental failures, perpetually dependent, unproductive, and non-reproductive. Rather, the representations of disabled girls and girlhoods that *Cripping Girlhood* critically analyzes function recuperatively and construct certain disabled girls as valuable and as the subjects best able to cope with and teach viewers lessons about how to survive in very precarious times. The figure of the disabled girl offers lessons about how to construct the ultimate flexible subjectivity, how to successfully engage in a process of endless capacitation, how to "brand" and profit off embodied difference, and when and how to die within the austere conditions of the US healthcare system. However, as I reveal throughout the coming pages, the disabled girls that ascend to spectacular visibility are welcomed home into the national imaginary as valuable subjects only under the condition that they reinforce the normative power structure. Touted as a post-ADA achievement, they insidiously signal the redundancy of disability as a political project. Let us return to the bus bench billboard one final time to continue to unfurl the workings of this new representational politics of disabled girlhood.

The Disabled Girl and Ablenationalism

Soon after I encountered the bus bench billboard, I looked up the text that was surreptitiously placed in the corner, "Love Has No Labels" and "#WeAreAmerica." I discovered that "Love Has No Labels" is a public service advertising campaign that was launched by the Ad Council[3] in 2015. "Love Has No Labels" describes itself as "a movement to promote diversity, equity, and inclusion of all people across race, religion, gender, sexual orientation, age and ability" and claims that "love is the most powerful force to overcome bias, discrimination and racism" (Ad Council 2022). As I saw firsthand, the figure of the disabled girl features hypervisibly in the campaign's visual messaging, and as I later learned, she also plays a pivotal role in their first two viral Public Service Announcements (PSAs), both available to watch on YouTube. Like the bus bench billboard, the figure of the disabled girl is intimately tethered to nationalism, visually mobilized to tell a new story about citizenship, inclusion, disability, and girlhood.

The campaign's first PSA, "Love Has No Labels," was among the ten most watched YouTube videos in 2015,[4] and in 2016 it was nominated and won an Emmy for best commercial. The eponymous PSA asks viewers to "rethink bias." The video takes place on a busy pier on Valentine's Day and spotlights skeletons dancing and embracing behind an x-ray screen, while a crowd of onlookers gathers. The skeletons—all who look the same behind the x-ray screen—soon reveal themselves, diverse couple by couple. The crowd cheers on each reveal. There is a lesbian couple who embrace and kiss, another is an interracial couple, and one couple is a disabled girl and her sister. Each reveal prompts a message on the screen, for example, the lesbian couple's message is "love has no gender." The disabled girl and her sister prompt a peculiar message, "love has no disability."

Their second PSA, which aired on Independence Day in 2016, was also nominated for an Emmy. "We Are America" stars professional wrestler and actor John Cena. As an extension of the "Love Has No Labels" campaign, its goal is to redefine patriotism. In the video, Cena walks through a nondescript, small town US main street, decorated with American flags. He recites a monologue, persuading viewers that "to have love for a country is to have love for the people who make up that country" ("John Cena" 2016). The monologue celebrates diversity as a valuable, defining feature of the nation; as Cena notes, "almost half the country belongs to minority groups," and asks, "After all what's more American than the freedom to celebrate the things that make us, us?" Cena ends his monologue with "to love America is to love all Americans, because love has no labels." The disabled girl makes an appearance in the last scene, smiling and waving goodbye, as if reminding the viewer, to love America is to love her.

Cutting across the three scenes in the "Love Has No Labels" campaign is an understanding of the disabled girl as an American *girl*, and as an invaluable subject from whom the viewer is to learn from. Rather than excluded from future visions of the nation-state because, as disabled, she is imagined as a "drain" on the economy or as a threat to the nation's health, she is constructed as integral to the construction of the United States as diverse, healthy, and inclusive. She functions to rehabilitate the presumably US citizen viewer from a place of ignorance about disability to a place of disability tolerance and even love. It is important to note that this campaign emerges at an incredibly divisive time in the history of the United States. It is the lead up to the election of former President Donald Trump. One could argue that the figure of the disabled girl is affectively mobilized to keep the nation together.

In *The Biopolitics of Disability*, Mitchell and Snyder (2015) track a distinct historic shift in the twentieth century from what they call "liberal to neoliberal disability," from eugenic exclusionist practices to neoliberal inclusionist practices, brought upon by the mainstreaming of disability rights, the recognition that incapacity is the "new normal," and the shift from production (Fordism) to consumption (post-Fordism), most evident in the "mounting cultural capital of the ever-expanding disability business" (41). Certain disabled bodyminds, like the disabled girls in the "Love Has No Labels" campaign, rather than parasitic, have come to symbolize a "certain kind of embodied value for contemporary nations," and "increasingly perform [. . .] representational work [. . .] as a symbol of expansive inclusionist efforts" (Mitchell and Snyder 2015 15; 19). To theorize the uneven pattern of inclusion for newly visible disabled identities, Mitchell and Snyder (2015) draw from Jasbir Puar's (2007) formulation of "homonationalism," which is a conceptual frame to help think through "how acceptance and tolerance for gay and lesbian subjects have become a barometer by which the right to and capacity for national sovereignty is evaluated" (Puar 2013, 336). Homonationalism considers how liberal, rights-based LGBTQ movements and forms of political inclusion are operationalized by the state as signifiers of modernity and social progress, and how this creates forms of exceptionalism and valuation, wherein certain, respectable LGBTQ subjects are deemed worthy of protection by the state, most often at the expense of and from the "regressive" racialized other. In the wake of "tolerance" and "acceptance," bodyminds that can't assimilate into newly normed standards of queerness fall even farther away from protection and find themselves on the outskirts of a recently assimilated community.

Similarly, ablenationalism is a conceptual frame that helps us think through how disability has been operationalized by the state to signify modernity and social progress in contradistinction to "regressive" nation-states. Mitchell and Snyder (2015) argue that both homonationalism and ablenationalism consider how treating crip/queer people "as an exception valorizes norms of inclusion" (13). In other words, ablenationalism also creates forms of exceptionalism and valuation. Certain disabled subjects, those who can "approximate historically specific expectations of normalcy" are celebrated and deemed worthy of protection by the state, while others who have been pathologized as too impaired to labor or consume in alignment with neoliberal expectations of productivity are rendered disposable (Mitchell and Snyder 2015, 2). Although outwardly appearing to value disabled subjects as a part of the multicultural tapestry of the United States, the project of ablenationalism in effect reifies existing values of able-bodiedness, heteronormativity, and rationality—or what Mitchell and Snyder (2015) call "normative modes of being" (2).

In the coming pages, *Cripping Girlhood* investigates other scenes, where like the "Love Has No Labels" campaign, the disabled girl emerges spectacularly and valuably. One major contribution of this book is its efforts building out the conceptual frame of ablenationalism by placing it in conversation with scholarship in girls' studies, such as Harris's (2004) theorization of the future girl. In doing so, I thoroughly explore the process by which certain disabled girl figures ascend to visibility over others. This allows me to consider the stakes of contemporary disability visibility. Rather than uncritically celebrate the fact that the disabled girl is at the forefront of the disability visibility revolution, I question, why and to what end? As we know, the contemporary production of the disabled bodymind "must also be thought of as a space of the contradictions of neoliberalism—it is at once privileged as a site of inclusion, but that inclusion is also the promise of its exclusion" (Sothern 2007, 146). Unsurprisingly, the disabled girl figures who ascend to visibility and who are exceptionalized as valuable disabled subjects in contemporary media culture are often the disabled girls who are positioned as best assimilating into existing cis-heteronormative, chrononormative, white supremacist, and ableist understandings of girlhood. Their inclusion into the national imaginary often works to depoliticize disability and make it less disruptive. The uncritical celebration of their newfound visibility—as a testament to the United States' purported disability excellence—insidiously works to obscure the fact that the inclusion and recognition of exceptional disabled girls relies on the exclusion, disposability, and even the debilitation of girls who are not intelligible as disabled or who cannot assimilate into new norms of disabled girlhood.

Integrating the Disabled Girl, Transforming Feminist Disability Studies

Despite recent claims about the critical mass of diverse, authentic, and empowering narratives about disability, *Cripping Girlhood* reveals that representations of disabled girls and girlhoods in popular media culture are still—more often than not—mired in and reproduce a medicalized understanding of disability. They are constructed using what countless disability activists and scholars have termed the medical or individual model of disability, which posits disability as a pathologized condition, an individual deficit, and a self-evident truth inhered in the bodymind. Within this paradigm, disability is understood as something that must be overcome, intervened upon, cured, or eliminated. It is perceived as a problem confined to the individual disabled person, thus requiring an individualized solution or treatment. Rather than the disabled person themselves, doctors, physical therapists, psychiatrists, geneticists, and other medical professionals are deemed the ultimate authority on the disabled bodymind, as they are the ones positioned to treat the individual. Absent in this model is any recognition of disability as a social justice issue, a culture, a source of knowledge, or even an identity. To this day, this is still the dominant understanding of disability in the United States (and much of the Global North). Featured heavily in the coming pages is the framing of disability as a common sense target for rehabilitation (chapters 1 and 3) and as a problem that must be fixed at all costs, even if it brings more harm (or even death) to the disabled person (chapter 4). As we will also see in the coming pages, grief, disappointment, anxiety, and even sometimes happiness coheres around medicalized understandings of disabled girls and girlhoods. For example, anxiety about disability's inherent potential to derail the disabled girl on her journey "growing up" is a lurking presence throughout many of the narratives that others—from journalists to documentarians—construct about the disabled girl.

Disability activists, scholars, and advocates have long pushed back against this myopic understanding of disability, arguing instead for the recognition of disability as multiplicitous: as an identity, as culture, and as valuable embodied human difference (Oliver 1990; Garland-Thomson 1997; Linton 1998; Clare 1999; Siebers 2008; Kafer 2013). A pivotal moment in the history of disability activism, and in turn, within the field of disability studies, was the development of the social model of disability. Positing a distinction between "impairment" (physical/mental/sensory difference) and "disability," advocates of the social model argue against the idea that the disabled body, in and of itself, is inherently disabling. Instead, they contend that disability is a product of exclusionary social relations. In conversation with Patty Berne, co-founder of disability justice performance project Sins Invalid, late disability justice activist Stacey Milbern, explains:

> If you and I go to a building, and there's no ramp, typically people think the problem is that we use wheelchairs. Whereas a social model of disability would say that the problem is that the building is not accessible. And, it doesn't seem like a radical concept, but it changes the fundamental way we think about disability, and the work that we need to do to include people with disabilities. ("My Body Doesn't Oppress Me, Society Does" 2017)

In other words, the social model asks us to examine how social, architectural, and economic barriers render certain non-normative bodyminds functionally disabled. Whereas the medical model looks to "solve" the problem of disability through correcting, normalizing, or rehabilitating the disabled body, in effect, bringing it closer to an able-bodied ideal, the social model re-defines the problem, and asks us to look instead toward the inaccessibility of the built environment, the lack of access for many to adaptive devices, and discriminatory attitudes that favor certain bodies and minds over others. In the words of Patty Berne, "My body doesn't oppress me. My body's fun. But, society, that can be incredibly oppressive" ("My Body Doesn't Oppress Me, Society Does" 2017). The social model provokes an analysis of power. It asks us to think through ableism as a system of oppression that favors able-bodiedness/mindedness at all costs, as well as produces certain bodyminds that fall away from a constructed ideal as disposable.

It was not until I was in graduate school that I came to understand disability from a critical perspective, as something more than what our medicalized imaginary evinces. It was through feminist disability studies that I began to learn more critically about disability, solidifying my academic interest in disability theory. In my first gender and women's studies graduate course, I was introduced to disability studies through Rosemarie Garland-Thomson's (2002b) field-defining article, "Integrating Disability, Transforming Feminist Theory." It was through this article that I started to make sense of my own experiences of disability in and beyond girlhood, intimately resonating with Sara Ahmed's (2017) adage, "theory can do more the closer it gets to the skin" (10). In "Integrating Disability," Garland-Thomson (2002b) calls out the lack of, as the title suggests, integration between feminist and disability theory, arguing that the methods, approaches, and perspectives of feminist theory have a lot to offer disability studies, and vice versa. She argues that disability is an ideology, "—like gender—[it] is a concept that pervades all aspects of culture: its structuring institutions, social identities, cultural practices, political positions, historical communities, and the shared human experience of embodiment" (Garland-Thomson 2002b, 4). She proposes disability as a cultural system—the disability/ability system—that operates to stigmatize particular bodies and minds that fall away from the norm—what she names the "normate"—defined as a composite identity, held by those in power (white, cis, heterosexual, Christian, able-bodied, male) (Garland-Thomson 2002b). Thus, rather than the myopic understanding of disability purported by the medical model, as a self-evident truth of the body—or a natural state of abject inferiority—, Garland-Thomson (2002b) positions disability as a "culturally fabricated narrative of the body" (5). It is historically, geographically, and socially contextual, and it operates to confer the distribution of unequal resources, status, and power. Most strikingly, for me, as a gender and women's studies student, was Garland-Thomson's attention to the ways in which gender, race, and disability intertwine. As she contends, the most nuanced and complex analyses of gender are intersectional or take into consideration the co-constitutive nature of systems of oppression. Thus, more than a monolithic material reality, race, gender, class, sexuality, geographic location, citizenship status, and age all come to bear on a person's experience of disability.

The title of this section, "Integrating the Disabled Girl, Transforming Feminist Disability Studies" is not only a play on Garland-Thomson's article, but it also calls to mind another field-defining article that builds on Garland-Thomson's, called "Integrating Race, Transforming Feminist Disability Studies," written by Black feminist disability studies scholar Sami Schalk and crip of color scholar Jina Kim (2020). In the article, they contend that the intellectual insights of feminists of color, who have long been writing about health and the body, but perhaps not under the sign "disability," have largely been excluded as contributors to the field of feminist disability studies. With this acknowledgement, they advance feminist-of-color disability studies as a framework that recognizes the contributions of and mobilizes critical race scholarship and feminist-of-color theories, refocusing the field's citational practices. As they write, "centering race in feminist disability studies [. . .] frames disability as a *method* [. . .] as lens to analyze the intersecting systems of ableism, heteropatriarchy, white supremacy and capitalist violence, particularly as they assign value or lack thereof to certain bodyminds" (Schalk and Kim 2020, 37–38). As I hope to make clear in the following section, and throughout the text, cripping girlhood as heuristic is indebted to this conceptualization. It is fundamentally intersectional, as it seeks to carefully consider how ableism, white supremacy, ageism, and heteropatriarchy seek to define and delimit disabled girls and girlhoods, rendering certain disabled girls valuable and certain disabled girls disposable. More generally, in integrating the disabled girl, I seek to provoke feminist disability studies to more carefully and meaningfully consider age and temporality (and its intersection with gender, race, and sexuality) within its analytical purview. In integrating the disabled girl, I also am suggesting that disabled girl knowledges have much to offer feminist disability studies, as most feminist knowledge still centers around adult's perspectives and experiences. In the coming pages, I contend that disabled girls have much to teach us about humor, interdependence, intimacy, and imagining and enacting a world otherwise.

With all that being said, *Cripping Girlhood* is indebted to the work of Garland-Thomson, Schalk, and Kim, and other feminist disability studies scholars, many of whom recognize the social model's political significance, but question its fixity as well as the utility of separating out impairment from disability (Wendell 1996; Shildrick and Price 1998; Corker and French 1999; Tremain 2001; Mollow 2015). According to Shelley Tremain (2001), impairment is not "value-neutral" or "merely descriptive," but it is "an historically specific effect of knowledge-power" (620; 617). Alison Kafer (2013) takes up this critique and similarly argues, "asserting a sharp divide between impairment and disability fails to recognize that *both* impairment and disability are social" (7). Or, in other words, both impairment and disability do not exist apart from social meanings and understandings. What we consider to be an impairment, like disability, is historically, socially, culturally, and geographically specific. It shifts over time, place, and space. Further, ideologies of ability and disability affect us all, even those of us who do not consider ourselves to have an impairment or be disabled. To illustrate this, I always ask students in my disability studies class to reflect on how they are all assumed to be able to sit at their desk the whole class period (and fit in their desk) and take tests within a certain allotted time slot—this comes out of an expectation of what a bodymind can and should be able to do.

The social model's focus on changing disabling barriers can unwittingly "render pain and fatigue irrelevant to disability politics" (Kafer 2013, 7). Again, as I explain to my disability studies students, building more accessible walkways on campus, although important and necessary, might not really do anything for a student who cannot come to class because of their debilitating endometriosis pain. Feminist disability studies scholars argue that we must make room for chronic pain, illness, and even the desire for cure. For example, Susan Wendell (1996) in discussing her experience living with myalgic encephalomyelitis (ME) writes:

> I want to have more energy and less pain, and to have a more predictable body; about that there is no ambivalence [. . .] Yet I cannot wish that I had never contracted ME, because it has made me a different person, a person that I am glad to be, would not want to have missed being, and could not imagine relinquishing, even if I were 'cured.' [. . .] I would joyfully accept a cure, but I do not need one. (83–84)

Wendell's (1996) curative ambivalence recognizes the simultaneity of ME's trouble and value. A feminist disability studies perspective asks us to hold all these things at once.

The analyses of disability in this project bear in mind feminist critiques of the social model of disability. Most specifically, though, I build off Alison Kafer's (2013) political/relational model of disability, introduced in her monograph *Feminist Queer Crip*. This model does not so much refute the medical model of disability as much as it argues for the "recognition of the political nature of a medical framing of disability" (Kafer 2013, 6). It asks us to consider who gets access to care, under what circumstances, and how lack of access to care can literally disable, while bearing in mind that medicine and medical knowledges and practices are imbued with ideologies and are informed by the culture in which we all live. For example, in chapter 4 I examine how racist, sexist, and ageist understandings of chronic pain could have led to inadequate care in the case of Jerika Bolen, and thus accelerated her desire to die. However, I also recognize her experience of pain as *real* and as *really bad* and explore what it would mean to read her choice to die as an act of cripping girlhood. The political/relational model, like its name suggests, recognizes that disability is always experienced in relation and that it is political, or implicated in relations of power. In my discussion of disabled girl handlers and their service dogs in chapter 3, we see clearly how disability is experienced in and through relationships—in this case through the relationship with a non-human animal—as the service dog becomes key to the disabled girl's experience of disability and construction of subjectivity. Throughout the text we also see how disability is most often experienced in and through the family. For example, in chapter 1, the figure of the disabled girl is represented as the (reluctantly) happy linchpin of a new post-ADA family formation. In chapter 4, Jerika's decision to die is cast as an act of love that relieves her mother of having to provide care.

The recognition of disability as political makes room for "more activist responses, seeing 'disability' as a potential site for collective reimagining" (Kafer 2013, 9). I explore the politicization *and* depoliticization of disability throughout the text, reading quotidian acts of self-representation as political, such as in chapter 2 where I read the practice of disability vlogging as an act that re-authors the meanings typically ascribed to disabled girl bodyminds. Exploring the depoliticization of disability is one of the central concerns of *Cripping Girlhood*, as I map how the figure of the disabled girl is wielded to shore up (somewhat counterintuitively) normative discourses of disability, advance US nationalism in the name of benevolence, and re-secure white supremacy under the guise of disability inclusion, all of which take the teeth out of a radical disability politics that fundamentally understands the co-constitution of ableism, racism, heteropatriarchy, and capitalism.

Before I move on to describe more closely "cripping girlhood" as a heuristic that I employ throughout the text, *Cripping Girlhood*, most specifically in its theorizations of ablenationalism and state violence, is also indebted to the work of transnational feminist scholars of disability. Prior to Schalk and Kim's critique, Nirmala Erevelles's transnational feminist disability studies perspective, advanced in her wildly under-cited text, *Disability and Difference in Global Contexts*, critiqued the whiteness of the field and questioned the lack of thoughtful consideration of disability in transnational feminist scholarship. In arguing that the violence of colonialism is inherently disabling, Erevelles (2011) poses a provocative question, one that complicates disability studies' perhaps over-emphasis on a celebratory or empowering understanding of disability: "How is disability celebrated if its very existence is inextricably linked to the violence of social/economic conditions of capitalism" (17)? Her question, one that chapter 4 wrestles with more definitively, gestures toward the limitations of disability visibility as a political tactic and provokes a greater consideration of how certain bodies are literally disabled through state violence, war, viruses, toxic pollution, and "natural" disasters.

In a similar vein, other scholars such as Kateřina Kolářová (2015) and Jasbir Puar (2017) who trouble the dominant Western alignment of disability and identity, have taken up Julie Livingston's concept, "debility," developed during her research in Botswana, where no word easily translates to "disability." Debility refers to "impairment, lack, or loss of certain bodily abilities" and encompasses "a range of chronic illness and senescence as well as disability, per se" (Livingston 2005, 113). Debility asks us to think through the question of who can claim disability and under what conditions, critically understanding that certain forms of disability and certain privileged disabled people—who Titchkosky (2003) would name the able-disabled—can be and have become incorporated into the nation-state at the expense of others (Kolářová 2015; Puar 2017). Those others, like I argue in chapter 4 about Jerika's foil—the "unruly Black girl"—may never be able to "claim" disability or access the same rights and privileges that the ADA attempts to confer to specific bodyminds that are intelligible as disabled. Debility thus begs the question, how do we account for the nuanced and various ways in which bodies are incapacitated, or alternatively, recapacitated under neoliberal capitalism, state violence, ecological rupture, and toxic pollution? I hold a political commitment to thinking through these politics of differential inclusion and investigate which disabled girl bodyminds are and can be recapacitated for the project of US empire.

Cripping Girlhood

Crip in all its variegated meanings has been integral to the conceptualization and execution of this project. Not only do I advance cripping girlhood as a heuristic to make sense of representations and self-representations of disabled girls and girlhoods in contemporary media culture, but I am also invested in the radical potential of *crip* as a term that seeks to unsettle, and *crip theory* as it exists in productive relation to feminist disability studies. As I said earlier in this chapter, I utilize crip throughout the text as a term that recognizes the political and cultural power of disabled girls and girlhoods, even in the most quotidian of scenes. Second, I mobilize *to crip* or *cripping* as a practice that interrogates assumptions about disabled girls and girlhoods. Cripping girlhood, then, holds within it an affirmation of the fact that disabled girls crip girlhood: in a range of cultural sites that I explore throughout the text, disabled girls upend what we think we know about them and their experience, recasting the meanings ascribed to their bodyminds in their own terms. Cripping girlhood is also an analytical practice, in which, throughout the text, I endeavor to uncover how normative discourses and affects collide and facilitate the figure of the disabled girl's ascendence into the economy of disability visibility, ossifying "the disabled girl" as a visible (and newly valuable) subject position.[5]

Crip as a noun is provocative, derived from the slur *cripple* and reclaimed by disability activists and groups to refer to themselves and their cultural and intellectual production. To those outside of the disability community, the "in-your-faceness" of crip can be wince inducing, as suggested by Nancy Mairs (1992): "people—crippled or not—wince at the word 'crippled' as they do not at 'handicapped' or 'disabled.' Perhaps I want them to wince" (9). Like queer, crip holds and ferries the vestiges of a painful history and now functions as an intra-group term that instead signifies pride and solidarity. It recognizes the political and cultural power of disability and affirms the inherent value of non-normative ways of being in the world (Sandahl 2003). In Eli Clare's (1999) words, "crip" and "cripple" are "words to help forge a politics" (70). Crip is fluid, stretchy, expansive; it can describe a range of non-normative embodiments that do not neatly sit under the signifier "disability." It is claimed by not only those who have physical disabilities, but by people who have mental, intellectual, or sensory disabilities, and people whose bodyminds have been labeled sick, mad, or fat. The capaciousness of the term ties it to understandings of disability that go beyond the rigidity of the social model, with its clear delineation of disability and impairment. Crip probes at the categorical edges of ability and disability, exploring where they blur and dissolve.

As a verb, *cripping* or to *crip* describes a couple of different but related analytic practices. It is an act that "spins mainstream representations or practices to reveal able-bodied assumptions and exclusionary effects" (Sandahl 2003, 37). To crip is also to uncover how normative affects and discourses of race, gender, class, sexuality, and age intersect and concretize categories of disability (Clare 1999; Sandahl 2003; McRuer 2006, 2018; Kafer 2013; Schalk 2018). I am particularly fond of how Mel Chen (2012) integrates both analytic practices in their "queer-crip approach to disability," which they describe as a "disentangling of discourses that contain and fix dis/abled bodyminds" and a "reworlding that challenges the order of things" (215; 237). Similarly, cripping girlhood toggles between these practices, as I illuminate the process by which disabled girls crip girlhood, as well as uncover how normative discourses and affects attempt to "contain and fix" the figure of the disabled girl. For example, in chapter 2, a chapter that examines disabled girls on YouTube, I am interested in how disabled girls' cultural production in the form of disability video blogging (vlogging) unsettles the non-disabled viewers' relationship to the disabled girl bodymind, as well as "reworlds," or creates new relations of disability affinity. In that same chapter, I am also interested in tracking how disabled girl vloggers' cultural productions become commodifiable. The ascendence into visibility as a social media influencer (or as I term, crip-fluencer), as well as the transformation of disability into a self-branding practice requires an investigation into how the disabled girl bodymind is contained and fixed, made marketable and monetizable. I see these two analytic uses of *crip* or *cripping* as two sides of the same coin, as this project is interested in the tension between the stories disabled girls tell about themselves and the stories that others tell about the figure of the disabled girl.

As I have stated already, this project is a feminist disability studies project. I see *crip theory* as a generative complement to feminist disability studies, and an integral part of my theoretical framework. Carrie Sandahl (2003), in an early writing about the potential of crip, suggests cheekily, "if I had my druthers, I would replace the term disability studies with crip theory or crip studies to represent its radical edge" (53). Robert McRuer (2006) expands on the relationship between crip theory and disability studies in *Crip Theory* and argues that crip theory is more "contestatory." It is more willing to explore how disability identity politics can be exclusionary, while also "perhaps paradoxically" "recognizing the generative role identity has played in the disability rights movement" (McRuer 2006, 35). This tension between crip's capacity to be both identarian and anti-identarian has much value for *Cripping Girlhood*, as I am interested in the limits of visibility as a tactic of political inclusion for disabled girls, and disabled people more generally. Visibility sometimes requires a fixing of identity to ensure legibility. What does it mean that "the disabled girl" has become a valuable subject position for disabled girls to inhabit? Who falls out of this? What does that mean for those who are excluded or illegible as disabled girls? I am also interested in exploring when and where "disability" and "disabled" fail to hold and when and where the binary constructed between able-bodied/minded and disabled is limiting. I see *crip theory*'s urge for generative trouble as an integral part of this project.

A Note on Affect

Cripping girlhood as a heuristic, is also, as I briefly mentioned above, invested in thinking through affect, something that has recently begun to gain significant conceptual traction within the broader field of disability studies. If we return to where I began, with the "Love Has No Labels" campaign and the explicitness with which the disabled girl is tethered to love, we see how the study of affect, or emotion, is integral to understanding the work that the figure of the disabled girl performs in contemporary media culture. Although there are competing definitions, and thus theoretical and methodological uses of affect—some scholars argue for the total separation of affect and emotion—for the purpose of this project, I define affect in terms of intersubjective feelings and intensities that combine the emotional and the somatic. My use of Margaret Price's (2015) notion of "bodymind," aligns with this, as I believe it is vital to underscore the imbrication of the body and mind. Affects work through and on the bodymind: feelings are bound up with cognitive processes, and what and how we know is bound up with what and how we feel. Here it is also of much importance to emphasize the political potential of affect. For example, throughout this project, I investigate how love can be quietly recruited by power in the service of white supremacy, ableism, and US empire. How "love" for disability can absolve one of fighting for meaningful structural change. But I also investigate how love can be generative, for example, how a disabled girl's love for her service dog can chart new possibilities for kinship outside of the violence of normative domesticity.

In some ways, this project answers the call that Elizabeth Donaldson and Catherine Prendergast issued in 2011 in their introduction to the special issue on disability and emotion in the *Journal of Literary & Cultural Disability Studies*, "There's No Crying in Disability Studies!" They write:

> We clearly want to push the analysis of the emotional in Disability Studies further [. . .]. We would argue that, ironically, Disability Studies, forged as it has been with physical impairment as its primary terrain, has inherited damaging ableist assumptions of "mind" that discourage a more robust consideration of emotion. (130)

They go on to discuss the political importance of considering emotion for disability studies and argue because emotion has become "squarely at the center of political life," political life has become "squarely at the center of emotions" (Donaldson and Prendergast 2011, 132). Although the critical consideration of emotion/affect is emergent in disability studies, Black feminists and feminists of color have long recognized the fundamental entangling of emotion/affect and politics, from Audre Lorde's (1978; 1981) writings on anger and the erotic, to Gloria Anzaldúa's (1987) writing about the mestiza's "psychic struggle."

My deployment of affect signals a politically engaged approach to the subject of feeling, and it is specifically informed by feminist cultural theorists, drawing most heavily on the writings of Sara Ahmed (2004; 2010), Ann Cvetkovich (2003), and Lauren Berlant (2008; 2011). My definition of affect is intentionally imprecise, as this project is not necessarily as concerned with what affect is, so much as what affect *does*, although I do hope the impreciseness reflects the slippages and ambiguity between feelings as embodied sensations and feelings as psychic or cognitive experiences (Cvetkovich 2003). Further, my use of affect attempts to get at the "texture" or qualitative, embodied experience that has the capacity to exceed social subjectification through discourse. Theorists of affect contend that "constructivist models leave out the residue or excess that is not socially produced, and this constitutes the very fabric of our being" (Hemmings 2005, 549). Affect offers another angle to conceptualize subject formation, emphasizing connected and relational modes over the oppositional binarism of power/resistance. An affective critique emphasizes the "unexpected, the singular, or indeed quirky" over the generally applicable, which "offers a different worldview than the rather narrow one governed by a repressive/subversive dichotomy" (Hemmings 2005, 550). I see affect as an integral part of "cripping girlhood" as heuristic, not only because it is important to uncover how affects such as love, optimism, and happiness can be wielded in the service of systems of power, naturalizing ableism as a matter of common sense, for example, but also because affect attends to the messiness of subjectivity construction and to the embodied quality or texture of disabled people's lives and experiences.

More recently, disability studies has approached questions of affect in relation to posthumanism and neomaterialism. For David T. Mitchell, Susan Antebi, and Sharon L. Snyder (2019), it is due time that disability studies scholars move beyond the constructivism inherent in the social model and turn back toward the materiality of the disabled bodymind and consider its active participation in the reshaping of the world. Calling on Karen Barad's (2007) understanding of matter as a "dynamic intra-active becoming," for Mitchell, Antebi, and Snyder, posthumanist approaches to disability allow scholars to attend to the agency of disability's materiality and the intra-activity between the disabled bodymind and its environment (152). Although not my primary orientation to affect, I do gesture toward this posthumanist approach specifically in chapter 3 when I discuss disabled girl handlers and their service dogs and the enmeshment of their identities and being, showing how the service dog, or the non-human animal, is integral to the disabled girls' process of *becoming* disabled.

An Archive of Ambivalence

Affect guided this project's archive. It was, in part, the ambivalent feelings generated after watching *Miss You Can Do It*, the documentary that spotlights a pageant for disabled girls, that provoked my sustained interest in seeking out other representations and self-representations of disabled girls and girlhoods. Something about the documentary *stuck* with me. I found myself unable to make quick or stock critiques of the film. The ambivalence forced me to reckon with the contradictions inherent in the film, and it also provoked me to sit with my own ambivalent feelings about the way that the figure of the disabled girl was deployed. As I have hinted at a bit, I understand now that my own experiences of girlhood and disability have long shaped what media I have interest in engaging with, and so I see the process of constructing the archive of this book as a deeply personal one. My writing "unfold[s] from the relational flux of feeling and thinking in close proximit[y] to the worlds [I] seek to understand" (Driver and Coulter 2018, 7). As I worked to refine my artifacts for this project, I always came back to the ones that, similar to *Miss You Can Do It*, stuck with me. These artifacts—documentary films, news stories, YouTube videos, TikTok videos, and television episodes—in the plainest of terms, evoked mixed feelings. There was always *something more* about the disabled girls than I could immediately get at. In viewing these ambivalent artifacts, I felt moments of elation—for example, when disabled girls' witty and nuanced ways of being-in-the-world took center stage, like when Tierney, who is five years old and is diagnosed with Spinal Muscular Atrophy Type II, describes in *Miss You Can Do It* that if she had one wish she could materialize it would be "a castle for [her] dreams." But I also felt moments of distress, when the figure of the disabled girl was insidiously, sometimes violently, deployed for the obvious purpose of shoring up ableism and anti-Blackness, such as in Jerika Bolen's story in chapter 4. Encountering this productive tension, which toggled between elation and distress, disruption and capture, guided me in both delimiting and analyzing the artifacts in the project's archive. The chapters that discuss YouTube and TikTok have even more of a personal genesis, as they come out of my own engagement with social media. The creators that populate the coming pages were, in some ways, decided upon with the help of my personal algorithm.

My ambivalence is connected to my ethical commitment to writing *Cripping Girlhood* with care. As I explore thoroughly in chapter 4 on Jerika Bolen, all too often, disabled girls are called forth in research, used as objects to forward the scholar's argument, rather than subjects who have a voice. I understand that even though this is my critique, this book cannot be divorced from the violent history and legacy of academia's extractivism. I follow the lead of other scholars of disabled childhood, like Harriet Cooper (2020) who incisively writes about the emerging field of disabled children's childhood studies, and its attempts to "reframe" the traditional mode of research about disabled children that too often is born out of adult agendas. Writing as a disabled adult who was once a disabled child, she instead asks us to consider what disabled children want to tell us about their lives. To consider the voices of disabled children, however, requires that we understand how disabled children and their voices have been "made," produced, or delimited by ideological, cultural, and psychological forces (Cooper 2020). This means that, as researchers, we must work to not only foreground the voice of the disabled child, but to defamiliarize tropes and untangle discourses and affects that have produced our understanding of "normal childhood" and "development."

My deployment of cripping girlhood as heuristic, in its duality, as well as my decision to toggle between representations and self-representations are all part of my ethical commitment to writing the disabled girl with care. I understand that this project is a project of re-presentation, so I endeavor to center, as much as possible, the disabled girls' voices and desires in each chapter. In foregrounding disabled girls as subjects and knowers, or as experts of their own experiences, I include many direct quotes in each chapter from disabled girls, themselves, even when it might get uncomfortable for the reader. One of the aims of this project is to explore the affective dimensions of our—the viewer's—relationship to disabled girls in a "post-Web 2.0" world. With that being said, there has been an emergent and growing discussion in digital media studies and digital humanities about the ethics of academically engaging with user-generated content.[6] To try and minimize harm, my archive does not include any videos that are now private and the videos that I selected to write about are oriented around educating viewers (so not produced for the sole purpose of in-community dialogue). In my analysis of comment sections, I have changed commentor usernames to pseudonyms. You might notice that this book is not one that purports generalizability. One chapter presents one disabled girl and her story, other chapters present just a few disabled girls and their stories. This affords me the time to write each disabled girl with nuance and detail. This focused approach and its slowness is intentional. I want us to stay with each disabled girl for a while. The way that Black studies scholar Christina Sharpe (2016) writes about Black girls, specifically, in her book, *In the Wake: On Blackness and Being*, has guided me during my writing. She asks so thoughtfully, "What happens when we look at and listen to [...] Black girls across time? What is made in our encounters with them? This looking makes ethical demands on the viewer; demands to imagine otherwise" (Sharpe 2016, 51). I don't include this quote to substitute "disabled girls" for "Black girls," but I include this quote as a reminder that, you, too, reader have a role to play in the project of cripping girlhood.

Cripping Girlhood does not purport to present an exhaustive study of the disabled girl. All research projects, as Cooper (2020) notes, are caught up in the desire to know. But *Cripping Girlhood* doesn't presume to know all that there is to know about the disabled girl, neither does it believe that we can know it all (and perhaps, instead, it suggests, the unknowability of "the disabled girl" as a subject position). The archive that I settled on is subjective. Many of the cultural texts that I analyze are obscure. However, the main cultural texts that I analyze in each chapter are always accompanied by other related ephemera, including comments from comment sections, film reviews, blog posts, and a GoFundMe campaign. I also situate my analyses of these artifacts within broader cultural debates and histories, for example debates about the "invisible" gendered epidemic of autism in chapter 1, debates about "free labor" and Web 2.0 in chapter 2, and the history of the service dog and its connection to US militarism in chapter 3. As an interdisciplinary project, I draw from a multitude of theoretical traditions and scholarly fields, from Black feminist theory to critical animal studies.

In analyzing representations and self-representations of disabled girlhood, I borrow qualitative methods from critical media studies, most specifically textual and discourse analysis. Although this project does not purport to do audience studies, throughout the book I engage in textual and discursive analyses of comments left by viewers in response to the representations and self-representations that I analyze. I do this to investigate more fully the meanings that viewers, themselves, ascribe to representations and self-representations of disabled girls and girlhoods. For example, in chapter 2 I look to the comment sections of Rikki Poynter and Charisse Living with Cerebral Palsy's vlogs, in chapter 3 I look to comment sections on YouTube videos and TikToks that feature disabled girl handlers and service dogs, and in chapter 4, I look to the comment section of Jerika's GoFundMe campaign.

Now a couple notes on terms. This book does not seek to define "disabled girl" or "disabled girlhood." How we understand girlhood, like disability, changes over time. It is historically, contextually, and geographically specific. For the purposes of this book, I understand girlhood as a bio-social construction and a temporal life stage. Although many consider girlhood to be a life stage that occurs up until eighteen years of age, when one becomes a legal adult, I am not so rigid in my conceptualization. Some of the disabled girls in the coming pages are over the age of eighteen, but still refer to themselves as girls. Similar to girlhood, I do not characterize disability in a definitive manner. My use of crip gestures toward this commitment, as I understand the meanings of disability and ability as shifting, contested, and open to transformation. Disability is not necessarily a self-evident category, but instead I imagine it as more akin to an affiliation, a mode of experience, and a political identity. I am inspired by Alison Kafer's (2013) use of Joan W. Scott's notion of "collective affinity" to describe disability, as "play[ing] on the identifications that have been attributed to individuals by their societies, and that have served to exclude them or subordinate them" (11). Throughout the book, I resist universalizing disability and the experience of being disabled. I attempt to always account for the different nuances of experience, both socially and corporeally, when discussing different disabilities, as the experience of and meaning we ascribe to an autistic girlhood is different than the experience of and meaning ascribed to a deaf girlhood, for example. This also affords me the opportunity to think through how ableism, as well as compulsory able-bodiedness/mindedness—as a system, according to McRuer (2006), that produces disability via the presumption that able-bodiedness is the "natural" and "normal" order of things—can look and operate differently depending on how different disabilities or diagnoses or impairments are understood and valued. As you may have noticed already, I use the identity first, "disabled girl," rather than the person first, "girl with disabilities." This is a political choice.[7] I also use the term "bodymind" rather than the singular "body" or "mind" to emphasize the fundamental imbrication of the body and mind (Price 2015). Because a multiplicity of disabled girls and girlhoods populate the text, you may also be wondering why the title is *Cripping Girlhood* rather than *Cripping Girlhoods*. My use of girlhood, as you will soon see, calls attention to the ways in which the disabled girls I analyze crip the singular, normative concept of girlhood.

Writing this book has forced me to think through disability in innumerable ways: conceptually and theoretically, of course, but also personally. After discovering Rosemarie Garland-Thomson in graduate school, as I briefly mentioned, I reflected on my own girlhood in a new light. Garland-Thomson gave me the language to think differently about my experience throughout early elementary school in speech therapy and the dread and shame I felt being pulled out of class. I was able to think about my "small ear" differently, as my mom lovingly refers to it, and my experience with mandatory hearing tests in school, and again, the shame and dread of failing them year after year.

And, now, I look back at other moments that are not distant memories but are very much still a part of my day-to-day experience. For me, the process of writing this book, in many ways, has also been a process of claiming crip.

Chapter Outline

In chapter 1, "The Futurity of Disabled Girlhood," I crip representations of disabled girls and girlhoods in two HBO documentaries from the 2010s to continue to explore a new representational politics of disabled girlhood, one that tethers the figure of the exceptional disabled girl to ideas about the future. The first documentary at the heart of my inquiry is *Miss You Can Do It* (2013), a film that chronicles eight disabled girls and their parents as they prepare for and compete in a pageant for disabled girls, called Miss You Can Do It. The second documentary, *How to Dance in Ohio* (2015), follows three autistic young women as they prepare for a spring formal that is organized as a capstone experience for participants in the Columbus, Ohio group therapy treatment program for autistics, Respons.ability Social Therapy™ (RST). I explore how both documentaries work to recuperate exceptional disabled girl subjects as disabled future girls, or valuable proto-citizens, who, rather than parasitic, are integral to the future of the United States and its purported post-ADA disability exceptionalism.

I explore how in *Miss You Can Do It*, the founder of the pageant, Abbey Curran, is constructed as the paradigmatic disabled future girl, and how her empathetic entrepreneurialism serves as an example for all viewers constructing their subjectivity under the auspices of neoliberalism. The eight young disabled pageant girls, on the other hand, are valued for their affective labor, or their ability to generate good feelings. I show how they are recapacitated as happy objects. The linchpin to the United States' ablenationalist project, the disabled pageant girls are mobilized to teach the value of disability, which the United States and its citizens are positioned as recognizing, as opposed to other "regressive" nations. Specifically, I explore the adoption story of Alina, a pageant contestant from Southern Ukraine, and show how the disabled future girl insidiously shores up the hegemony of the white, US American nuclear family as the ideal site of care for disabled children.

As a chronological complement to *Miss You Can Do It*, *How to Dance in Ohio* explores the anxiety and uncertainty of coming of age as an autistic young woman and showcases how each protagonist—through their progress with Respons.ability Social Therapy™ (RST)—is actively, successfully cultivating a future for themselves. The film's underlying message is that the psychological, emotional, and behavioral "growth" and "progress" of the three protagonists attests to the fact that exceptional autistic young women—similar to Abbey Curran in *Miss You Can Do It*—can be folded into the national imaginary as disabled future girls. They are on a path toward a better future. They, too, *can* do it. Through inviting viewers to gaze at the autistic and become a good advocate, *How to Dance in Ohio* also attempts, with urgency, to tackle the "invisible" gendered epidemic of autism that emerges at the beginning of the twenty-first century. Within the film, the protagonists are mobilized to quell national anxieties about the epidemic's unchecked growth and what that means for the future of the United States. In both documentaries, I uncover how neoliberal ideals of productivity, heteronormativity, and compulsory able-bodiedness/mindedness collide and facilitate the inclusion of certain disabled girls into the nation over others. Excluded from the visions of the future that these documentaries construct are disabled girl bodyminds that are deemed too disabled or are cast as permanently "out-of-time."

At the same time that *Miss You Can Do It* and *How to Dance in Ohio* were circulating these emergent representations of disabled girlhood, disabled girls, themselves were quietly producing and uploading videos online, broadcasting their lived reality and re-authoring the meaning of their disabled bodyminds, in effect, *cripping* girlhood. In chapter 2, "From Disabled Girlhood 2.0 to the 'Crip-fluencer,'" I shift my focus to these self-representational practices, examining the accounts of two disabled vloggers on the social media video sharing platform YouTube. Specifically, I look to deaf vlogger, Rikki Poynter, and Charisse Hogan of Charisse Living with Cerebral Palsy. Both Charisse and Rikki created their channels when they were in high school in the mid-2010s at the precipice of what cultural commentators term the "disability visibility revolution." In other words, before the ubiquitous cultural presence of disability content and disabled creators on YouTube, Instagram, Twitter, and TikTok.

In the first part of this chapter, I track Rikki and Charisse's emergence on YouTube in relation to the Web 2.0 "revolution," showing how both Rikki and Charisse in the nascent days of their respective channels carved out a new space for disabled girlhood online. From reconfiguring the able-bodied "stare," to claiming disability, Rikki and Charisse's public narrativization and visual documentation of the disabled quotidian participated in charting a new genre of video on YouTube: disability vlogs. I read their practice of disability vlogging as labor, more precisely as political labor, to reveal how in the early days of YouTube, disabled content creators, like Rikki and Charisse, re-choreographed visual and affective relations between disabled people and their non-disabled audience.

In the second part of the chapter, I examine how Rikki and Charisse cultivate intimacy between themselves and their disabled viewers through harnessing negative affects such as shame, which in turn creates digital disability intimate publics that are grounded in anti-ableist solidarity. I also show how their digital disability intimate publics are co-opted by their non-disabled viewers. Paradoxically, their knowledges and experiences become taken up as instructive and tools to rehabilitate able-bodied viewers into tolerant neoliberal citizens, which participates in securing the myth that "overcoming ableism" is a matter of individual action.

In the last part of the chapter, I map Rikki and Charisse's transition from disabled content creators, or "disabled girls 2.0," to crip-fluencers. I show how Rikki and Charisse's immaterial labor—the labor of filming, uploading, and generating intimacy with their followers—has gradually become valuable and remunerable within the influencer economy, and more precisely under the intersecting conditions of post-feminist brand culture and post-ADA neoliberal inclusionism. I explore how the girl crip-fluencer constructs a self-brand out of disability and contend that branding disability is more than simply transforming disability identity into a commodity to be bought and sold, but rather it is a process of packaging *and* circulating an affective narrative of post-ADA disability exceptionalism. As the category of disability is recruited by state *and* corporate discourses of inclusion, to tolerate and even "love" disability becomes a matter of good business.

The disabled girl's furry companion, the service dog, shares the page in chapter 3, "Domesticating Disability: Crip Girls and Their Dogs." In this chapter, I analyze representations of disabled girl handlers and their service dogs in popular media culture, juxtaposing them with representations that disabled girl handlers construct and upload themselves on the short form video app, TikTok. In the late 2010s, the service dog (and to a lesser extent their disabled handlers) captivated the national imaginary, ushering in a critical mass of popular media and academic discourse documenting and evaluating the service dog as an exceptional tool of rehabilitation. I look to an episode of the 2018 Netflix docu-series *Dogs* that centers two disabled girl handler/service dog dyads (Corrine and Rory and Meghan and Strax), and a viral story of a disabled girl handler and service dog (Bella and George), and show how these spectacularly sentimental representations of the service dog/disabled girl dyad work to reproduce an insidiously harmful rehabilitative logic that position the service dog as the "last resort" for the disabled girls' integration into the strictures of normative society. Perhaps unwittingly, these representations re-secure compulsory able-bodiedness, chronormative understandings of girlhood, and capitulate the "good dog trope." I explore the history of the service dog and its connection to the variegated legacy of the dog as a "love machine" to contextualize the ablenationalist positioning of the service dog as simultaneously a cuddly companion and capacitating tool of mobility. Ultimately, I show how the affectivity of these representations take the teeth out of disability, so to speak, through forwarding a privatized understanding of care alongside a depoliticized understanding of disability, facilitating the uneven patterning to disabled girl subjects marked for life.

On TikTok, however, the story that disabled girl handlers construct and broadcast about their relationship with their service dogs is quite different than the story constructed in popular culture and academic discourse. On service dog tok, we witness the process by which the service dog and the concomitant relationship between the service dog and the disabled handler is integral to the construction—or shaping of—the disabled girl handler's subjectivity. In other words, rather than a rehabilitative tool that facilitates a disavowal of disability, the service dog is positioned as integral to the disabled girl handler's process of *becoming* disabled. Through proclaiming their desire for and delight in their interdependent and (non-innocent) loving service dog companionships, disabled girl handlers on TikTok *crip* girlhood by upending the assumption that the desire for independence and autonomy is a "natural" part of growing up.

In the final chapter, I explore the limitations of representation and the potential dangers of visibility as a political tactic of disability inclusion. "The Crip Afterlife of Jerika Bolen" centers the story of Jerika Bolen, a disabled, Black, gay, fourteen-year-old girl who in 2016, with the support of her mother, made the decision to cease ventilator treatments, enter hospice, and die. In this chapter, I examine the national fascination with and affective attachment to the figure of Jerika and demonstrate how more than just the spectacular star of a heart-wrenching human-interest story, Jerika becomes folded into the national imaginary as a privileged subject of ablenationalism: a pedagogue of death who affectively orients her audience toward good dying as a practice of good citizenship. In the mainstream media's narrative, Jerika's decision is framed as both tragic and aspirational. Living on for Jerika is naturalized as the choice that is inconceivable: the choice of death becomes a matter of common sense and an act of love for her mother.

In analyzing online news articles that document Jerika's decision and her death, and the GoFundMe campaign that her mother, Jen Bolen organized to pay for Jerika's final wish, a last dance, I uncover how racialized discourses of pain, girlhood, and disability coalesce with neoliberal discourses of bodily sovereignty and individualism and shape Jerika's value—in death—as an exceptional disabled girl. I show how the affective attachment to Jerika's spectacular story obscures the racialized debilitation, the bodily exclusion, injury, and slow death that is endemic to the contemporary United States. Unlike Jerika, the Black girls who are not intelligible as disabled, those whose disability is non-apparent or intermittently apparent, those whose bodyminds fall away from the normative, neurotypical standard and are interpellated as disruptive or unruly, or those whose debilitation is not recognized as producing a disabled subjecthood, remain outside of the available paradigms for inclusion that a post-ADA disability rights imaginary proffers. I end with tending to the crip afterlife of Jerika Bolen, asking what would it mean for us to read Jerika's decision as an enactment of her desire, or as an act of cripping girlhood.

The coda, "Cripping Disability Visibility in Fascist Times," provides one last opportunity to think about disabled girlhood, specifically in the context of the COVID-19 pandemic. I end with the story of nineteen-year-old Grace Schara who died in 2021 after being admitted to the hospital in Appleton, Wisconsin—the same place where Jerika lived—after contracting COVID-19. Grace was unvaccinated and on her death certificate it lists COVID-19 as the cause of her death. Her parents, however, allege that Grace was killed by the hospital, as she was wrongly coded a Do Not Resuscitate (DNR). Grace's story of death, however, is mobilized by her father on a memorial website to prop up anti-vaxxer conspiracy theories and discourses of Christian nationalism and white supremacy. The coda discusses the ongoing disposability politics of the COVID-19 pandemic and calls for feminist disability studies and scholars of girlhood to wrestle with Christian nationalism and anti-vaxxer logics and how they often recruit disability and girlhood. I ask, what does cripping representations of Grace's death and her afterlife tell us about contemporary disability politics? What can only Grace tell us?

One

The Futurity of Disabled Girlhood

In 2013, HBO aired *Miss You Can Do It*, a documentary film that chronicles eight disabled girls and their parents as they prepare for and compete in a pageant for disabled girls. The pageant at the center of the film, the Miss You Can Do It pageant, was founded in 2004 by Abbey Curran. Abbey has cerebral palsy, is a former Miss Iowa USA, and was the first disabled young woman to compete in the Miss USA pageant. In toggling between different perspectives—the parents', the disabled girls', and Abbey's—the film attempts to portray the quotidian realities of twenty-first century disabled girlhood. The film also revels in the glitz and glamour of beauty pageantry. It visually dazzles with the sparking brilliance of youthful femininity. In a review for the *New York Times*, questionably titled "Challenged, but Determined to Compete for the Tiara," Neil Genzlinger (2013) describes the film as "sweet" and argues that its strength lies in its intentional showcasing of the day-to-day and the "rewards and struggles" that disabled girlhood portends for the family. On his decision to showcase a pageant for disabled girls, the director Ron Davis notes in an interview with HBO:

> I go for inspiring stories, stuff that makes you cry out of happiness. [. . .] Everyone comes to the table with notions about people with disabilities. Notions meaning fear. How do you talk to them, what do you say? [. . .] I wanted to hear about their experiences and why they do it. (2013)

Two years later, in 2015, HBO acquired the rights to distribute another documentary film about girlhood and disability, the Peabody Award-winning[1] *How to Dance in Ohio*. The film follows three autistic young women for three months leading up to a spring formal, organized as a capstone experience for participants in the Columbus, Ohio group therapy treatment program for autistics, Respons.ability Social Therapy™ (RST). Similar to the praise for *Miss You Can Do It*, news outlets laud *How to Dance in Ohio*'s focus on the "real"—the mundane, day-to-day lives of disabled young women. Rather than a sensationalized take on autism, argues *Hollywood Reporter*, the film presents a refreshing portrayal of autistic young women and their families, where "no one gets bullied, no one is a savant, and there's no mention of the debate around vaccines" (Felperin 2015). The review goes on to say that unlike other documentaries about autism, *How to Dance in Ohio* is "heartening" because it "accentuates the positive so much" (Felperin 2015). The *New York Times* goes so far as to characterize the film in contradistinction to the ubiquitous human-interest stories that paint touching pictures of the "special needs child"[2] who scores a touchdown or is crowned prom queen. They write that the "piercing documentary" may seem like a "variation on this evening-news staple," but, the director and producer Alexandra Shiva, "goes so much deeper [and] though it too has feel-good moments, ultimately paints a portrait of young people whose futures are full of anxiety and uncertainty" (Genzlinger 2015). As Shiva clarifies, her desire with *How to Dance in Ohio* was to create "some sort of bridge of understanding" (Genzlinger 2015).

Curiously, the narratives that both documentaries construct about disabled girlhood are not overwritten by tragedy or pity. And although the documentaries are saturated in and generate *good* feelings, like happiness, optimism, and hope, they are not one-dimensional, inspirational accounts of overcoming disability. This chapter explores how *Miss You Can Do It* and *How to Dance in Ohio* exemplify a new representational politics of disabled girlhood, one that I began to unravel in the previous chapter. Similar to how the figures of disabled girls in the "Love Has No Labels" campaign are mobilized, *Miss You Can Do It* and *How to Dance in Ohio* work to recuperate the disabled girl subject as a valuable proto-citizen, and, rather than parasitic, position her as integral to the future of the United States.

My exploration of what these two documentaries have to say about contemporary disabled girls and girlhoods is animated by Alison Kafer's (2013) discussion about the disabled child. As queer theorists remind us, the child is a "dense site of meaning" (Dyer 2017, 291) that is often tied to notions of futurity (Berlant 1997; Edelman 2004; Berlant 2011). Recall Lee Edelman's (2004) oft quoted theorization: "the Child has come to embody for us the telos of the social order" (11). The child is the "preeminent emblem of the motivating end," moving us forward toward better futures (Edelman 2004, 13). For Kafer (2013), however, the child that Edelman describes is necessarily white and non-disabled. In an ableist society, the disabled child becomes a symbol of an undesired future. This is because, as Kafer (2013) reasons, "disability is [normatively] conceptualized as a terrible unending tragedy," so, "any future that includes disability can only [be imagined as] a future to avoid" (2). This chapter, wonders, however, what happens when certain disabled children, namely disabled girls, are brought into visions of the future? And, what do these visions of the future that include disabled girls look like? The title, "the futurity of disabled girlhood," gestures toward these two related inquiries.

It is telling that both Davis and Shiva emphasize the pedagogical merit of their documentaries. As Shiva specifically articulates, one of the goals of *How to Dance in Ohio* is to "generate an understanding of empathy among mainstream viewers" (Felperin 2015). The documentaries are explicitly positioned as re-orientation devices, not only do they teach contemporary viewers about disability, but also how to *feel* about disability. This makes sense, as documentary film has long been the dominant representational mode of disability, attempting to define and give meaning to disability (Brylla and Hughes 2017; Ben Ayoun 2021). Many of film's earliest experiments, according to Lisa Cartwright (1995), directly emerge from the "fascination with visibility that marked [. . .] nineteenth century Western science," and the desire to see, know, and control the human body (87). As such, disability documentary historically—and most specifically that which has been created by non-disabled filmmakers—has often tended toward the objectification of the disabled body by way of a medicalized gaze, or through practices of "enfreakment," wherein the disabled person's impairment becomes the "target for a [. . .] ridding of the existential fears and fantasies of non-disabled people" (Hevey 2013, 445). Somewhat more optimistically, Mitchell and Snyder (2015) point out that documentary can also offer the potential to re-orient non-disabled viewers toward a capacious and less pathologized understanding of disability, as perhaps Davis and Shiva gesture toward in interviews about *Miss You Can Do It* and *How to Dance in Ohio*.

In what follows, I examine how *Miss You Can Do It* and *How to Dance in Ohio*, separately and in conjunction, weave a complex narrative about contemporary disabled girlhood and the disabled girl's role in the stories we tell about post-Americans with Disabilities Act (ADA) United States. I show how both documentaries attempt to recuperate disabled girls as exceptional proto-citizens, or disabled "future girls," privileged disabled subjects who have been deemed productive, valuable, and integral to the future of the United States and its purported post-ADA disability exceptionalism. In both documentaries, anxieties about the future that disability portends for the disabled girl protagonists, their families, and the nation are continually managed by the disabled girl, herself. She is constructed as a resilient and resourceful subject, an object of happiness and optimism, and a pedagogical figure who has much to teach us about how to manage the precarious reality of our own futures. Specifically, in *Miss You Can Do It*, Abbey Curran, the founder of the Miss You Can Do It pageant, is constructed as the quintessential disabled future girl. She is lauded for her ability to take her future into her own hands and seize her goals while giving back to her community. The young pageant girls, as the judges in the pageant remark, have much to learn from Abbey. Although they are too young to enter the labor market, or really take their futures into their own hands as such, the documentary constructs the eight pageant contestants as happy objects, valued for their affective labor, or their ability to generate good feelings. The young pageant girls are mobilized within the space of the documentary to teach the value of disability, which the United States and its citizens are positioned as recognizing, in effect becoming the linchpin to the United States' ablenationalist project. Similarly, *How to Dance in Ohio* constructs its disabled young women protagonists as autistic future girls. The documentary explores the anxiety and uncertainty of coming of age as autistic young women and showcases how each protagonist—through their progress with Respons.ability Social Therapy™ (RST)—successfully cultivates a future for themselves. In raising awareness and serving as a "bridge of understanding," *How to Dance in Ohio* also attempts to tackle the "invisible" gendered epidemic of autism. The autistic future girl protagonists are mobilized in the film to quell national anxieties about the epidemic's unchecked growth and what that means for the future of the United States.

However, in *cripping* representations of disabled girlhood in both documentaries, I uncover how neoliberal rationality, heteronormativity, and compulsory able-bodiedness/mindedness facilitate the inclusion of certain disabled girls into the national imaginary over others. Not all disabled girls can become disabled future girls, and those that do must assimilate into heteronormative gender roles and perform proper affectivity. Some disabled girl bodyminds are necessarily excluded from the visions of the future that these documentaries construct: those who are deemed too disabled or are cast as permanently "out-of-time."

Before I move on to my analysis of *Miss You Can Do It*, it is important to point out that *Miss You Can Do It* and *How to Dance in Ohio* are part of a larger ground swell of disability documentary, and specifically documentary that explores the intersection of disability, childhood, and youth, ushered in at the beginning of the twenty-first century. Global in scope, these films range from the experimental, such as the 2008 Canadian documentary *Antoine* that chronicles the real and imagined life of Antoine Houang, a five-year-old blind boy, to the observational, such as *Body and Soul (De Corpo e Alma)*, a 2010 Mozambican documentary that chronicles the day-to-day trials and tribulations of three physically disabled young Mozambicans. One could argue that in the United States, HBO led the charge, producing and acquiring a notable repertoire of documentaries about disability, childhood, and youth; for example, *I Have Tourette's, But Tourette's Doesn't Have Me* (2005); *Autism: The Musical* (2007); *I Can't Do This, But I CAN Do That* (2010); and, *Life According to Sam* (2013).

It is no coincidence that both documentaries that are at the heart of this chapter were produced and/or acquired by HBO. Sheila Nevins, the former president of HBO Documentary Films (2004–2017) notes that during her tenure she was most interested in producing and acquiring films that showcase the human struggle and reflect "the challenges of surviving a difficult world" (Mascaro 2008, 241). Many of her documentaries "focus heavily on those that are living with disabilities," because, according to Nevins, "being born with a disability [...] puts people in crises and races of their own" (Mascaro 2008, 241). One could read this as an incitement of "narrative prosthesis," as one way Nevins appears to mobilize disability is as a metaphoric stand-in for the "human struggle" (Mitchell and Snyder 2000). There is also a personal catalyst for her focus on disability. In an interview with her alma mater, Barnard College, Nevins spoke of witnessing her mother's experience living with a limb difference. She recalls one incident when her mother was once angrily asked to cover up her arm in a café. Nevins said that this "moment of concealment caused her great pain and thus inspired her to make it her life's mission to show disabilities instead of hide them" (Liebman 2016).

"Accomplishment Begins with Two Words, I'll Try": The Disabled Future Girl

Miss You Can Do It opens sonically with the uplifting rustic twang of a clawhammer banjo melody, as a waving American flag quickly pulls away to reveal the idyllic Midwestern town of Kewanee, Illinois. Within the first minute of the film, the viewer is introduced to Abbey Curran, the founder of the Miss You Can Do It pageant. Putting on make-up and looking at her reflection in a vanity, she remarks assuredly:

Accomplishment begins with two words: I'll try. I mean, seriously, what is the use of living if you don't have a dream, or you don't have hope? And I knew that there was something better in my life than just being a student, or just being a girl from Kewanee—that eventually, um, something had to be magnificent 'cause I think we are all sent here for a reason or a purpose.

It is clear that the Miss You Can Do It pageant—described as an exceptionally inclusive space for girls of all "different disabilities and nationalities"—is Abbey's purpose, born out of the desire to, as she articulates, "pass the dream onto someone else."

Diagnosed with cerebral palsy as a child, Abbey started competing in pageants at age sixteen. In 2008, she was the first disabled young woman to compete in the Miss USA pageant after being crowned Miss Iowa. Although CP impedes her ability to walk in pageants without an escort, she positions her disability as something that has driven her to participate in pageants, not necessarily something that has limited her. Abbey explains that she was driven to do pageants because it is "something different, maybe, for a girl with a physical disability. We also want to be looked at as beautiful [. . .] and accomplished." She recounts that her desire to participate in pageants galvanized after a conversation with another disabled girl who felt that the severity of her disability prevented her from competing. Evoking the rhetoric of overcoming, she notes that "being born with cerebral palsy was definitely something that I had to overcome. While others saw me as different, I simply saw myself as having more challenges."

The documentary constructs Abbey as the paradigmatic disabled future girl, a kind of young woman, who, according to Anita Harris (2004) is lauded for her confidence, gumption, and willingness to "take charge of her life, seize chances, and achieve her goals" (1). One might deem the disabled future girl an ontological impossibility, as disability has historically signaled a future foreclosed, or, in Alison Kafer's (2013) words, a "future no one wants" because it is one that "bears too many traces of the ills of the present to be desirable" (2). But, as I began to discuss in the previous chapter, in post-ADA times, certain disabled bodyminds have become newly valuable and available for incorporation and inclusion into late modern national imaginaries and neoliberal capitalist economies. Abbey is constructed as one of the privileged few, capacitated as an "able-disabled" subject that is self-enterprising and entrepreneurial. She is held up as an example of the enduring potential that all disabled individuals possess to "overcome" the purported limitations of disability to "fit into normal society" (Titchkosky 2003, 527–30). Despite the hesitations of her parents, Abbey attended and graduated college and has successfully entered the labor market through founding the Miss You Can Do It pageant (which is also a non-profit organization). What is most interesting is that the creation of the Miss You Can Do It pageant comes out of her disabled knowledge and experience—that which has, for many, been historically deemed valueless. The pageant takes disability as its raw material and generates value, both in a financial and affective sense, for various stakeholders (including the viewer). Throughout the film, Abbey is celebrated for her productivity, her innovativeness, and her ability to self-manage, just as the non-disabled future girl is lauded in Harris's (2004) formulation.

Emphasized in these opening scenes is not only Abbey's perseverance, as she explains she competed countless times before winning a crown, but also her benevolence—her desire to pass the dream on to someone else. Implicitly we understand that this "someone else" is another disabled girl. Jodi Melamed (2011) argues that neoliberal multiculturalism privileges those subjects who "learn to do good, to feed the poor, to uplift women, [and] learn to play their parts in the civilizing/disqualifying regimes" (45). Through the creation of the pageant, as an endeavor of "uplift," Abbey becomes luminous—not only does she literally shimmer throughout the documentary—but she is narratively put under a spotlight and interpellated into the cultural imaginary as a "metaphor for social mobility and social change" (Ringrose 2007, 472). The prominence of the flag in the opening scene visually signals to the viewer that Abbey's story, and concomitantly the story of the Miss You Can Do It pageant, is not just an individual tale of triumph, but it has significance to how we imagine the nation and what we understand about what it means to be an American in post-ADA times.

Abbey's status as a pageant queen is significant, as it illustrates how the recuperation of disabled girls as disabled future girls involves the ossification of ideal norms of heteronormative gender, specifically what Amanda Apgar (2023) terms "compulsory hetero-ablebodiedness." Apgar (2023) argues that binary gender is always premised on the proper enactment of able-bodiedness/mindedness (and as McRuer reminds us, heterosexuality) and that the "presence of disability may disrupt the discursive and/or material structures by which gender is made intelligible—through atypical body shape, movements, or speech" (119). If one understands gender as a product of citational practices—the reiterative enactments of gender norms—then the disabled bodymind is always at risk of gender failure via the literal inability to enact or *do* gender. Disability, then, is imagined as a threat to living an ordinary life and cultivating a future, not only because of impairment itself, but because impairment can reveal the unnaturalness of gender, "thereby risking its intelligibility" (Apgar 2023, 119). Immediately as the documentary opens, the viewer sees Abbey sitting at a vanity putting on make-up—literally *doing* a gendered ritual of normative femininity, visually pushing back against the dominant understanding of disabled women and girls as non-feminine, non-sexual, non-reproductive, or even permanently infantilized (Siebers 2008; Mollow 2012). Abbey's triumph, being crowned Miss Iowa and competing as the first disabled young woman in the Miss USA pageant, signals her success *doing* (and perhaps even mastering) gender.

Her successful assimilation as a disabled subject into normative ideals of young womanhood must also be understood as it is connected to dominant, or "chrononormative," understandings of development (Freeman 2010). Developmental progress—"becoming adult"—is tied to a conceptualization of "growing up" that presupposes a linear understanding of time and requires proper temporalization of bodyminds (toward maximum efficiency). For girls, growing up is understood as march forward from the dependence of girlhood to the independence of womanhood, defined by "marriage and reproduction," and in neoliberal times, productivity (Kafer 2013, 35).

At the end of the film, after the winner is crowned the announcer praises Abbey for creating a "special event" for disabled girls and expounds:

> I've always thought, if I was a parent, and one day the doctor comes up to me and tells me that I have a special child, I know I could've handled that, because I love these special, special children. But when you were told you had a special child, did you think about things such as maybe there wouldn't be too many sports for this child. Maybe—maybe there wouldn't be a wedding. Maybe there wouldn't be a prom. I don't know. But we're going to make the most of it.

The judge's remarks reflect and naturalize feelings of disappointment and loss that saturate the ableist assumption that to have a disabled child, or a disabled girl in this case, is to have a child with no future. However, Abbey's narrative—its successful alignment with the dominant understanding of girl-becoming-woman's chrononormative temporality—ultimately signals the possibility of a future for disabled girls that disability is presumed to foreclose. And if other disabled girls can't achieve that future, they at least have a space and a literal stage, provided by Abbey and her Miss You Can Do It pageant, to act out a futurity that once was assumed to be inconceivable.

The representation of Abbey's life and experiences, and her story of "overcoming," not only offers a possibility model for other disabled girls, but it also compels non-disabled viewers to imagine their own subjectivities and lives as works in progress, or as projects that require consistent evaluation. In asking, "what's the use of living if you don't have a dream," she demands that the viewer evaluate their own life project and adjust accordingly. If she can do it, why can't I? Her disability, rather than being positioned as an impediment to her future girl status, becomes what makes her stand out as exceptional, as a subject worth listening to and aspiring to be like. Within the space of the documentary, Abbey becomes a powerful representational symbol.

Although the construction of Abbey as a disabled future girl serves to re-orient the non-disabled viewer toward disability as something more than a pathologized or parasitic existence, in emphasizing Abbey's extraordinary and individual capacity, attitude, and perseverance, the film works to cover over the structural realities that ableism portends. In one scene where she is driving her adapted car, tricked out with a vanity license plate (MISS IWA 8) and equipped with a steering wheel spinner knob and a handbrake, she remarks that when people hear that she has cerebral palsy, they automatically think that she is going to encounter "lifelong challenges." This is true, she explains, but it is not necessarily because of her impairment, like many people intimate. For her, what is most difficult to contend with are the stares, judgements, and low expectations that are foisted upon her. Abbey calls out the low standards that ableist culture projects onto disabled people, but in a post-ADA twist, the film marshals Abbey's experience as a disabled young woman to orient the viewer toward the neoliberal and post-feminist myth that hard work, determination, confidence, and perseverance is key to a successful and hopeful disability future.

Abbey's whiteness, her class privilege, her citizenship status, her beauty, and the extent to which her non-normative bodymind can approximate norms of ability, both in terms of the body and mind, are all things that are never really mentioned in *Miss You Can Do It*. According to Mitchell and Snyder (2015),

> Ablenationalist inclusion models involve the treatment of disabled people as exceptional bodies in ways that further valorize able-bodied norms as universally desirable and as the naturalized qualifications of fully capacitated citizenship to which others inevitably aspire. (44–45)

In other words, the inclusion of a privileged minority of disabled subjects—the "able-disabled"—into the nation operates to further mark out and exclude those disabled subjects who are unable to "approximate historically specific expectations of normalcy" (Mitchell and Snyder 2015, 2). There is no mention of the structural and corporeal barriers to access in terms of Abbey's dream—how expensive it is to participate in pageants, what role the "mildness" of Abbey's CP (as the film emphasizes repeatedly) played in her ability to participate, and how the privilege afforded by her whiteness and normative attractiveness aided in her success.

Abbey symbolizes what the disabled pageant girls *could* become. The pageant judges and parents consistently remark that she is "good example" for the disabled pageant girls. As one pageant judge specifically states, "Abbey can show these girls that the sky's the limit. And, ultimately, you can overcome whatever obstacles life might throw your way and do whatever you want to do." Her success is attributed to sheer will power, her big heart, and her ability to step out of her comfort zone and take a risk. This is framed as something anyone can do; thus, securing the myth that success is out there and available to all. She articulates this as such in a speech near the end of the film:

> This pageant is based off my life, in hopes of giving these beautiful ladies fire, determination, and the realization of if they run towards their dreams, they will get there. All they need is someone to push them, someone to believe in them, and someone to simply say, you can do it.

Rather than a socio-political issue or political identity, Abbey's narrative works to individualize disability. Disability is abstracted into a personal (reflexive biographical) project that disabled people must consistently work on and through and that non-disabled people are primed to learn from.

The Disabled Girl as Happy Object

As Abbey's story unfolds, it becomes clear that she is not only constructed as a disabled future girl—a possibility model for all disabled girls—, but her narrative is an affective template for the disabled pageant girls that the film chronicles. Abbey and the disabled pageant girls are each introduced first through the lens of their parents, who recount a harrowing birth and diagnosis story, replete with visuals of the disabled pageant girls as babies hospitalized and hooked up to various monitors. Abbey's story includes footage of grainy childhood home movies. Her parents, like the others throughout the film, recount that they did not know what to expect from their daughter's life post-diagnosis. Evoking a common adage said by parents of disabled children, they remark, "Nobody ever told us what her life would be like. You know, what we could expect." Fantasies of their daughter's future are shattered by a disability diagnosis. However, the film does not dwell in the "bad" feelings generated by the trouble of disability (anxiety, nervousness, grief, betrayal). Instead, each girls' narrative goes on to center their determination, bubbliness, and youthful sparkle as reprieve from the bad feelings, potential crises, and foreclosed futures that disability traditionally evokes. Throughout the film, the young disabled pageant girls generate good feelings, most explicitly happiness, for both the viewer and the people they encounter within the documentary itself.

The representation of the winner of Miss You Can Do It, seven-year-old Delaney illustrates the peculiar process by which the young disabled pageant girls are recapacitated into and circulate the documentary as happy objects. Like Abbey and the other young pageant girls, Delaney is constructed through discourses of overcoming, determination, and courage. As the winner of the pageant, she is exceptionalized, positioned as *the* miss you can do it, or as the ideal young disabled girl proto-citizen subject. Explaining how they choose the winner, Abbey and the judges state that it is "not about the outfits" or "about the hair." Rather, it is "about the girl on the inside." They elaborate that they "want the girl who is just so happy, so excited, who is truly going to make a difference in her life [and a] difference in other people's lives." Ultimately, they are "looking for the biggest heart and the most sparkle, and someone to represent all the disabled girls."

When we are first introduced to Delaney, her parents note that she gets frustrated at times because of her "lack of independence"; she is "strong willed" and wants to do everything herself. Delaney has a spastic form of cerebral palsy, which causes her muscles to stiffen and cross, affecting her mobility. Her mother explains that it is "almost like she is fighting herself." However, her parents emphasize the fact that she does not "show" her frustration: "She is the happiest little girl, and very rarely do we get to see that point where she is really angry at things. She just tries no matter what—it doesn't matter if it takes fifteen times to get her shoes tied." The juxtaposed scene that forms the backdrop to this description of Delaney is a visual representation of her "strong will" and "independence." First, we see Delaney, with her blonde hair in a bouncy side ponytail, confidently stroll into the interview room holding on to her walker for balance. Delaney smiles and the judges greet her enthusiastically. The scene then abruptly cuts to baby Delaney in pigtails practicing walking with a gait trainer. This scene is comprised of two cells, the first is a zoomed-out view, where the viewer can see Delaney in her entirety and a woman who is guiding her. The second is a zoomed-in view, abstracting her disabled body through closely spotlighting her impairment. We see Delaney's limb's cross as she shakily takes steps forward. The scene transitions back to present day Delaney, and as she attentively answers questions from the judges, she attempts to navigate herself into a chair.

The juxtaposition of scenes works to contain anxious or bad feelings by highlighting Delaney's developmental achievements. Her strong will and capacity for hard work is visualized in the difference between shaky baby Delaney's slow movement forward and bouncy girl Delaney's ability to glide into the room and attempt to sit herself in a chair. Delaney captivates the judges with her eloquent responses to their questions and her general excitement for the pageant. The judges are affected by her effervescence, and they bombard her with more questions while laughing and smiling. In contradistinction to the cultural history of disgust, pity, and fear that disabled people have most often been associated with, and even more so, the tragedy and grief that stick to disabled children, within the space of the interview, Delaney circulates joy and delight (Hughes 2012). Proximity to Delaney is pleasurable for the judges.

Delaney is a happy object. According to Sara Ahmed (2010), happy objects are simply objects—not limited to physical and material things, but also values, aspirations, and practices, that direct us toward happiness. Happiness, she clarifies, "involves affect (to be happy is to be affected by something), intentionality (to be happy is to be happy about something), and evaluation or judgment (to be happy about something makes something good)" (Ahmed 2010, 21). Happiness is a promise that orients us toward some things (those that cause pleasure and are hence deemed "good") over others. Certain bodies, more than others, bear the promise of happiness. Calling on Black, feminist, and queer scholars on the political uses of happiness to justify oppression, Ahmed (2010) points out that happiness has historically been wielded as a technology of governance, one that often "redescribe[s] social norms as social goods" (2). Connecting happiness to disability, Kelly Fritsch (2013) writes about how positive affects structure the contemporary production of disability: from the hope that cure demands to the inspiration of overcoming. As one example, she writes that disability objects, like the International Symbol of Access (ISA) have become a site of "affective happiness within neoliberalism," functioning to contain and manage the "problem" of disability through circulating good feelings of "having

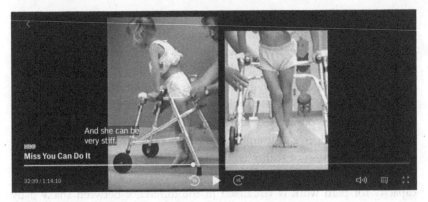

Figure 1. Delaney using a gait trainer (*Miss You Can Do It* 2013)

done our duty for the disabled" (144). In this scenario, disability "appears to disappear," as good feelings distract, individualize, and depoliticize the "problem" of disability or, specifically, in this case, the latent inaccessibility of the built environment (Fritsch 2013, 145).

As a happy object, Delaney performs affective labor that is valuable, and this labor provides the conditions of possibility for her intelligibility as a disabled future girl. She orients the judges and viewers toward disability, but it is toward a specific idea of what disability, and specifically disabled girlhood, looks like. Delaney is represented as excited, as optimistic, as eloquent, and as hard working. Through the affective labor of happiness, she contains the anxiety of disability, orienting judges and viewers toward disability as it is conceptualized through these positive affects. Rather than represented through a vision of a tragic future, she is imagined as actively transforming the future, positioned as someone who will "make a difference." Here we see how happiness dovetails with ideas about ability, neoliberal rationality, and normative ideas of futurity, specifically as they relate to discourses of productivity and self-betterment. As Apgar (2023) argues, "the imperative to improve upon the present is refracted through neoliberal injunctions for individualism, self-management, self-care, and self-improvement, which are 'rationalized as an investment in the self towards a more normal, if not better, future'" (8). Returning to the visualization of Delaney's developmental progress—the juxtaposition of baby Delaney and present-day Delaney—we can read this as a metonym for a grander vision. It signals the potential promise of a futurity—if one works hard enough—that has "improved upon the present" (Apgar 2023, 8). As a disabled future girl, Delaney performs representational labor as an affective pedagogue of ideal neoliberal citizenship, teaching the viewers that they *too* can (and should) do it.

However, the subtle contrast between the atmosphere of Delaney and Kenna's interview, a pageant girl who has an intellectual disability, makes clear how the construction of the disabled future girl unwittingly relies on and reproduces the logic of compulsory able-mindedness. We first meet Kenna and her family in their big suburban backyard, where they are playing a rousing game of baseball. Kenna's dad describes their family as "happy-go-lucky," as a family who "works hard, has fun, and enjoys their kids." Kenna and her sister Tasha, both of whom are competing in the pageant, are disabled. Tasha is fourteen and has cerebral palsy, and Kenna is seven and her disability is never made completely clear, but her parents characterize her disability in terms of "comprehension." She asks the same question over and over, they note, and they have given her the nickname "repeater" because she repeats most things that she hears. Kenna's interview is far less conversational than Delaney's. She says "hi" and answers "yes" to a couple of the judges' questions. During the interview the camera cuts to Abbey, who states that "kids who can't speak obviously have a harder time. It's difficult because you do fall in love with the girl who is going to talk your ear off." Kenna's inability to talk someone's "ear off" positions her as unable to "represent all the disabled girls," as potentially "unable to make a difference."

Her disability positions her as *too* disabled; she is figured as permanently outside a narrative of collective progress toward "better more perfect" lives and bodyminds (Apgar 2023, 37). Intellectual disability has a robust history of being linked with childhood; in the nineteenth century, people classified as "idiots were seen as remain[ing] at an early stage of development" (Carlson 2010, 30). Intellectual disability is thus often tethered to discourses of infantilization, and the intellectually disabled white girl is often imagined as an eternal child (Desjardins 2012). Kenna is young and time rich. But, because of the "severeness" of her intellectual disability, she is cast as always, already outside of chrononormative understandings of development—of progress—that insidiously undergird the construction of the disabled future girl. Because chrononormativity demands properly temporalized bodyminds, or at least ones that can approximate or attempt a smooth movement along a linear telos of events: birth, schooling, labor, marriage, reproduction, and death, Kenna's future is not as readily apparent as Delaney's. Instead, what viewers witness is the unrelenting, "permanent non-futurity" of intellectual disabilities (Apgar 2023, 43).

The Disabled Girl as the Linchpin of the Future Family

The disabled girls' happy object status also functions within the space of the documentary to shore up an ablenationalist narrative that constructs the United States as exceptionally inclusive, characterized as a nation where there is a future for disabled children. We see this in the representation of the Hollis family and their story about the journey adopting one of their daughters Alina, a disabled girl from Southern Ukraine. The viewer is first introduced to Alina's sister, Margaret (Meg), a shy girl with Down syndrome, in her interview with the judges. We see Meg's shyness dissipate as the judges start playing a game of peek-a-boo with her. The documentary lingers in this pleasurable moment, and the judges and Meg laugh together while playing the game. The documentary then shifts to Elmwood, Illinois, where a suburban house sits squarely in the frame. A family is playing t-ball in lush, green grass, and we see that a little girl is up to bat. The carefree, playful mood evoked by this American family's summer ritual quickly dissipates as we hear Anne, the matriarch, begin to recount the story of the birth of her first daughter:

> Originally, they thought they heard a heart condition, so they took her to evaluate her. About two hours later the doctors came in and said that they had great news that the heart condition that they suspected wasn't there. We were very excited about that. And I will never forget what the resident said: 'You guys really dodged a bullet—most babies with Down syndrome have a heart condition.' And that was the first time anybody had even mentioned those words to us. I remember in those moments being completely devastated and thinking about all the things that I thought I wouldn't have. One of the things that I remember from that day [is that someone] said 'remember it's okay to grieve the child that you thought you were going to have. Because in grieving that it helps you celebrate the one you have been given.' It's been an amazing gift, but we did not know she was coming with this extra chromosome.

After the emotional recounting of Meg's "devastating" diagnosis, her story diverges from the other disabled girls in the documentary, with Anne explaining that Meg's disability prompted a decision to adopt another girl with Down syndrome. She explains that she wanted to have a "constant" for Meg because she knew that "with the developmental delay, and as Meg got to be twelve, and maybe wouldn't be invited to every sleepover" she would "be sad for her." For the Hollis family, the crisis of having an unexpectedly disabled girl, and the attendant crisis of the girl's bleak future is assuaged through the Inter-Country Adoption (ICA) of Alina.

ICA as a practice has grown exponentially in the late twentieth and early twenty-first century (Eng 2003, 2006; Marre and Briggs 2009; Raffety 2019). David Eng (2003) observes that ICA has "become a popular and viable option for [. . .] hetero[normative] couples seeking to (re)consolidate and (re)occupy" conventional family structures (1). Overwhelmingly, the economy of ICA is structured by the transnational flow of children, disabled and non-disabled alike, from poor countries to wealthy (most often Western) countries and families. Discussing the global disability politics of ICA, Erin Raffety (2019) builds on Eng (2003) and contends that ICA has become a neoliberal tool for the reproduction and maintenance of the white, middle-class, heteronormative, and *ableist* nuclear family (n.p.). The practice perpetuates moral, social, and economic hierarchies between the West and "abroad through a marginalizing care of the Other" (Raffety 2019, n.p.).

In their search for a child with Down syndrome, Anne and Todd participate in a "rehabilitative mission" on behalf of the West (Rafferty 2019). Recounting the process of ICA, Anne and Todd explain that when they contacted an international Down syndrome adoption agency, they did not care where in the world the little girl came from; they just wanted to provide Meg with a sister of the same age. Specifically, they could not "look at the list and pick," so Todd and Anne agreed to start with the first little girl, and "if that didn't work out, then [they] would go to number two." An article in *The State-Journal Register*, "Adoption Completes Family Touched by Down Syndrome," elaborates a bit more on the Hollis' family search for a sister for Meg. The idea to adopt a child with Down syndrome, allegedly "became a mission when [Anne and Todd] learned that children with developmental disabilities and no mother or father usually are placed in an institution if not adopted by age 4. It's a formula for a short, unhappy life" (Hilyard 2009). In the article, Todd explains,

> We got involved with Reece's Rainbow (a self-described international Down syndrome orphan ministry), and they showed us pictures of 20 kids that were available for adoption and said if we didn't see one we wanted, they'd show us 20 more, then 20 more after that. [. . .] Alina was the first one we saw. (Hilyard 2009)

Figure 2. Alina in Ukrainian orphanage (*Miss You Can Do It* 2013)

Within Anne and Todd's narrative, the "orphan child with Down syndrome" is abstracted, objectified, and rendered future-less, and Anne and Todd, and the broader nation of the United States, are positioned as the child's saviors in waiting. This narrative extends "child saving discourse" that both maintains moral hierarchies between the (implicitly white and Christian) West and the "rest" and conceals a tacit ableism that perpetuates disabled children as always, already helpless and in need of rescue (Raffety 2019, n.p.). The abandonment and disposability of disabled subjects, specifically children, is positioned as a problem "out there" and not within the spatial geography of the United States.

As saviors, Anne and Todd are further constructed throughout the documentary as unwaveringly American vis-à-vis their valuation of disabled children, unlike Ukraine, who, as a country, is positioned as "backwards" vis-à-vis their disability politics. The visual juxtaposition of the sunny, idyllic Hollis suburban backyard with the cold, dilapidated Ukrainian institution for disabled children is an aesthetic choice made by the producers to affectively elicit sympathy and a feeling of superiority from the non-disabled and presumably American audience. The two sites function mimetically as stand-ins for *Ukraine* and the *United States*, which operates to shore up US exceptionalism through a fantasy of American disability benevolence. The United States is figured as generous and, in some ways, the "fixer" as Mitchell and Snyder (2016, 53) would posit, for those who geopolitically and morally "lag behind" its post-ADA achievements in disability valuation. After the scene with the institution, Anne recounts that the "worker at the orphanage said to [her], 'You stupid Americans, you have all these perfect kids to pick, and you pick this one of no value, you stupid Americans.'" Todd adds, "They don't understand why you're in their country to adopt this child who has no worth in their eyes." The camera shifts back to Anne, and with tears welling in her eyes, she says, "She's perfect in her spirit, and that's what we've always focused on." Alina is positioned as available for recapacitation as an exceptional and thus valuable disabled girl subject. Through her "perfect spirit" she is a happy object for Meg and her parents alike. With intervention, she is able to be brought forward in time: into the ablenationalist modernity of the United States in order to be given a chance at a disability future. We see this made even more clear in a scene from the pageant, wherein on the glittery stage a judge helps Alina explain to the audience that when she was adopted, she "left several friends in the orphanage" and that she wishes that all her friends could find "loving families because any[one] who is differently abled did not have a good future waiting for them" in Ukraine. This narrative both presumes and perpetuates that fantasy that a disability inclusion or integration project "at home" in the United States is one that is "complete" (Mitchell and Snyder 2016, 49).

Anne and Todd explain that they have faced some pushback "at home" with their choice to adopt a child, who, like Meg, has Down syndrome; to some of their family members they are "crazy," but to others, they are "saints." Anne clarifies that they are neither crazy, nor saints, and that "anybody could do it, it's whether or not you choose to." Implicitly, the construction of Anne and Todd as average yet exceptional parents reproduces a "class-based model of appropriate and 'deserving' parenthood" which obfuscates structural barriers to adopting and parenting disabled children under the guise of individual choice (Cheney 2014, 257). Their narrative also serves to shore up, in Eng's (2006) words, the "psychic boundaries of the white middle-class nuclear family—guaranteeing its social and ideological integrity as well as its affective ideals" (56–57). In some ways, the adoption of Alina is positioned as what holds the family together. Or, more precisely, according to the title of the article in *The State-Journal Register*, it "completes" the Hollis family. The ICA of Alina resecures the family as a "happy object," in that the family, as Ahmed (2010) argues is itself, "a myth of happiness, of where and how happiness takes place, and a powerful legislative device, a way of distributing time, energy, and resources" (45). Through the Hollis family's narrative, the disabled girl comes to symbolize the United States' purported tolerance of disability as well as shores up the hegemony of the white, US American nuclear family as the ideal site of care for disabled children.

The final point I want to make in relation to the Hollis family's narrative is about the two sons, Noah and Caleb, and how both Alina and Meg, as happy objects, are framed as rehabilitating their brothers from a state of passive, innocent ignorance about disability to advocates of tolerance for their sisters. Through their parents' retelling of a horrific hate crime, it becomes clear that Alina and Meg occupy the position of a compliant disabled body in service of their brothers' flexibility. This use of flexible refers to what Robert McRuer (2006) describes as the flexible subject of late modernity, or a subject who "tolerates a certain amount of queerness" and can weather subjective crises (12). Anne and Todd explain that their house and car were recently vandalized, spray painted with ableist phrases (e.g., "get outta town retards" and "retodds"). Although the girls were too young to read and understand the hate-speech, the boys, Noah and Caleb, could read, and they had to explain to them that "retard is not a good word. People out there might not like your sisters. Because of ignorance, because they don't like people who are different," and that the boys "might have to stick up for [their] sisters one day." This scene ends with both parents crying in the middle of the frame; they explain that after this incident, they "realize[d] how much better Noah and Caleb are because of Meg and Alina. [They] couldn't have raised them to be that great without them. So the benefits of being a parent—just realizing how strong they are going to be—it makes it worthwhile."

We see here that in the framing of Meg and Alina as "gifts" to the family, disability, rather than being understood as a burden, is transformed into something that is valuable because it "serve[s] as a catalyst [. . .] for others' self-improvement" (Apgar 2023, 85). The disabled girl bodymind is recuperated as "productive" in an economic sense because of how "disability functions as the 'price' for others' personal enrichment" (Apgar 2023, 85). Therefore, disability's inherent value is obscured, and instead it is measured in relation to the growth of Noah's and Caleb's (and their parents') "spiritual or moral standing" (Apgar 2023, 84). After the incident, a YouTube video on the "Everyone Matters" YouTube Channel titled, "The Hollis Boys, 6 and 7, 'Speaking up for our sisters' with Down Syndrome" went viral. The video serves to educate the public about Down syndrome and features the two boys holding up a series of notecards that read: "Our sisters are realizing that with some hard work and help they can do anything." Not only are Noah and Caleb represented as flexible, ideal post-ADA proto-citizen subjects, who are tolerant of disability, but we can theorize the Hollis family as attaining a similar flexibility. The family, as an ablenationalist achievement, weathers several crises including the birth of Margaret and the hate crime, and in both cases, the crisis is managed through Alina, whose transnational adoptee subjectivity is contained and safely consumed through her happy object status as a compliant, recapacitated, disabled girl.

How to Dance in Ohio and the Anxiety of Autistic Girl Futures

The autistic future girl is at the center of *How to Dance in Ohio*, another documentary about disabled girlhood acquired by HBO two years after *Miss You Can Do It*. Alexandra Shiva's coming of age documentary explores the anxious liminality and the attendant trials and tribulations of autistic young womanhood. The spring formal, which serves as the climax to *How to Dance in Ohio*, is eerily similar in context to the pageant that is at the heart of *Miss You Can Do It*. Reviews of the film de-emphasize the significance of the dance, for example, Genzlinger (2015) states that the dance is "merely a device for examining the myriad challenges the three girls and their parents face as adulthood nears." *How to Dance in Ohio* seeks to explore "bigger" questions about the futures of each protagonist, specifically defined as their ability to "go to college, live independently, make friends, [and] hold jobs" (Genzlinger 2015). The parents of Caroline, Jessica, and Marideth—the three young women the film chronicles—all express fear that their daughters have no future waiting for them, or if there is a future for them, it is bleak. Aging, although inevitable, is constructed throughout the film as a high stakes enterprise. In a scene when Caroline and Jessica are getting their hair styled at a salon prior to the dance, Caroline's mother, for instance, explicitly expresses the potential foreclosure of a future that disability portends. She says worriedly:

> Any time there's something different about your child, along the way, it's almost as though this huge world slowly . . . the opportunities slowly close in. And you're thinking, oh, did another door close for her? Did another door close for her? Or did it open for her?

Like *Miss You Can Do It*, disability throughout the film is figured as potentially disrupting common sense ideas about growing up. In this scene, endless opportunity is understood as what happens when one smoothly moves forward through time, or "up" in the telos of development: from birth, to school, to college, to work, to marriage. Despite the uncertainty about doors closing, Caroline's mother ends on an optimistic note, exclaiming, "It's just so exciting to see her interact, and have hopes, goals, [and] dreams that other kids have."

Because of Caroline's participation in Respons.ability Social Therapy™ (RST), optimism and hope bloom in anxiety's wake. Created by clinical psychologist Dr. Emilio Amigo, RST is designed, according to the website for Amigo Family Counseling, to address the "social deficits" for "individuals with an autism spectrum disorder diagnosis." RST groups "aim to improve clients' abilities to initiate, maintain, and sustain social relationships, to develop social-emotional reciprocity, and to enhance the verbal and nonverbal aspects of social engagement." RST markets itself as offering important, life building "tools" to autistic young people. However, as a therapeutic intervention, RST is undergirded by a rehabilitative logic that seeks to "return" the autistic to neurotypicality and its attendant proper affectivity (or at least an approximation of such). Throughout the documentary, we see that to "return" the autistic to an approximation of neurotypicality requires a "straightening" out of development, or a temporal disciplining of autistic bodyminds as a way of animating autistic futurity. The film's underlying message is that the psychological, emotional, and behavioral "growth" and "progress" of the three protagonists attests to the fact that exceptional autistic young women—similar to Abbey Curran in *Miss You Can Do It*—can be folded into the national imaginary as disabled future girls. They are on a path toward a better future. They, too, *can* do it.

Two years prior to the release of the film, in 2013, the American Psychiatric Association (APA) published the fifth edition of the Diagnostic and Statistical Manual of Mental Disorders (DSM-5), which made significant changes in criteria for the diagnosis of "autism spectrum disorders." One addition was their "gender-related diagnostic issues" subsection, which states that "the male-to-female ratio of autism diagnoses is 4-to-1 and that this may reflect an underdiagnosis of autistic girls and women, particularly those without intellectual disability" (Mandy 2018). The authors suggest this occurs "perhaps because of subtler manifestation of social and communication difficulties in girls on the spectrum" (Mandy 2018).[3] Countless other news articles emphasize the urgency with which the autistic girl must be diagnosed: as the autistic girl ages out of childhood, she is at higher risk for anxiety and depression, bullying, self-harm, and eating disorders (Mandavilli 2015; Neustatter 2015; Szalavitz 2016). The promotional materials for the film evidence the film's intervention in this overlooked, gendered "crisis" of autism—one that must be managed and contained before it is too late. For example, in multiple news stories and on the Peabody Award website it is noted that although "autism is one of America's fastest growing developmental disorders" affecting "1 in 68 children," according to the Centers for Disease Control and Prevention, "boys are almost 5 times more likely to be diagnosed than girls" (Peabody Awards 2015; Dunlap 2015). Shiva remarks explicitly that she was drawn to telling Marideth, Caroline, and Jessica's stories because "there was something about the invisibility of girls on the spectrum" (Dunlap 2015).

In these narratives about autism and gender that circulate alongside and frame *How to Dance in Ohio*, autism is understood solely as an invisible threat that is growing in epic proportion. It is something that must be identified in the population, as well as within the specific autistic girl bodymind before it is too late. This understanding relies on and reproduces what Ebben (2018) has characterized as "autism-as-epidemic," a structural metaphor that conceives of autism as an out-of-control threat to the individual, the family, and the nation. Within this frame, "hyperawareness of deviance is encouraged" and early intervention is positioned as key to the "maintenance of the social order" (Ebben 2018, 144). In the context of this contemporary autism discourse that paints the picture of the invisible gendered epidemic, not only is the individual girl, to use Berlant's (2011) words, an "embodied liability" if she goes undiagnosed, misdiagnosed, or has a delayed diagnosis, but the family, the economy, and the nation are too at risk unless adequate "gender sensitive" screenings are widely implemented, research on gender and autism funded, and early intervention for girls made priority. In some ways, the film, itself, functions to intervene into this epidemic, as it participates in creating "awareness." It invites the viewer to gaze at the autistic and become a good advocate through "learn[ing] to see autistic nonnormativity, to worry about it, to read it as danger, [. . .] and to act as a defender of normalcy" (McGuire 2016, 102). In doing so, the film attempts to secure a vision of a national future that includes properly rehabilitated autistic young women: autistic future girls.

The discourses of autism that the film is informed by and participates in constructing—autism as disorder, as epidemic, and as a threat to the nation— troublingly, make sense. As Anne McGuire (2016) notes in her genealogy of autism, "contemporary understandings of autism emerge out of a psychiatric/biomedical history of identifying and diagnosing its disorder [. . .]—as some 'thing' that one could be found to 'have'" (27–28). She goes on to explain that in 1943, Dr. Leo Kanner and his contemporary, Nazi sympathizer, Dr. Hans Asperger, both (separately) defined autism as a disorder, a central pathology characterized through the exhibition of non-normative behaviors (many of which are still found as diagnostic criteria in the DSM-5) that need improvement or correction (McGuire 2015). It is important to note the historical context in which Kanner and Asperger's "discovery" was rooted— one characterized by the ubiquity of eugenic ideologies of "racial purity, fitness, and hygiene" (McGuire 2016, 32). It was a time of "increased public and private surveillance of normal and abnormal behaviors," especially necessary in childhood (McGuire 2016, 32). Although an individual pathology, autism was conceptualized as a larger threat to the nation, as the "fitness, health, or hygiene of the individual was understood as absolutely inseparable from that of the state as a whole" (McGuire 2016, 33).

Contemporary conceptualizations of autism are often marked through an understanding of a potential transformation or *return* to an approximation of normalcy (Yergeau 2018). Cognitive paradigms suggest a "model of the human mind/brain that is not only fluid, changing, unfixed, but is even much like behaviorist conceptions of human behavior, *improvable*." (McGuire 2016, 50). Neurosciences, too, have introduced the conception of the brain as "plastic," which proposes that the brain (and the mind, as McGuire reminds us, these two concepts are intertwined) is "not simply 'hard-wired' [. . .] but [. . .] can change over time" (Nadesen qtd. in McGuire 2016, 50). This idea of improvability is also mobilized in contemporary autism advocacy discourse, which emphasizes that with proper individualized, biomedical intervention comes the promise of "any body's full potential for human development" (McGuire 2016, 100).

In contemporary autism research and advocacy, autism is not only understood in terms of improper communication and behavior (or improper sociality, according to RST), but it is also commonly understood as a "state of too slow development" (McGuire 2016, 7). In the case of all three autistic young women protagonists, their parents express a temporally oriented fear: they fear that their daughters will not be able to smoothly move through the transient stage of young adulthood, a stage understood as a pivotal transition from childhood/dependence to adulthood/independence. More specifically, they fear that their daughter's bodyminds are "out-of-time" and will remain so, foreclosing an autistic future worth living for. For example, in a scene where twenty-two-year-old Jessica and her parents are meeting with Michelle Seymour from the County Board of Developmental Disabilities to discuss the prospect of Jessica's eventual move out, her father explains to the viewer: "When she was young, I thought, okay, well, she'll be like an adult child, living with us until the day we pass. I kind of accepted that. But I can see that she can—that's not the case." Although Jessica expresses to Michelle that she does not feel ready to move out of her parents' house because she is afraid that she will forget to take her medication and does not have enough money saved to move out, her parents smile and interject: "she's working on it . . . she's working on it." Similarly, Caroline's mother, Johanna, expresses anxiety at the fact that Caroline "looks younger" and "sounds younger" than other nineteen-year-old young women. In a scene where she picks up Caroline from community college, she says, "It's scary entering this next place, this big world, it's terrifying," and goes on to state that Caroline "could be such a target." However, with the social skills that she is learning in RST, Caroline's mother is hopeful that her body and mind will align once again.

Here we see how the autistic girl-becoming-woman's bodymind is located within a temporally, and even more frightening for Caroline's mother, corporeally liminal space. Jessica's parents articulate how they once anxiously imagined future Jessica as "out-of-time," her future body imagined as "fully developed" thus locatable in the future, but her future mind "located in the perpetual past" (e.g., developmentally 'too slow' and always late) (Kafer 2013; McGuire 2016, 142). Rather than a crip reimagining of disabled interdependence, Jessica's parents' evocation of the grotesque potentiality of an "adult child" living at home is affectively managed by the promise of RST: anxiety shifts to hope ("That's not the case") and frustration shifts to a recognition of perseverance ("She's working on it"). Caroline's mother's fear of "slowness" is figured through the specter of sexual violence. As Erevelles and Mutua (2005) contend, it is within the liminal space of young womanhood that "physiological transformations (e.g., breasts, menstrual periods) can no longer sustain dominant constructions of the disabled adult" as non-sexual and infantilized (254). Not only does RST offer the promise of social skills, but it aids in capitulating the autistic young woman into time through aligning the autistic body and mind. In other words, it offers the promise of proper temporalization, as the autistic young woman is now able to move through the normative stages of young adult development: moving out, going to college, and entering the "big world."

Dancing into Time: Rehabilitating Autistic Young Womanhood

In *How to Dance in Ohio* Respons.ability Social Therapy™ offers the possibility and promise that if the autistic puts in the work to "become a student of people," according to Dr. Amigo, they can and will *return* to an approximation of normalcy. The name is telling. Fusing "response" and "ability" into "responsibility," "Respons.ability," sediments the intertwining of compulsory able-bodiedness/mindedness and neoliberal norms as a precondition for inclusion into society. In explaining RST to the viewer, Dr. Amigo asks the group, "Don't you guys agree, that when you have Asperger's and autism, it's probably easier when you're a kid, but when you become a teenager, then you realize, 'Oh, this social thing's kind of challenging,' right?" As she transitions from childhood to adulthood, the autistic girl-becoming-woman is compelled to work hard and quickly in RST to transform and save herself from a bad future: a future that is stalled or without opportunity.

In the case of sixteen-year-old Marideth, this self-work is framed in relation to her lack of interest in boys and her improper hygiene, as much of her storyline revolves around her parents' anxieties about her "lagging" development. The corrective interventions that viewers witness are attempts to contain ability trouble *and* queerness, as Marideth's leaky autistic bodymind not only falls outside of neurotypical norms of sociality and behavior, but outside of heterosexual and cisgender norms of young womanhood. To be clear, although Marideth does not express queer sexual desire, per se, as Yergeau (2018) argues, autism is a neurology of a queer nature, and according Groner (2012), "autistic sexuality is always necessarily queer, even if the people involved are not gay, lesbian, bisexual, or transgender" (265). In emphasizing the disabled girls' and young women's participation in a youthful femininity most often reserved for non-disabled girls, *How to Dance in Ohio*, similar to *Miss You Can Do It* attempts to claim disabled girls as "girls." But, unfortunately, instead of opening up "girl" as a capacious category of experience and being, the films fold the disabled girl protagonists into the already established bounds of a rigid, essentialist understanding of girl that is tethered to stereotypical embodied rituals and norms of hegemonic, white, heteronormative femininity.

Near the beginning of the film, right after the viewer first meets Marideth, the RST participants are practicing what happens at a dance, walking around the room with music in the background. A voice-over of Marideth says, "I'm not good at interacting with others. Sometimes I feel like I have to socialize." Students are coupling off to slow dance, and the creative social arts director, Ashley, couples Marideth with Chris. She places Marideth's hand on Chris's shoulder, and they start to dance. Dr. Amigo comes up to them, stops them, and tells them, "Okay, you guys are like marching to the beat of your own drum." He puts his hands on their shoulders and moves them together "like a metronome," and says, "you know part of connecting with somebody is to move in similar patterns. [. . .] Dance is like life. It is a way of communicating." Not only is Marideth reluctant to interact and socialize, but in another scene, she expresses not being interested in finding a date to the formal, which is positioned as another important exercise leading up to the dance. Dr. Amigo intervenes and attempts to convince her otherwise. At an RST meeting, he removes Marideth and another student, Drew, and expresses to them that they have indicated a fondness for each other. Drew is then prompted to ask Marideth to the dance. She says yes, and the camera zooms in on them holding hands for a moment. As they walk away from the camera, Marideth subtly but forcefully pulls her hand away.

Throughout the film, learning how to dance functions both as a metaphor and a practice for, as Dr. Amigo articulates, "overcoming the crippling experience of autism." According to Dr. Amigo, the spring formal serves as a major "step in the group participants' social development." It is the "ultimate test" because it is "loud, fast, confusing, [and] complicated" and a "collection of the worst possible sensory experiences that people living with autism encounter." In other words, it is positioned as an opportunity for the autistic protagonists to exercise the skills they have attained through their time at RST. In the film, passing this "test" is not only dependent on the successful ability to steel oneself and change one's behavior and response to sensory overstimulation (the capacity to perform normalcy), but because this is a dance, success also depends on one's ability to conform to the normative temporal rhythms of cisgender and heterosexual development. As Amanda Apgar (2023) argues, the "legibility [of a] future depends on [. . .] familiar, normative scripts of cisgendered development" (158). Learning how to dance, as Dr. Amigo emphasizes, is about communicating with your partner, which is visualized throughout the film as happy heterosexual coupling. For Marideth and Drew, their coupling is celebrated as not only common sense, but as an achievement for Marideth. The clasped hands symbolize a momentary temporal return to the "dominant social order," to "straight time," more specifically, wherein the transitory stage of young womanhood is most often understood as a time to learn how to be a desirable subject according to the logic of heteronormativity (Apgar 2023, 120). The clasped hands also evoke good feelings, as heterosexual love is a device that directs us toward "what gives life direction of purpose"; it is evoked as a promise of the good life and of a happy future (Ahmed 2010, 90).

In another scene, we learn that Marideth often forgets to rinse the shampoo and conditioner out of her hair. She does not seem particularly fussed about forgetting, but this a major concern for her mother. Marideth's mother explains that they've created a system to remind Marideth the proper procedure for washing her hair. They've tasked Marideth's sister to print out and laminate signs for the shower that visually describe each step in the hair washing process, with one that explicitly reminds Marideth to rinse her hair. Immediately after this scene, Marideth and her sister are sitting in Marideth's room, Marideth is sitting at her desk scrolling on the internet. Her sister takes Marideth's hair (clearly not rinsed) down from a ponytail and starts brushing it. The conversation abruptly shifts and Marideth asks her sister what she thinks about long hair on guys. Her sister responds, "I don't like long hair on guys." Marideth then says, "it's okay." The scene shifts to a family dinner at an Indian restaurant. Marideth brings up guys with long hair one more time, asking her dad if any men at his work have long hair. He says no, laughing. The conversation meanders and ends with Marideth, who reveals that she might not want to marry or have children, to which her parents remark to the viewer, "she is just not there yet. I think she likes the idea of a boyfriend or a date, but she's not quite ready to have that experience."

The juxtaposition of the hygiene intervention and Marideth's questions and comments about long hair is thought provoking. As we know, disabled girlhood challenges "heteronormativity [...] and simultaneously disrupts and flirts with patriarchal norms of 'girlhood'" (Erevelles and Mutua 2005, 254). I am not trying to make the point that hygiene rituals are inherently oppressive, but rather that in the context of the film, the anxiety around hygiene is, again, an anxiety about proper heterosexual and gender development. Because hair is so bound up in ideas about femininity and womanhood, for Marideth, to achieve good hygiene is to achieve and enact a properly feminine, gendered embodiment. Her comments about men with long hair express some curiosity about gender expression, perhaps highlighting the strangeness and arbitrariness of gender norms. Her sister's and her parents' response, however, shut down this curiosity. These blips of queerness are continually positioned as Marideth's quirks and as things that she will eventually "grow out of." This recenters cisgender and heterosexual development as the natural, desirable, and probable outcome of work in RST, as well as illustrates, once again, that compulsory hetero-ablebodiedness undergirds the production of the autistic/disabled future girl.

Jessica's story illustrates how rehabilitation and thus the transformation of the autistic protagonists into autistic future girls is contingent on the ability to conform to neoliberal (and neurotypical) norms of labor. For example, in one scene, the viewer tags along with Jessica to work, a bakery/job training program that employs autistic people called Good Food for Thought. As she starts her daily tasks—mixing flour and other cupcake ingredients—she narrates: "It's harder for people with autism to find jobs because we don't know the social rules like everybody else does." An emotionally charged scene occurs next. Owner and psychologist Dr. Audrey Todd calls Jessica in her office, and it is revealed to the viewer that there was an "incident" where Jessica did not heed the instructions of an allistic employee (she explains she wanted to do things "her way") and she also asked the allistic employee to not stand behind and watch her as she works (it makes her uncomfortable). Dr. Todd firmly says to Jessica: "Well, the first thing, you really have to watch your attitude, because you act like you're superior to others. [. . .] It's very disrespectful." Jessica interjects, pleading: "I feel like . . . there are times where we don't understand each other. [. . .] I wasn't trying to be mean." Dr. Todd responds: "I really don't necessarily have to understand you because you're an employee, and your function is to work." Jess looks down and replies, "But if you don't understand me, how can I work?" Dr. Todd goes on, "You don't need to be always understood in the work setting. You have to work." Jessica is crying and profusely apologizing at this point, and Dr. Todd appears indifferent and eventually ends the conversation with: "Keep a neutral tone, even though you may not feel neutral inside. You're actually a very—you have a very good work ethic. [. . .] And what you're learning from us is part of work etiquette. Okay?"

As she ages into adulthood, Jessica's employability takes on new urgency. Her employability, however, is dependent on her ability to internalize proper work etiquette, which according to Dr. Todd is about proper affectivity—not coming off as superior, watching one's attitude, and keeping a neutral tone. Many scholars have written about the relationship between affect and labor within the growing service sector under neoliberal capitalism. Most famous is sociologist Arlie Hochschild's (1983) theorization of "emotional labor," or the management of one's emotions during social interaction in the labor process that is required of specific professions. So, although Jessica is hired to and is paid to bake, or perform physical labor, she is also being monitored for her capacity to manage and produce a feeling, or for the work of facial comportment, tone, and atmosphere. The focus on the individual autistic's natural, but improvable affective deficiencies ("not knowing the social rules"), obscures ableism as a structural force that excludes autistics from the workplace. Even though Good Food for Thought is a workplace for autistics, rather than bend the expectations of work to fit the autistic, it is the autistic that must bend to the expectations of work.

Interestingly, for Dr. Todd and Good Food for Thought, autism is good for business. Not only does the bakery run off autistic labor, but its business model capitalizes on the social capital garnered through its inclusionism and focus on job training for autistics. As part of the autism-industrial-complex, Good Food for Thought both serves to manage the "epidemic" as well as profit off it.

The job training at Good Food for Thought complements and mirrors

RST's intervention; for Jessica, learning how to be a good worker—and successfully attaining good work ethic—manages the anxiety of the autistic girl-becoming-woman's protracted (and potentially stalled) development. To master the affectivity of a good worker is to be brought back into time, as productivity is not only integral to the construction of neoliberal subjecthood, but to chrononormative conceptualizations of young womanhood. Employability is key for the disabled future girl, as her transformation from parasitic to productive is contingent on her eventual inclusion into the market as a producer and a consumer. Recalling the earlier scene with Jessica and her parents, imagining a future for their daughter requires the promise of independence, which for Jessica can only become possible if she can save up enough money to support herself. Perhaps paradoxically, Jessica's tense "lesson" circulates good feelings, as, like Delaney, it serves to illustrate her rehabilitative potential and her progress. She too *can* do it, and implicitly, she teaches the viewers that we can, too.

Cripping the Present

This chapter's aim is not to paint a one-dimensional picture, wherein the documentaries only work in the service of constructing a disabled future girl whose sole function is to shore up heteronormativity, neoliberalism, or the project of US ablenationalism. In turning to the stories that the disabled pageant girls and the autistic young women have to tell about themselves and their experiences, we see that the disabled girl and young women subjects in *Miss You Can Do It* and *How to Dance in Ohio* often exceed the imposition of futurity. As two brief but notable examples, I turn to Tierney and Teyanna, two disabled pageant contestants from *Miss You Can Do It*.

Diagnosed with Spinal Muscular Atrophy type 2 (SMA type 2), the insight and knowledge that Tierney shares with the viewers from her perspective as a disabled girl provokes a visceral contemplation of the present. When viewers are introduced to five-year-old Tierney, her mother emphasizes the fact that her future is tenuous at best: "she's never walked, she's never been weight bearing. It's progressive, so it happens over time. [. . .] She has less movement than she had a year ago. [. . .] She only has a 40% chance to live to be seven." As her mother is delivering this somber story in the foreground, Tierney is in the background zooming around in her powerchair gleefully shrieking. As she comes forward into focus more, the viewer sees that she is attempting to catch butterflies with a butterfly net. It is a jarring juxtaposition of sorrow, laid bare the progressive nature of SMA and the probability of no future, and crip joy, as Tierney zooms around in the sun, remarking, "a beautiful day to catch some butterflies." Later in the film, when she is getting ready to meet the judges for her interview, Tierney's mom asks her, "If you had one wish come true, what would it be and why?" Tierney responds, "I want a castle for my dreams."

In making room for pleasure and stillness, Tierney sidesteps the forward movement imposed by a curative and neoliberal temporal imaginary. Both scenes emphasize a visceral and imaginative present-ness. Tierney's joyful experience of her body, her chair, and the butterflies provoke viewers to attend to a felt temporality of stillness: of an embodied here-and-now. This contrasts with the tempo of neoliberal capitalism, saturated with a feeling of rapidity as it dovetails with the felt rhythms of a curative imaginary that compels its subjects perpetually forward in search of a treatment or cure. Instead of moving forward, Tierney gleefully stays in place, or more accurately, zooms in circles in search of butterflies, the fullness of her embodied joy butting up against the grief of the imagined future loss of her body. In desiring a castle for her dreams, Tierney again sidesteps an imposition of neoliberal futurity—as a dream is usually considered an affective device that orients us toward the future. The viewer could read her wish as a recognition and understanding that her future may never bear, as the progressiveness of her SMA type 2 has rendered her outside of the normative temporality of girlhood. But I suggest that her imaginative envisioning of a castle for her dreams draws attention to the pleasure and luxuriousness of dreams as a felt experience in the present. Her wish makes plain the largeness of her desires here-and-now, destabilizing the common sense value of perpetual movement forward.

As I have gestured toward throughout this chapter, the future orientation of these films depoliticizes disability. The construction and celebration of these exceptional disabled girls—disabled future girls—operates in the service of a post-ADA US narrative, an ablenationalist narrative, to be specific, that purports to understand and recognize the value of disability, or at least of certain disabled people. Disability is rendered as a problem of the past—symbolized, for example, by baby Delaney's shaky steps, Marideth's struggle learning how to dance, and Alina's "past" life in Southern Ukraine. In these documentaries, disabled girls and girlhoods also symbolize a futurity where disability "appears to disappear" (Fritsch 2013, 145). Disability is transformed into a tool to teach the able-bodied Other lessons about tolerance and about how to cultivate the proper affective orientation demanded by ablenationalism.

Teyanna's speech, however, through calling attention to the present, is a direct affront to *Miss You Can Do It*'s attempts to depoliticize disability. The speech portion did not get as much airtime as the formal wear or interview portion, but Teyanna's speech, the one speech that they did choose to air in its entirety was a powerful theorization of ableism from the perspective of a Black, disabled girl, called "Am I disabled?":

> My name is Teyanna Alford. I am twelve years old and I have cerebral palsy. Most of the time people look at me like I am not expected to do anything. I want to be treated like everybody else. The meaning of disabled is not having any power. But I have the power to do anything I am willing to try. That makes me able.

In speaking about her experience being looked at like she is "not expected to do anything," Teyanna critiques what Eddie Ndopu (2013) would call an "able-normative supremacist culture" that imagines disabled bodyminds—and specifically Black, disabled girl bodyminds—as inherently lacking agency and power (and we will see this again in chapter 4 with the case of Jerika Bolen). An interview earlier in the documentary reveals that when Teyanna was a baby, doctors recommended placement in an institution because of the "severity" of her cerebral palsy. The only Black girl contestant that the documentary chronicles, her story is the only one that includes the specter of institutionalization. Teyanna's experience underscores the violent power of disability as a taxonomical category that intersects with other systems of oppression, such as racism and classism, imposed on those that able-normative supremacist culture seeks to define as disposable. In theorizing her lived experience, Teyanna crips girlhood, recasting the meanings ascribed to her bodymind in her own terms. She politicizes disability, resists disposability, and asserts her humanity and value: as a Black, disabled girl who has the power.

Two

From Disabled Girlhood 2.0 to the "Crip-fluencer"

On October 1, 2014, white, deaf makeup vlogger[1] Rikki Poynter uploaded a Q&A video on her YouTube channel.[2] This was not a typical question and answer video for Rikki, but was, rather, a video in honor of Deaf Awareness Week. In the closed captioned *Q&A: Deaf Awareness Week* Rikki juxtaposes a personal narrative of coming to understand her disabled subjectivity—through the eyes of a non-disabled classmate in sixth grade—with a brief critique of institutional barriers for d/Deaf people.[3] Self-identified deaf and disabled girls flooded Rikki's comment section. An astounding number of viewers thank Rikki for creating an accessible video to which they can intimately relate. For example, KittyAim writes,

> Thank you, thank you, thank you for your video! I don't have the guts to do what you are doing, it's really great. I love that you have your own subtitles too, I was able to understand a WHOLE youtube video for the first time in my life!

Many of the 400 comments detail instances of feeling isolated and fundamentally misunderstood by the hearing world, analogous to what Rikki describes in the video. For example, in their comment, Pepper Malley recounts their own experience of living with severe hearing loss:

> rikki thank you SO MUCH for making this video. i can relate to you so much. I have severe hearing loss, and i usually just say im deaf, but people are always surprised whenever i mention it because i speak 'normally.'

Not only were deaf and disabled girls affected by Rikki's video, but many other commenters were also in awe over intrepid Rikki, emphasizing the value they found in the video's educational content. For example, DuneLover commented, "I definitely learned something today. Very educational video-thank you!" SmoopyBoopy similarly noted that the video "was Amazing. Thank you for putting this out there and educating people. [. . .] Also, I enjoyed your sass in this video." *Q&A* went viral, circulating on the internet beyond the reach of any of Rikki's previous beauty videos. Moved by the success of the video as well as viewers' affective responses, Rikki made the decision to change the direction of her YouTube channel from its focus exclusively on beauty to a focus on deaf culture, activism, and the everyday experiences living as a disabled girl in an ableist world. Although perhaps not Rikki's intention when she transitioned her channel in 2014, she has now become a disabled micro-celebrity, a spectacularized social media influencer who has affectively and effectively put her disabled subjectivity to work on the internet: a girl crip-fluencer.

Moving from the previous chapter's discussion of representations of disabled girls and girlhoods constructed and produced by others, this chapter takes a closer look at disabled girls' self-representational practices on the video sharing social media platform, YouTube. I juxtapose a close analysis of a selection of Rikki Poynter's YouTube videos (ranging from the inception of her channel to present day), the comment sections, and her broader social media presence with another girl crip-fluencer, Charisse Living with Cerebral Palsy. Charisse, who was diagnosed with low tone cerebral palsy and ataxia[4] as a child, has like Rikki created a full-fledged social media career out of documenting her lived reality as disabled. Both created their YouTube channels in high school, in the 2010s at the precipice of what cultural commentators term the "disability visibility revolution." In other words, before the ubiquitous cultural presence of disability content and disabled creators on YouTube, Instagram, Twitter, and TikTok. I explore Charisse and Rikki's cultural productions and focus in on how Charisse and Rikki utilize YouTube as a vehicle to construct their disabled subjectivities and create disability community. I also trace the process by which Rikki and Charisse transform into girl crip-fluencers. Most simply, the girl crip-fluencer is a disabled girl social media user who channels her everyday life and identity into flows of content made available for consumption. Although this characterization may read redundant, the remarkable thing about the girl crip-fluencer is that she has put the very "stuff" of her disabled girl subjectivity to work on social media. She generates capital, both social and financial, vis-à-vis the public documentation and narrativization of her embodied difference. As I will go on to explain, the girl crip-fluencer has cultivated a self-brand out of disability, and in the process, she has helped facilitate the "re-branding" of disability. An emergent twenty-first century subject position and cultural figure, the girl crip-fluencer represents a post-ADA "fantasy of achievement accomplished by good ideas, hard work, and self-confidence" (Sarah Banet-Weiser 2012, 56).

As I detailed in the last two chapters, the disabled girl has been left out of theorizations that propose the girl as the privileged subject of neoliberal capitalism because as disabled, she is imagined as inherently *unproductive*, "at-risk," and unable to enter the future labor market. The girl crip-fluencer belies this conceptualization. She is, using McRobbie's (2009) words, a "highly efficient assemblage of productivity" (59). The girl crip-fluencer has successfully entered the labor market, and in doing so, she comes to embody "hopeful future possibilities and potentialities" (Harris and Dobson 2015, 146). For example, at the time of writing this in 2022, Rikki's YouTube channel has morphed into just one arm of her networked social media presence. She now describes herself as a "YouTuber, writer, streamer, and public speaker" and is represented by C Talent, a talent management company that describes itself as representing "high-profile Deaf and Disabled artists, athletes and influencers with the goal of changing the way the world views and defines disability utilizing the massive reach and power of the entertainment and media industries." Rikki has also since partnered with multiple brands, including AT&T, Google, the skincare brand Youth to the People, and has helmed multiple hashtag activism campaigns, including #DeafTalent and #NoMoreCraptions. One can even buy Rikki Poynter merch: shirts and face masks emblazoned with "Do I look Deaf Now?" or "My Accessibility, My Choice," a riff on the feminist slogan "my body, my choice." Rikki, as a girl crip-fluencer and as a formerly abandoned "subject of recognition" is not only called to broadcast online her alternative mode of being-in-the-world, but she is now paid for it (Povinelli qtd. in Mitchell and Snyder 2015, 104).

My use of "crip" in girl crip-fluencer, however, signals the paradoxical nature of this subject position/cultural figure. In tracing the evolution of Rikki and Charisse from disability content creators to crip-fluencers, this chapter uncovers how on YouTube, disabled girls *crip* girlhood. They use the platform as a tool to "unsettle" or "make strange and twisted" what we think we know about girlhood and disability (McRuer 2018, 23). The opening vignette illuminates the fact that disability vlogging (video blogging), as a self-representational practice, is political work, as it holds the affective capacity to create "new relations of affinity" outside the hegemonic strictures of ableist domination (Coté and Pybus 2007, 104). In other words, Rikki's *Q&A* generates disability intimacies between herself and other deaf and disabled girls, and in effect, carves out space for a disability community to bloom. Disability vlogging pushes back against the erasure disabled girls face in a larger cultural imaginary that ignores the ordinary "pleasures and frustrations" and the "day-to-day" goings on of disabled youth (Alper 2014, 3). Ultimately, my fusion of crip and influencer is my attempt to resist simple dichotomies and instead dwell in the tension that exists between social media—YouTube specifically—as a vehicle for developing disabled subjectivity, community, and activism *and* as a vehicle that answers to the neoliberal capitalist demand for and monetization of disability visibility.

In what follows next in the first part of the chapter, I track Rikki and Charisse's emergence on YouTube in relation to the Web 2.0 "revolution," showing how both Rikki and Charisse in the nascent days of their respective channels carved out a new space for disabled girlhood online. From reconfiguring the able-bodied "stare," to claiming disability, Rikki and Charisse's public narrativization and visual documentation of the disabled quotidian participated in charting a new genre of video on YouTube: disability vlogs. I read their practice of disability vlogging as labor, more precisely as political labor, to reveal how in the early days of YouTube, disabled content creators, like Rikki and Charisse, re-choreographed visual and affective relations between disabled people and their non-disabled audience.

In the second part of the chapter, I examine how Rikki and Charisse cultivate intimacy between themselves and their disabled viewers through harnessing negative affects such as shame, which in turn creates digital disability intimate publics that are grounded in anti-ableist solidarity. I also show how their digital disability intimate publics are co-opted by their non-disabled viewers. Paradoxically, their knowledges and experiences become taken up as instructive tools to rehabilitate able-bodied viewers into tolerant neoliberal citizens, which participates in securing the myth that "overcoming ableism" is a matter of individual action.

In the final part of the chapter, I map Rikki and Charisse's transition from disabled content creators, or "disabled girls 2.0," to crip-fluencers. I show how Rikki and Charisse's immaterial labor—the labor of filming, uploading, and generating intimacy with their followers—has gradually become valuable and remunerable within the influencer economy, and more precisely under the intersecting conditions of post-feminist brand culture and post-ADA neoliberal inclusionism. In charting their social media evolution, from building community in relative obscurity on YouTube to partnering with corporate brands—and in Charisse's case, starring in a streaming series on Facebook—I elucidate how both Rikki and Charisse create a self-brand out of disability, which ultimately evinces a defanging of the radical potential of disability in the service of capital.

Before I move on, I want to quickly explain my use of "girl" in relation to Rikki and Charisse, as it may be less obvious than in the previous chapter. In tracing their journey on YouTube, this chapter toggles between a discussion of Rikki and Charisse's early days on YouTube, when they are in high school, up until a few years ago, when they are well into their 20s. To many, then, they are no longer girls, and have not been for quite some time. However, like I note in the book's introduction, not only do I understand girlhood as a biosocial construction and as an elastic life stage, but as a capacious category of analysis. Rikki and Charisse's youngness is an integral part of their disabled subjectivity and their self-brand, and their experience of deafness and disability is acutely shaped by how others read them as young, feminine, subjects. In many of their videos they reflect on their girlhood, and many of their viewers (or at least the ones that comment) identify themselves as teenage girls. I see "girl" then as a productive lens for understanding and analyzing Rikki and Charisse's experience of disability and social media at the intersection of gender and age.

Rikki, Charisse, and Social Media's "Disability Visibility Revolution"

To be honest, I came across and became interested in disabled girl YouTubers somewhat accidentally. At the time, I was in graduate school and watching YouTube was one of my pleasure practices (and it still is, as my friends can attest). I stumbled upon Rikki Poynter's channel organically as I was searching to expand my repertoire of beauty channels to watch and subscribe. Her channel was like many of the others that I watched at the time, a profusion of "Chit Chat Get Ready with Me," "Monthly Favorites," and "Empties" videos. Her deaf identity was not the focus of her channel when I clicked the subscribe button—it was never completely unacknowledged—but, rather, it was just not foregrounded in the content of her videos. I was already writing about representations of disabled girlhood in other media spaces, so it was a bit serendipitous when I looked in my subscription box in early October 2014 to find her video *Q&A: Deaf Awareness Week*. Poynter's transition piqued my interest in this genre of YouTube videos, and from there I stumbled across the burgeoning genre of disability vlogs, or videos that document and broadcast

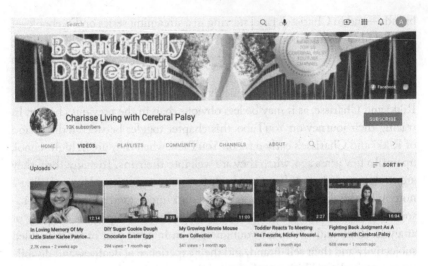

Figure 3. Charisse Living with Cerebral Palsy's YouTube Channel

the embodied reality of disability from the "sit-point" of a disabled person (Garland-Thomson 2002b). Soon after subscribing to Rikki, I found Charisse.

Charisse started her channel in the early 2010s as "Jazzygirl585." In the description of her channel, she explains that "After battling a childhood full of bullying, judgement, and misunderstanding due to my disabilities I began sharing my life with the world, starting when I was a very shy, lost, lonely 16 year old girl." The goal of her channel, as she clearly states in her most viewed video, *Charisse's Story—My Life Journey with Cerebral Palsy*, is to "spread awareness and understanding of disabilities" and show that "people with disabilities can do what other people do, just in their own unique way." At the time of writing this in 2022, Charisse has amassed just under two million video views and 10,000 subscribers (characterized as a "micro-influencer" in influencer marketing parlance),[5] and she has uploaded over 400 videos, ranging from the mundane *Baking Cupcakes with Cerebral Palsy*, where she quite literally bakes cupcakes, to the confessional *What I Want the World to Know*. The content of Charisse's channel has not changed much in the decade-plus since it was created. Her videos have a distinctly lo-fi aesthetic. She favors natural lighting, and the videos feature a generous amount of Microsoft WordArt, noticeable jump cuts, and are often spliced with still images. Instead of utilizing a professional filming room, Charisse often sits in her living room, or takes her viewers with her to the park or on vacation. In this way, the videos are suffused with the charm and intimacy of home movies.

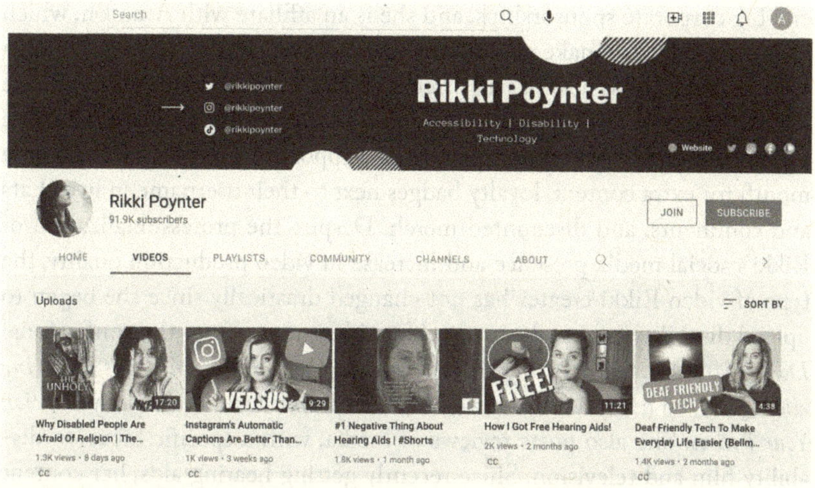

Figure 4. Rikki Poynter's YouTube Channel

Like Rikki, she has also taken her career beyond YouTube and now brands herself as a public speaker, advocate, and content creator. Her social media presence has expanded, and she also has an active Instagram and Facebook page. In 2020, Charisse became pregnant and made her streaming debut on the Facebook Watch docu-series, "9 Months with Courteney Cox." She now sprinkles in videos that document her journey as a disabled mother. She too has had several brand partnerships—most recently with a cleaning products company—reflecting the domestic turn in her channel's content.

Returning to Rikki, her channel experienced exponential growth post-*Q&A*. She has since amassed over 90,000 subscribers and over six million video views (characterized as a "mid-tier influencer" in influencer marketing parlance). Soon after being featured on *The Huffington Post*, she was interviewed by *Upworthy* and the *BBC*. She was also invited to VidCon 2016 (the flagship influencer conference) to speak about audism on YouTube, invited to Apple's headquarters for global accessibility day, and invited to Google's headquarters to speak about captioning on YouTube. Over the years her channel's aesthetic has become more professional. Her videos are now increasingly slick with a higher production quality and feature studio lights instead of natural lighting, bright, well-composed thumbnails, and a professionally designed title slide. Her social media presence has a farther reach than Charisse's: she has an active TikTok, Instagram, Facebook, Twitter, and she had a stint of live streaming on Twitch. Rikki has had several big corporate sponsorships, and she is an affiliate with Amazon, which means that she can make commission from viewers if they use her Amazon affiliate links. Rikki also has a Patreon, where "Patrons" can pay to become members and receive exclusive content. In addition, she recently launched a YouTube channel membership, where supporters can pay up to $9.99 a month for extra content, loyalty badges next to their username in live chats and comments, and discounted merch. Despite the professionalization of Rikki's social media presence and increase in video production quality, the type of video Rikki creates has not changed drastically since she began to upload disability centered content. Her videos range from the confessional *Do I Regret Getting Hearing Aids? Pros and Cons of Hearing Aids (Hearing Aids Q&A)* to the informative *#NoMoreCraptions: How To Properly Caption Your Videos*. She also posts reviews of media, with a specific focus on disability film and television. Since recently getting hearing aids, her content has veered toward focusing a bit more on disability technology.

When they first launched their channels, Rikki and Charisse were on the precipice of what cultural commentators have recently named the "disability visibility revolution." Most tout social media as the driving force of this revolution, which has been characterized in terms of a critical mass of new, purportedly authentic representations of disability identity and experience. For example, in a 2020 *Forbes* article, "Is the Social Media Generation Transforming Disability Representation?," the author juxtaposes the COVID-19 pandemic and its intensification of "disability crises worldwide" with the power of a "new narrative" of disability espoused by the voices of a new generation of online disability activists (Casey 2020). Explaining this new narrative, Casey (2020) writes that online:

> The voices of this new generation of disabled influencers ring loud and clear; their ownership of who they are, their rejection of the old stereotypes of what it means to be disabled, and the way they are replacing them with something so humanly compelling, relatable, exciting, informed and real.

This "new narrative" is contrasted with disability representation of the past, which, according to the article, was like a "tumbleweed across the desert," most often evoking pity, inspiration, or sympathy (Casey 2020). Unsurprisingly, the article rearticulates a cultural politics of diversity that apprehends visibility and recognition as, what Herman Gray (2013) would posit, the end itself. In other words, *Forbes* understands social and political progress for disabled people as tethered to their visibility. The article ends with what appears to be a call to action: "global disability inclusion will never be a reality without [disabled people] being able to recognize [themselves] in the images and stories of our time" (Casey 2020).

Social media platforms, like YouTube, the internet's second most visited website[6] and second most popular social media platform (as of writing in 2022), are now teeming with "voices of this new generation." One can search "day in my life disability" on YouTube and hundreds of videos pop up, uploaded by a range of users—from amateur content creators to professional disability rights organizations. Some of the most trafficked YouTube vlogging channels are helmed by disabled content creators, and long gone are the days that "disability" and "social media influencer" contradict each other. Take Molly Burke, mentioned in the *Forbes* article, a twenty-something blind lifestyle vlogger and social media influencer who has just under two million subscribers on YouTube. She describes herself in her YouTube "about" as "a typical sushi and makeup loving millennial girl who just so happens to be blind!" She goes on further to explain the mission of her channel and invites her audience to join her: "Even though I can't see, I know that there are bright spots in everything we face. Let's find them together! Subscribe to join the Killer Bee Club. Let's learn and grow together!:)" Molly has had countless high-profile brand sponsorships: Disney, Dove, the Bill and Melinda Gates Foundation, and Netflix, to name just a few. She even has her own forum on "Guru Gossiper," a platform for gossip about social media influencers. Fifteen-year-old Adalia Rose, who sadly passed away at the time of editing this in 2022, is another example of a highly visible and successful disability vlogger. She has cultivated an audience of just over three million subscribers on YouTube and over fifteen million across her socials through producing videos about her life with Hutchison-Gilford progeria, a disability that causes the body to age rapidly. She describes her YouTube channel as a place "to make you laugh." Like Rikki, Adalia has a merch shop where one can buy t-shirts and thermoses emblazoned with "Boss Bae" and her personal catchphrase, "Oh Shimmy." It almost goes without saying, then, that the ecology and economy of social media has changed tremendously between now and when I began this research in 2014. In 2014, disability vloggers and disability content on YouTube was few and far between. Disabled influencers, as we know them now, did not exist. Channels like Rikki's and Charisse's, in broadcasting their intimate day to day, were the forerunners of the purported "disability visibility revolution," carving out space and paving the way for the Molly Burke's and Adalia's of the internet.

Disabled Girlhood 2.0: Web 2.0 and the Power of Disability Vlogging

As scholars of new media persuasively argue, social media has facilitated the opportunity for youth to "mess around," "hang out," and construct and "perform their identities in ways that are not possible elsewhere" (Chau 2010, 65; Nakamura 2008, 207; Alper 2014; Ellis 2015). In the early aughts, the emergence of social media platforms that relied on ordinary user-generated content was dubbed in mainstream media as part and parcel of the Web 2.0 "revolution." Web 2.0 marked a new paradigm of the internet, and at first, many media studies scholars and cultural pundits alike optimistically envisioned Web 2.0's tools as eventuating the democratization of knowledge (Jenkins 2006; Burgess and Green 2009; Marwick 2013). Media studies scholar Henry Jenkins (2006) spoke of burgeoning "participatory cultures," new patterns of media consumption characterized by contribution or production, made possible by Web 2.0's infrastructure and its concomitant low barrier to artistic expression and civic engagement. Narratives of Web 2.0 emblemized the user using the portmanteau prosumer: a user who simultaneously produces and consumes. Youth, especially, flocked to early social networking sites like Facebook, Bebo, and Myspace, accessing and participating in mediated publics of their own making, forming connections with other youth regardless of geographical location, and shaping the web as they desired (boyd 2007). Sharing facets of their identity via their profiles, on these early social networking sites youth could "try out" constructing various "digital bodies" that transcended the corporeal (boyd 2007).

YouTube's first slogan, "Broadcast Yourself," in inviting its everyday users to carve out their own space on the internet, exemplified participatory culture's ethos. Its platform architecture—merging both the technical aspects of media production and circulation as well as the community and networking aspects of social media—was thought to engender the possibility for the democratization of content creation and knowledge distribution, as well as the potential for the playful construction of self and community (Burgess and Green 2009; Chau 2010). YouTube did not require familiarity with "complex coding languages or other technicalities" (Labrecque et al. 2011). To start a channel, one just needed access to a digital camera or webcam (now, a smartphone), the internet, and a creative vision. Rikki and Charisse built their channels through "broadcasting" their intimate day-to-day, often sitting in front of a camera in their childhood bedrooms. In these early, lo-fi disability vlogs, both Rikki and Charisse carved out space on the internet, sharing their experiences and knowledge gleaned specifically from their perspective as disabled girls.

Just as quickly as Web 2.0 animated feelings of utopian optimism it also invited skepticism, and critiques were soon leveraged against the "free labor" that social media platforms like YouTube appropriated from their visitors, users, and content creators (Terranova 2000; Cammaerts 2008; Andrejevic 2011; Marwick 2013).[7] The practice of disability vlogging—of "broadcasting yourself," as the early YouTube slogan invited—, is *labor*, albeit perhaps more slippery to comprehend as labor, as it seemingly blurs boundaries between leisure-as-work and work-for-pay. This work of "broadcasting yourself" was soon theorized as a value-generating activity that is not immediately perceived as labor, or what Italian autonomist Maurizio Lazzarato (1996) named immaterial labor: activities that produce the "cultural content of the commodity"—for example, knowledge, communication, aesthetics, services, and affective relations.

Rikki and Charisse's work cultivating their YouTube channels—ranging from the technical work producing and uploading videos to the affective work sharing intimate parts of their lives as flows of content for consumption—can all be classed in terms of what Mark Coté and Jennifer Pybus (2007) call immaterial labor 2.0. Although this labor—and more so at the beginning of their YouTube channels—is often "freely" given, pleasurable, politically meaningful, and endows them with cultural and social capital, it is also simultaneously exploited. Under what some scholars have named "platform capitalism" or "digital capitalism," the commodity has become the most subjective and intimate "non-economic" parts of ourselves—our intellectual and emotional capacities, our aesthetic preferences, and our very identities. On sites like YouTube, consumption is also a productive activity. Watching and sharing videos, liking, commenting, and subscribing are all activities that generate value—material/economic and social/affective—for YouTube (or post-2006, its parent company Google), its corporate partners, and the users and creators who engage with the platform. Thus, capital expropriates surplus value from Rikki and Charisse's flows of content (their intimate lives, embodied experiences, and identity) and from the affective states and relations they generate. For example, Charisse and Rikki's content, their interactions with their viewers, and viewers' interaction with their content are all used to train YouTube's algorithm. YouTube also generates profits through advertisements that play before and during their videos. Another more nebulous example, and one that I will elaborate on later in this chapter, is how the immaterial labor of intimacy creates knowledge about and affective responses to disability, which in turn can be expropriated in the service of neoliberal inclusionism and used to generate social capital for the average non-disabled viewer of Charisse and Rikki's channel.

However, it remains that via their channels, disabled girlhood became visible in new and unexpected ways. Rikki and Charisse's disability vlogs, as affective tools for understanding the self, function as technologies of disability subjectivity. In "broadcasting" the self of their own making, they re-choreograph the visual and affective relation between themselves and their non-disabled audience. In many of Rikki and Charisse's early vlogs, they invite viewers into the private space of their bedrooms, a pivotal space for the "formation and representation of [. . .] female adolescent identity" (Berryman and Kavka 2017, 6). Their content was similarly intimate, akin to what one would expect to find housed inside a teenage girl's diary. Some of Charisse's earliest vlogs, *I have cerebral palsy*, *Cerebral Palsy Poem*, *Me With Cerebral Palsy*, and *Talking about School*, clearly evince what Tobias Raun (2012; 2018) has theorized as early social media's turn toward therapeutic or confessional culture. Writing about trans vloggers, he notes that vlogs can be conceptualized as "therapeutic tools" that allow creators to "release powerful emotional energy in ways that are not possible off-screen" (Raun 2012, 165). The camera functions as proxy for a trustworthy and non-judgmental "external interlocutor," and the vlog, itself, becomes an archive of feeling: a method for coping with the oppressive gaze and trauma imbued by dominant culture (Raun 2012, 165; Cvetkovich 2003).

Rikki Poynter's corpus of videos that document her journey learning American Sign Language (ASL) is a poignant example of how the disability vlog functions as a vehicle for the construction of subjectivity. These videos where she is practicing, learning, or discussing ASL, for example, *Do I Want My Hearing Back? (ASL Vlog)*, *30 Second Sign Language No Facial Expression Challenge (ASL Vlog)*, and *Learn ASL with Me: Days of the Week*, are some of her most intimately reflective, and consequently, they are some of her most viewed. Rikki has firmly stated that she does not identify as "big D, Deaf," or culturally deaf, and these vlogs in particular are one place where she comes to understand and reckon with her disabled subjectivity, her deafness, and her place in the community, specifically as an "outsider." In her video, *Learning Sign Language As A Deaf Adult*, she recounts her childhood experiences. She was unable to afford hearing aids even though she "qualified" for them, consequently she was raised orally, mainstreamed, and then not allowed to learn ASL. She reveals that she was ashamed of being deaf in middle school and high school because "no one knew": she felt like the "odd kid out" because

Figure 5. Rikki Poynter in her YouTube video, *Learning Sign Language as a Deaf Adult* (2016)

she believed something was "wrong" with her. In the video she emphatically reassures her audience that after she found the Deaf community on Tumblr, she was able to reject the pathologization of her deafness and the shame it engendered. However, Rikki admits that although at that point she had been learning ASL for one and a half years, she was nervous to create ASL videos because she was still "awkward" at signing. She admits: "I'm basically a hearing kid in a deaf person's body." Despite her professed hesitancy, or perhaps because of it, she alerts her audience that more "ASL vlogs" are coming. She confesses to her audience that she cannot fathom switching her channel over fully to ASL because she sees herself as "living in two worlds." Not only do the ASL vlogs push back on "compulsory speaking," but they simultaneously operate as a tool through which Rikki shifts the conceptualization of herself (Mauldin 2018). She "comes home" to her bodymind in a publicly vulnerable and radical way, feels out her disabled subjectivity, and embraces the liminality of her deaf identity (Clare 2010). In the process, she carves out space for others who embody the zone beyond the binaries of Deaf/deaf, deaf/hearing, and able-bodied/disabled.

In Rikki's vlogs (and Charisse's too, as I will soon discuss), she intentionally puts her disabled bodymind on display through "claiming and naming

Figure 6. Charisse in her YouTube video, *Walking & running with Cerebral Palsy* (2010)

her impairment before the audience can" (Sandahl 2003, 43). Whether it is through putting "deaf" in the title, or signing at the beginning of the video, this repeated practice of self-disclosure upends the visual logic of compulsory able-bodiedness through disrupting the normative conceptualizations of what disability looks like. Because she is deaf, her bodymind is not always interpellated immediately by the audience as anomalous—her disability is intermittently apparent depending on if she is signing, or if her hearing aids are visible. This repeated practice of re-presenting the self as deaf/disabled, "catapults disability into the public sphere" from the vantage point of the disabled person (Garland-Thomson 2002a, 58). This practice reconfigures what Rosemarie Garland-Thomson (2002a) has named "the stare." According to Garland-Thomson (2005), staring is a visual and embodied exchange. She explains, "staring at disability choreographs a visual relation between a spectator and spectacle. A more intense form of looking [. . .] staring registers the perception of difference and gives meaning to impairment by marking it aberrant" (Garland-Thomson 2005, 56). Thus, staring is an intersubjective act of sense-making that can provoke mutual transformation.

Charisse's disability vlogs also reconfigure the able-bodied stare. In videos that showcase Charisse "doing being ordinary," or demonstrating quotidian tasks for her viewers, such as *Walking & running with Cerebral Palsy*, *Making Pancakes with Cerebral Palsy*, and *Putting on Makeup with Cerebral Palsy*, Charisse visually spotlights "impairment effects"—her shaky legs and arms, most specifically (Sacks 1984). In this practice of disability vlogging, the camera explicitly functions as proxy for the stare. For example, in Charisse's second most viewed video, *Walking & running with Cerebral Palsy*, in her drawn out and slightly slurred speech she narrates her mobility aid journey, from using a walker as a child, to forearm crutches in second grade, to just one forearm crutch in the third grade, and then ultimately, to walking unassisted in the fourth grade. The last half of the video is an extended clip of Charisse, as the title suggests, walking and running. Walking away from the camera in what looks to be an idyllic suburban backyard, with a slight sway of her arms, drag of her feet, and occasional knock of her knees, she pulls a dog on a leash behind her. She reaches a tree a few feet away from where the camera is located, and then she turns around and walks back toward the camera with a huge grin on her face. As she gets closer to the camera, she quickly turns around with the dog galloping behind her, her body undulates slightly left to right as she runs back toward the tree, her hair swishing with the momentum of her body.

This video authorizes the stare by inviting her viewers to watch her walk and run. Conceptualized as an act of self-disclosure akin to Rikki's, Charisse puts the "ragged edges and blunt angles" of her disabled embodiment on display (Siebers 2001, 747). The video archives a powerful visuality and visceral-ness of the disabled bodymind, a "new realism" that does not hold back on provoking a matter-of-factness about CP and ataxia (Siebers 2001). This matter-of-factness is also generated through Charisse's narration: her in-depth explanations about different mobility aids and how her CP and ataxia have, over the course of her life, affected her movement. In this way, disability vlogging becomes a practice through which Charisse films herself into being, constructing her disabled subjectivity and re-authoring her audience's experience of her bodymind difference (Siebers 2001). In the act of sharing her experience and embodied knowledge, Charisse pushes back against the sexist, ableist and ageist assumption that she does not know or understand her own disabled bodymind.

Instead of a passive specimen to behold by the able-bodied gaze, the platform architecture and intra-activity of YouTube facilitates the possibility for disability vloggers to "broadcast" the self of their own making. For both Rikki and Charisse, disability vlogs function as narrative-affective spaces through which they "move through" and "enter into new sociopolitical meanings" of their embodiment (Mauldin 2018, n.p.). Disability vlogging, then, is also a practice of archiving knowledge and feeling—a cripistemology of disabled girlhood—as a resource for others.

Digital Disability Intimate Publics

Through their practice of disability vlogging, Rikki and Charisse both generate disability intimacies that are integral to building online disability communities that are grounded in anti-ableist solidarity. Their YouTube channels become a space where we see the blooming of digital disability intimate publics. As media studies scholar Shaka McGlotten (2013) argues, intimacy is a force. It describes a feeling of connection, or a sense of belonging. More specifically, intimacy names "the affective encounters with others that often matter most, while also functioning as a juridical form, an aspirational narrative, and therapeutic culture's raison d'etre" (McGlotten 2013, 11). On social media, intimacy has been described as immaterial labor that produces social relations, affective attachments, and a perceived interconnectedness between users (Senft 2008; Abidin 2015; Dobson et al. 2018). On YouTube, Rikki and Charisse craft intimacy in a multiplicity of ways. One way is through their consistent direct address to their audience. Sometimes this takes the form of beginning videos with "hey guys welcome back to my channel," or soliciting feedback from their viewers about a certain video topic. Sometimes they directly address their audience in the comment section, writing back to audience questions and suggestions. Intimacy is also crafted vis-à-vis the confessional quality of their disability vlogs, as they facilitate the impression of viewers' unmediated access to their private feelings and inner thoughts. Both Rikki and Charisse consistently upload videos where they self-disclose traumatic incidents, express feelings of isolation, and reflect on experiences of ableism. Often, in their disability vlogs, Charisse and Rikki perform radical vulnerability, productively harnessing negative affects such as sadness, loneliness, and shame as a method to build a politicized community of fellow feeling.

Via this immaterial labor of intimacy, Rikki and Charisse cultivate digital disability intimate publics. An intimate public according to Lauren Berlant (2008) is a "porous, affective scene of identification among strangers that promises a certain experience of belonging" (viii). Digital disability intimate publics provide their disabled participants with an affective frame for being in the world, perhaps one they would have not arrived to offline due to social or geographical isolation. Remarkably, an intimate public "creates *situations*" where qualities or lives that have been deemed "puny or discarded" can "appear as luminous" (Berlant 2008, 2). Digital disability intimate publics are spaces where the public and private overlap, where the "illusion" between the separation of politics and emotional life visibly breaks down (Dobson et al. 2018).

In the next section, I close read two videos and their comment sections, one each from Charisse and Rikki, to explain the mechanisms by which they both craft disability intimacies that in turn generate the affective conditions of possibility for digital disability intimate publics. My first example is Charisse's most watched video, *Charisse's Story—My Life Journey with Cerebral Palsy*. In this video Charisse carves out space for fellow "misfits" through the recounting of psychic pain and ableist isolation. In my second example, *Shit Hearing People Say (Things You Don't Say to Deaf & Hard of Hearing)*, I show how Rikki leverages crip humor as a method to affectively re-route pain into pleasure as a practice of solidarity building. In both these videos we witness the collective political work of disability intimacy, as it coheres community and engenders recognition through a mutual process of claiming crip.

Charisse's Story: Fellow Feeling "Misfits"

Charisse's Story—My Life Journey with Cerebral Palsy is Charisse's most watched YouTube video. This seventeen-minute video uploaded in 2012 during the early days of her YouTube channel has amassed over 260,000 views, 830 comments, and 2,900 "thumbs up." Alternating between video footage of present-day Charisse and still photographs of her as a baby, she narrates her "life journey" with cerebral palsy and ataxia. Charisse begins the video sitting on the ground with her face off-center in the frame, in what viewers can assume is her childhood bedroom. Behind her is a makeshift backdrop comprised of two Americana style patchwork quilts. The lo-fi, amateur aesthetic—the make-shift backdrop, dim lighting, and spliced in photographic footage—reads as "real," as less manufactured, or overly staged (Paasonen 2005). The stylistic qualities, form, and content of the video lends credence to the perception of authenticity, and this augments the feeling of closeness, both affectively and spatially, as the camera becomes a proxy for the viewer.[8]

Figure 7. Charisse in her YouTube video, *Charisse's Story—My Life Journey with Cerebral Palsy* (2012)

A slide show of baby pictures moves through the frame as Charisse describes her birth, and viewers learn that her umbilical cord was wrapped around her neck, cutting off oxygen for seven minutes. Halfway through the video, Charisse confesses that she did not realize she was disabled until someone at school started bullying her in the second grade. She recounts, "When I was little I really didn't see myself as different from all of the other kids. I didn't see myself with a disability. I thought I was just like them, so I would try to do everything my classmates would do." With a furrowed brow, she pushes her hair behind her ears and adds, "I guess when I found out how different I really am, I was near the middle of second grade because some of my classmates started bullying me because I was different." Here the audience is let in on the fact that Charisse came to a violent recognition of herself as disabled through the hostile gaze of the non-disabled other. The video ends on an optimistic note, however, as Charisse resolutely declares that her YouTube channel is what changed her life, as her peers began to treat her differently after watching her videos. With a huge grin on her face, Charisse explains that her senior year of high school was "so much better": she started helping students who have mental disabilities, she was on the varsity basketball team and cheer squad, and she is currently dating the boy who asked her to prom.

Throughout the video, Charisse recounts painful memories of feeling ostracized and misunderstood by her non-disabled peers. However, through the immaterial labor of recollection, she constructs a politicized understanding of herself as a disabled girl, as well as generates space for others to come to their own politicized understanding of their disabled experiences and identity. Let us take a closer look at one of the most vulnerable moments of the video, when Charisse recites a somber poem that she wrote in eighth grade about her experiences with her peers. Locking eyes with her viewer, she recites:

> As others treat me, how people look at me / sitting by the lonely tree, looking at others wishing that was me. / As others come, think I would never know / telling things about me, 'that she never knows.' / Oh what they say, makes me cry. / Saying, 'She's not our type,' / 'Have you heard her talk.' / 'Look how she acts.' / But they don't really know my type. / I know I can't swim. / I know I can't speak right. / I know who I am, and I know people treat me the wrong way.

In the poem, Charisse vividly describes her experience feeling cast out, isolated from, and misunderstood by her able-bodied peers. Her peers' perceptions of her disabled bodymind—specifically how she "talks" and how she "acts"—gives way to her literal segregation from them—she sits by the "lonely tree" looking at others. But, in "wishing" she was those others she also articulates the desire for intimacy—a sense of belonging and closeness to her peers. From her peers' perspectives, it is Charisse's disabled bodymind that forecloses the possibility of intimacy. However, Charisse declares that she realizes she "can't swim" and "can't speak right," but she does not express a desire to change her bodymind. Rather, she "knows who [she] is" and realizes that people treat her the "wrong way." Here Charisse comes to recognize that the problem is not her disabled bodymind: it is the able-bodied other's inability to "know her type."

This poem effectively (and affectively) theorizes ableism through Charisse's experience of misfitting, which denotes an incongruent encounter between flesh and the world (Garland-Thomson 2011). Charisse describes the discrepancy between the particularities of her embodiment—her speech and her movement—and the world, between "that which is expected and that which is" (Garland-Thomson 2011, 593). Here it is not only the discursive construction of disability as lack, pathology, or flaw, that constitutes Charisse's outcast status, but it is also the materiality—the "stuff"—of her disabled bodymind as it comes into friction with the built and arranged environment (both spatial and temporal) of girlhood. In Charisse's recognition that "she knows who she is" and "she knows that people treat her the wrong way" we see the blooming of an "oppositional and politicized" consciousness and identity (Garland-Thomson 2011, 597). Indeed, Garland-Thomson (2011) argues that "subjugated knowledge" is another "potential effect" of misfitting, as well as the potential for the formation of a community of misfits (597). Her performance of vulnerability generates an affective bloomspace in the comment section, allowing others to reflect and ruminate on their own experiences and subsequent feelings of misfitting.

We see Charisse's desire for belonging and closeness reciprocated in her comment section. The commentors call Charisse into subjectivity through an "exchange of mutual recognition," or a mutual process of claiming crip (Alcoff qtd. in Garland-Thomson 2011, 596). For example, Livia Rodriguez writes in response, "I have cerebral palsy as well, I know it can be hard, and that there just no cure for it. But you are right God made US like this for a reason. My mom tells me that it means we are stronger then [sic] other people." SusieMiss2007 also resonates with Charisse's story and comments, writing:

> Charisse, thank you so much for sharing. I have Spastic CP & I know how hard it can be. Although I can walk without assistance I still walk differently & remember all the crap I went through. I graduated back in 2010 but sometimes you just need to know that there is someone else out there & that you aren't alone. Please keep making your videos & stay strong!

Both Livia Rodriguez and SusieMiss2007 directly address Charisse, relating to how "hard" it can be to have CP. Livia Rodriguez laments the fact that there is no cure, but then takes heed of her mother's and Charisse's interpretation of disability, repositioning her disabled bodymind as valuable. It is a "gift" that endows her with a strength that able-bodied people do not possess. Livia Rodriguez's comment rejects the normative positioning of the disabled bodymind as inherently undesirable. Further, her capitalization of "US" reflects and produces an emphatic feeling of connection between herself and

Charisse. Similarly, SusieMiss2007 self-reflexively offers up her own pain—the "crap" she went through in high school. In reminding Charisse (and all others who read her comment) that what is most important is the knowledge that there is "someone else out there," SusieMiss2007 affirms the importance of crip kinship and the healing power of community. SusieMiss2007 also expresses a desire for continued proximity to Charisse, as she encourages her to continue to make videos. Countless other commentors who note that they have CP respond similarly to SusieMiss2007 and Livia Rodriguez, offering their gratitude, declaring a feeling of recognition, recounting their own experiences, and pleading with Charisse to continue making videos. Through the immaterial labor of vulnerability, Charisse cultivates a digital zone of intelligibility for fellow misfits, a "place where they can [too] take up space, [. . .] break open, and be seen and held in community" (Kafai 2021, 44). The digital disability intimate public that blooms is characterized by the emotional reciprocity among its participants and a shared re-orientation toward disability as inherently valuable.

Shit Hearing People Say: The Political Power of Crip Humor

"Do I look deaf now?" Rikki asks incredulously in *Shit Hearing People Say (Things You Don't Say to Deaf & Hard of Hearing)* as she slaps a sticky note with "DEAF" written in all caps on her forehead. Although different in tone than *Charisse's Story*, in Rikki's most watched video, *Shit Hearing People Say*, she also productively harnesses negative affect and performs a radical vulnerability that carves out space for other deaf and disabled people to be "seen and held in community" (Kafai 2021, 44). In the video, Rikki's acerbic crip comedy functions as both a "shield and weapon" (Berlant and Ngai 2017). It refracts the shame so often born out of audist and ableist experiences. In inviting her viewers to laugh along in the comment section, in shame's place blooms anti-ableist, and specifically anti-audist solidarity. Posted on November 5, 2014, in the early days of Rikki's channel, *Shit Hearing People Say* clocks in at a tight three minutes, and has amassed over 551,000 views, 14,000 "thumbs up," and an astounding 2,546 comments. The visual aesthetics of this video match *Charisse's Story*: Rikki, with her signature side-swept hair, sits squarely in the center of the frame, a NASCAR cladded comforter decorating the bed directly behind her. We can imagine that this is the private space of Rikki's bedroom. The video is mostly lighthearted in tone and Rikki directly addresses the audience, inviting viewers to "play a game called 'Things you shouldn't say to people who are deaf or hard of hearing.'" It bears

Figure 8. Rikki Poynter in her YouTube video, *Shit Hearing People Say (Things You Don't Say to Deaf & Hard of Hearing)* (2014)

a similar confessional quality to *Charisse's Story*, as Rikki divulges that she has been on the receiving end of these "things you shouldn't say."

In her signature deadpan tone, Rikki begins the video by stating: "This is going to be such a fun game. There are no prizes. Just shits and giggles." "Is deafness contagious?" she leads with. She looks up from the notebook she is holding, stares intensely through the camera, and responds to the question with "I don't know but come over here. I'll cough on you and tomorrow we will find out." Rikki moves on to the next: "Why do you need subtitles for this? You've already seen it." "Well," she throws back bitingly, "in that case, we'll just mute it while you're watching it. We'll see how well you understand it then." She moves on to the classic "You're too pretty to be deaf." She forgoes a verbal response to this comment and instead offers up her embodied reaction. Rolling her eyes and whipping her head directly backwards, she hits herself in the face with her notebook. She shakes her head and offers another in a deadpan tone: "You don't look deaf." This is when she slaps the DEAF sticky note onto her face. After looking back down at the list, she asks "Can you hear me now?" She walks behind her bed and crescendos into a yell: "CAN YOU HEAR ME NOW?" "Ladies and gentlemen," she commands, "this is not a Verizon wireless commercial. Let's not do this." "And last but not least," Poynter says, "What do deaf people sound like when they are having sex?" Shaking her head and looking playfully to the side, she responds, "I don't know, but when I have sex with somebody, I'll be sure to get you a front row seat!" She ends the video inviting her viewers to play along: "d/Deaf/HOH viewers leave comments below of the ridiculous things you've been told! We can laugh during ROUND 2!"

In crafting jokes out of her own personal experience—out of the banality of everyday ableist and audist microaggressions—Rikki pokes back at dominant society, and "undermines the people who" laugh at her and others in her community (Reid, Stoughton, and Smith 2006, 635). Her performances—from making the "DEAF" sticky note and slapping it on her forehead to backing up behind her bed to yell "CAN YOU HEAR ME NOW?"—operate as a hyperbolic mirror, reflecting the hackneyed ridiculousness inherent in the "shit" hearing people say. On the affective labor of the comedic, Lauren Berlant and Sianne Ngai (2017) write, "comedy helps us test or figure out what it means to say 'us'" (235). Disability scholars, too, have theorized humor as a mode of communication that cements community (Albrecht 1999; Corker 1999; Shakespeare 1999; Reid, Stoughton, and Smith, 2006; Milbrodt 2018). In the case of self-deprecating humor, it facilitates the twisting of position from "victim to perpetrator," from the butt of the joke to the one wielding it (Reid, Stoughton, and Smith 2006, 635). For example, Rikki's ending bit about sex, specifically her invitation into the room when she eventually has sex with someone, rebels against the ableist, ageist, and sexist myth that disabled girls do not experience sexual desire or have a "sexual culture" (Siebers 2012). The joke's construction and delivery thwarts the imposition of innocence and instead offers an uncomfortable proposition for those who dare ask what deaf people sound like having sex. Rikki's comedy performs important political work by disrupting the ageist and sexist ideologies that often insidiously govern the day-to-day existence of girls like herself, as well as exposing the insidious and deadly nature of compulsory hearing/able-bodiedness.

Rikki's performance of acerbic crip humor affectively re-routes pain into pleasure, generating an intimacy between herself and her audience. Like with *Charisse's Story*, the comment section of *Shit Hearing People Say* is illustrative of the political potential of disability intimacy. Disability studies scholar Mairian Corker (1999) argues that crip humor can operate as an "emancipatory practice," but context matters greatly (81). The audience, joke teller, as well as the specific ways in which disability is joked about are key factors that delineate crip humor's transformative potential. In the case of *Shit Hearing People Say*, it is clear that Rikki's intended audience is deaf and HOH people, as she directly addresses this audience at the end of her video by soliciting material for "round two." The audience is invited to become an active participant in Rikki's comedy. This is not just because they are presumed to "get" the jokes, but they become part of the comedy act itself. In recounting the "ridiculous" things hearing people have said to them in the comment section, viewers are afforded a space to self-reflect and critically engage with the banality of everyday ableism and audism. Transforming their experiences of structural oppression, harm, and shame into the raw material for jokes becomes a pleasurable practice, and an act of solidarity. This requires a performance of vulnerability on the commentors, end, too.

For example, Lizardyou writes "I'm deaf in my left ear, and the most annoying thing ever is when I ask someone to repeat something and they just say, 'nevermind' . . .-_-." Lizardyou's comment clearly resonated with others, as it has 368 thumbs up and 37 comments. In response, xyzKittiepaws writes, "Awww, I'm so sorry. Have you told anyone it bothers you? You should pull the same thing on Hearing offenders:P When they ask for a repeat just say nevermind [sic] too:P." Lizardyou responds back to xyzKittiepaws and says, "They usually just laugh if I confront them about it hahah so I tend to just ignore it haha (:." Bearing witness to Lizardyou's experience, xyzKittiepaws twists the "Hearing offender" into the butt of the joke and offers a comedic response as an anti-ableist rhetorical tactic. Other commentors emphatically write that this scenario is the "BANE OF THEIR EXISTENCE," that they "relate to this shit so hard," and ask, "What goes through people's heads?" Amelia Wright offers a common intrusive question: "so . . . deaf people have babies?—True story." CampKid playfully responds, "There's several ways to make babies, but none include hearing being crucial in any way:-P." Many other commentors are aghast but not surprised at the hearing person's suggestion that deaf people's reproductive capacities are somehow affected by their disability.[9] Rikki's deaf, disabled, and HOH followers reposition the ableist presumption of reproductive incapacity as a joking matter, re-routing the suffering and pain of gendered audism into raw material for the construction of an affective scene of belonging marked by laughter. Rikki's comment section becomes a pleasure space. The construction of this digital disability intimate public is marked by a process of mutual recognition—of "relating"—or coming to realize that their experiences are not isolated incidents that point to a pathological truth of the disabled and/or deaf bodymind. En masse their experiences are evidence that reveal the true problem: the disabling effects of an audist society. Humor is not only a technique to blow off steam, but a crip consciousness raising tool. By divulging their own experiences being the "butt of the joke"—ranging from shameful to annoying—deafness transforms into "grist for the mill," as commentors come to a collective understanding that being deaf or HOH is just an alternative and viable way of life, not one that is shameful, tragic, or pathological (Milbrodt 2018, n.p.).

. . .

Rikki and Charisse's disability vlogs "create an immediate emotional response (sadness, rage, pain, compassion, joy)—an affective charge of investment, of being 'touched'" (Cvetkovich qtd. in Kuntsman 2012, 3). The comment sections of both *Charisse's Story* and *Shit Hearing People Say* illustrate how the disability intimacies that Rikki and Charisse craft engender a sense of connection for all who watch the vlogs. Non-disabled people, too, express feeling moved. "I am crying this really touched my heart," reads a comment Raph Neer left in response to *Charisse's Story*. Book945 concurs, "This video made me cry it's so beautiful and inspiring." In response to *Shit Hearing People Say* Emon F. writes, "This was really enlightening and pretty funny! Thank you for such a great video." Lizzie's Second Account similarly responds, "I loved this video! I think it would be great for more hearing people (like myself) to watch it and learn something. I had a really awesome science teacher who was deaf, spoke very well and knew no sign language." Comments like this, that express feeling inspired, touched, and enlightened are ubiquitous, woven throughout the comment sections on Rikki and Charisse's channels.

If we look closer at the comment sections, we find that the disability intimate publics that bloom have also become instructive for able-bodied viewers, facilitating their rehabilitation into tolerant, neoliberal, post-ADA citizens. Many comments specifically refer to the pedagogical value of disability vlogs as affective tools of re-orientation. For example, in response to Charisse's confessional *What I Want the World to Know*, Fern Mallow writes, "One of my classmates said that people that have disabilities are stupid when I heard it I went over and hit him and said u wach dis video and then he relised what he did." In that same vein, in response to Rikki's *Q&A*, Bug-Catch93 writes,

> You are an amazing person. Thank you for informing hearing people, like me, about what it is like to be deaf. You helped me understand some of the hurdles deaf people have to jump through in life. I am not a YouTuber, but if I ever start uploading videos I will be sure to Closed Caption them. Keep doing what you're doing—you are helping make the world, and the Internet, a better place.

As disability educators, both Rikki and Charisse move or re-orient their viewers from a place of disability ignorance to one of "understanding," as BugCatch93 puts it. The disability intimacies that Rikki and Charisse craft are, in some ways, co-opted by their able-bodied viewers, moving them toward enacting individual acts that symbolize "overcoming ableism." Their YouTube channels thus also participate in an *affective* project of able-bodied rehabilitation through provoking commenters to turn inward. For example, AppleJuice writes in response to *Charisse's Story*:

> My professor just showed this video in one of my Speech Pathology classes. Thank you for being vulnerable and sharing your faith. I hope I can be like you in the future, and I'll remember you when I encounter people with Cerebral Palsy in the future, whether in the clinic or everyday. We're about the same age; I hope we would've been friends in high school if we'd gone to the same school.

One of the most common refrains in Rikki's comment section is that the video has inspired the viewer to learn ASL. For example, Sam Worthington in response to *Q&A*, referencing the dangerous lack of disability training for the police, writes:

> Damn, I had no idea about the police thing. Just goes to show what you don't understand until you've been in someone elses shoes. That's so sad. And seeing you get choked up about it was hard to watch. I couldn't imagine what it'd be like. You inspire me to want to take ASL [American Sign Language] classes.

Both AppleJuice and Sam Worthington articulate feeling moved by Rikki and Charisse's vulnerability and note that they have been "inspired" to imagine that they will now take an alternative course of action in the future regarding their encounter with disability. For AppleJuice, this looks like holding Charisse in mind when they encounter people with CP "in the future" in the clinic and in their everyday life. For Sam Worthington this looks like possibly taking ASL courses. Within the space of Charisse and Rikki's channels, affective re-orientation relies on imagining a "future-oriented" version of tolerance wherein we all imagine "a good society yet to come" (Brown qtd. in Elman 2010, 285). Tolerance, although it "has been constructed as a transcendent virtue," historically functions as a "protean [. . .] vehicle for producing and organizing subjects" (Brown qtd. in Elman 2014, 91). Tolerance emerges out of a "civilization discourse" that positions both tolerance and tolerant subjects with the West in opposition to the "barbarous" Other, and in the United States, it operates as both a "universal value and impartial practice" (Brown 2008, 6–7). Disability intimacies, then, are apt to become co-opted and mobilized in the creation of an ideal subject of neoliberalism, and even more specifically, in the service of ablenationalism. The ideal non-disabled subject of the ablenationalist project is self-actualized through the constant performance of proper feeling toward disability, in contradistinction to the "uncultivatable poor and racialized populations who are reduced to their base instincts and impulses" (Haritaworn 2015, 89). One has to imagine that Rikki and Charisse's whiteness, too, plays an immeasurable role in the receptivity of the commentors. The docility of their white femininity shapes their message as non-threatening, as a gentle reminder to "love thy neighbor."

Similar to the disabled *Miss You Can Do It* pageant girls I discuss in the last chapter, Rikki and Charisse are re-capacitated as exceptional disabled girl subjects vis-à-vis their ability to teach their able-bodied audience how to properly harness feeling (e.g., to affect and be affected). However, as the comments attest, this good society to come born out of a new emotional habitus of ablenationalism is not necessarily one in which ableism is eradicated, or disability is desirable. But rather, it is defined by an inclusionism that hinges on the institutionalization of the goodwill of the able-bodied. Although I do not fault any of Charisse and Rikki's able-bodied viewers and commenters for their wish to construct a more accessible world, we must remember that the transformation from hearing and/or able-bodied viewer into tolerant ASL teacher and/or speech pathologist is an individual act, not a collective response to the ableist, hostile, economic, social, and political conditions with which deaf and disabled people must contend. Disability is at once fetishized and envisioned as a simple problem that can be taken care of by self-growth, personal reflection, and an enlightened career.

The qualities of disability intimacies more broadly, as politically "transgressive" and intensely affective, are the very same qualities that make them commercially valuable. Feminist and digital media scholars argue that we must understand digital intimate publics "as part of larger historical shifts toward the rendering of intimate life, emotions, care, and social relations, into private capital" (Dobson et. al 2018, 15). In other words, Charisse and Rikki's digital disability intimate publics are, too, subject to co-optation, commodification, and capture by private capital—as disability has become a lucrative niche market as well as a brand (which I will discuss more fully later in this chapter). More insidiously, though, digital disability intimacies are subject to a larger ideological and symbolic capture, wherein they fuel the process of the gradual depoliticization of disability as it is incorporated into the national imaginary as a valuable part of the "multicultural" tapestry of the United States. This process disaggregates disability from intersectional projects of social justice, as a method of containing potentially disruptive bodyminds.

The Girl Crip-fluencer: Branding Disability

Soon after establishing and growing their channels and respective audiences, Rikki and Charisse began to harness their "microcelebrity" status—cultivated through their intimate engagement with their followers—into brand deals and paid partnerships (Senft 2008). As crip-fluencers, they now monetize their flows of content, putting their disabled and deaf subjectivities to work in new and profitable ways. Their career success as crip-fluencers is contingent on, as you would expect, their capacity to influence their audience. But also, fascinatingly, their success is also connected to their ability to cultivate a compelling and sellable brand out of disability. In exploring Rikki and Charisse's process of self-branding, it becomes clear that for the crip-fluencer, strategically toggling between presenting oneself as a disability activist and disability entrepreneur is valuable and thus remunerable within the context of post-/popular feminist, neoliberal, and ultimately, ablenationalist brand culture. Before discussing the specific contours of Rikki and Charisse as crip-fluencers and their strategies of self-branding, it is first necessary to give a bit of context on influencing.

Soon after YouTube's acquisition by Google in 2006, everyday content creators gained the ability to monetize their videos through YouTube's partner program. In allowing advertisers to play ads before or after one's videos, content creators became eligible to receive ad revenue payments from YouTube—a share of YouTube's profit from the advertiser.[10] Corporate brands soon began to approach content creators, establishing arrangements—called influencer marketing—where they directly compensate creators for endorsing the brand's product or service in their YouTube videos (and usually across other social media platforms). This paved the way for the birth of the social media influencer: an everyday internet user that amasses a large following through the visual documentation of their everyday life (Marwick 2013; Abidin 2016, 2021; Duffy 2017). Social media influencing transcends content creation as a hobby; through the monetization of cultural production, content flows, and intimacy, influencing has become an established career.

For the corporate brand, influencer marketing promises the potential acquisition of a targeted demographic to advertise to, as well as an influential and trusted mouthpiece for their product or service. For the content creator-cum-social media influencer, influencer marketing promises the potential to cultivate a career out of "doing what you love," where leisure and labor are fundamentally intertwined (Duffy 2017).[11] For disabled people, many of whom have been shut out of the traditional labor market due to structural ableism and discriminatory hiring practices, social media influencing offers an enticing possibility for a career that appears to be outside the normative, oppressive, and often inaccessible strictures of work.[12] YouTube affords a new opportunity to put the very "stuff" of disabled subjectivity to work; it is a tool that can facilitate the transformation of the disabled bodymind from that which has historically been deemed unproductive, a drain, and surplus into the raw material for the generation of capital. However, as Brooke Erin Duffy (2017) cautions, success comes to very few who attempt to construct a career as an influencer. Gendered precarity undergirds the shiny promise social media influencing offers, as the influencer economy is mostly powered by underpaid and undervalued immaterial labor, much of which is performed by girls and women (Duffy 2017; Rubio-Licht 2022).[13]

Cultivating a successful career as a social media influencer, requires, literally, the capacity to *influence*. With that being said, the generation of disability intimacies, of creating a trusted and connected relationship with one's audience, can also be envisioned as a key strategy of establishing one's value to corporate brands. Most often, these corporate partnerships are intended to operate synergistically, where a perceived alignment occurs between the corporate brand's message, aesthetics, and values and the content creator's values, aesthetics, and, most importantly, their identity. Another strategy to gain the interest of and establish value to potential corporate partners is to have a clear and compelling, or marketable, self-brand.

As Charisse and Rikki have transformed their social media presences into their full-time careers, they have increasingly engaged in intentional strategies of branding the disabled self. Most simply, self-branding is about packaging the self as a product to be sold. It is a transposition of a brand relationship—one traditionally cultivated between consumers, marketing, and a product—into a model for constructing one's identity, relationships, and day-to-day existence (Banet-Weiser 2012; Khamis et al. 2016). The social media influencer is the apotheosis of the branded self, as they are packaging and selling their identity, values, and aesthetics to potential corporate partners and their viewers. Self-branding is about constructing, marketing, and selling a compelling and cohesive narrative of the self that flexibly responds to the demands of the market, and it is a method to establish visibility in an increasingly crowded and precarious digital economy.

For Charisse and Rikki, their hashtag campaigns, #BeBeautifullyDifferent and #NoMoreCraptions exemplify the internalization of market logic in the production of their own cultural content. Hashtag campaigns, although conceptualized as tools for the new generation of social media activists, are also technologies of "self-professionalization" (van Driel and Dumitrica 2021, 67). Charisse and Rikki's hashtags distill a narrative derived out of the commoditization of their disability identity and facilitate the circulation of their self-brand within and beyond the digital ecosystem of social media. Their hashtag campaigns evince not only the process by which the girl crip-fluencer constructs her own self-brand as a disability activist and entrepreneur, but they also demonstrate how disability has become a brand within the context of neoliberal brand culture. To be clear, branding disability is more than simply transforming disability identity into a commodity to be bought and sold, but rather it is a process of packaging and circulating an affective narrative of post-ADA disability exceptionalism. As the category of disability is recruited by state *and* corporate discourses of inclusion, to tolerate and even "love" disability becomes a matter of good business.

#NoMoreCraptions

In 2016, Rikki launched her first hashtag campaign: #NoMoreCraptions. The hashtag campaign sought to make visible the dearth of accurate and well-formatted closed captions on YouTube, exposing the ubiquitous lack of accessibility for deaf and hard of hearing users. At the time, YouTube's automatic closed captioning was, as Rikki playfully argues, "crap." For creators on YouTube who desired accurate and well formatted captions, they either had to caption the videos themselves or outsource the labor to their viewers. For viewers who needed captions, if the creator did not take initiative with captioning the videos, the viewers were stuck with undecipherable automatic captions. From Rikki's crip sit-point, this was an unacceptable access issue. Rikki partnered with Ai-Media, a transcription, captioning, and audio description company for the launch of her campaign on September 1, with a video on their channel, "Rikki Poynter—My No More Craptions Campaign." On September 25, Rikki uploaded her own video. With over 19,000 views and 870 likes, *#NoMoreCraptions: How To Properly Caption Your Videos*, is a step-by-step tutorial that teaches creators and viewers how to caption videos on YouTube. Rikki emphasizes the importance of formatting captions in an accessible way—for example, by not cluttering the frame and being realistic with how much text to place on the screen at once—and she reminds viewers that they, too, can caption their favorite creators' videos and submit the captions through the community captions feature (which, it is important to note was removed September 28, 2020 by YouTube who cited it was "rarely used and had problems with spam/abuse"). Rikki ends her tutorial reiterating the hope that "together we can make a positive change in the community." She clarifies that she means,

> All communities. For deaf and hard of hearing people. For those with auditory processing disorder. For those who are learning English or whatever language that they are watching the video in. For those that want to watch Gilmore Girls or Brooklyn 99 without waking up their neighbors or their roommates.

"Don't worry, I have your back!" she playfully adds. The video ends with a montage of different people, who the viewer can only assume are Rikki's subscribers and YouTuber friends, signing #NoMoreCraptions. Over 40 YouTube videos were uploaded with the "no more craptions" hashtag.

As it reverberates throughout the internet, #NoMoreCraptions does political-affective work by uncovering insidious spaces of ableist and audist exclusion as well as begets feelings of outrage, belonging, and justice. But it also aids in building Rikki's self-brand as an online disability activist, one whose cripistemological knowledge is available for purchase. By tweeting #NoMoreCraptions or posting a video tagged with #NoMoreCraptions, disabled and non-disabled creators and viewers alike are transformed into vital parts of the campaign's interconnective tissue. As a strategy of self-branding, hashtags stimulate recognition as well as aid in the construction of an influencer's cohesive narrative of the self. A hashtag, according to Akyel (2014), is "always already incomplete [. . .] a rhizomatic form that connects diverse texts, images, and videos" (1102). This rhizomatic quality allows Rikki to traverse the internet flexibly and affectively. Indeed, the functionality of the hashtag, what Clark (2016) calls a "discursive intervention" into dominant narratives, as well as its functionality as a nodal point of a larger digital ecosystem, works to facilitate the girl crip-fluencer's circulation and spectacularization. Every time #NoMoreCraptions is evoked in a YouTube video or linked on another social media site, it builds a network of support for the campaign, and ultimately points back to Rikki, engendering her visibility as the founder of the campaign. The cripistemological knowledge that undergirds the campaign is

Figure 9. An LGBT No More Craptions t-shirt from Rikki Poynter's merch store

most literally commodified through Rikki's line of merch. The hashtag here, takes a different aesthetic form, traversing offline on bodies. Rikki's hashtag merch, like many other influencer's, signifies more than the hashtag; the wearer is intelligible offline as part of a digital community, they are hailed as part of the #NoMoreCraptions ecosystem. For the wearers, #NoMoreCraptions becomes part of *their* self-brand.

Two years after the launch of the campaign, in 2018, Poynter wrote an article in *Medium* reflecting on the campaign and the subsequent discourse that emerged around captions and accessibility in light of deaf YouTuber Rogan Shannon's twitter thread calling out Netflix's incorrect captioning practices. Relaying her frustration with the audist/ableist statement, "there are more important things to complain about than lack of captions," the title of Poynter's *Medium* article counters with, "captions, are, in fact worth complaining about." Rikki calls forward the ADA to support the mission of her hashtag campaign. As she emphasizes in the article, "it became a law for a reason." She closes with mentioning the 2011 complaint that the National Association of the Deaf (NAD) filed against Netflix for their lack of closed captioning, which is in violation of the ADA. "Of course, the ADA won, Netflix added captions, and people were getting access," Rikki writes, "Accessibility for deaf and disabled people is important. It's mandatory."

Rikki, like Charisse, walks a fine line between disability activist and entrepreneur. And, like Charisse, her self-brand pivots on the strategic toggling between both. #NoMoreCraptions evokes the affectivity of disability rights, and the campaign illustrates how Rikki's ascendence into the economy of disability visibility as a girl crip-fluencer is both dependent on and reproduces post-ADA discourses of disability exceptionalism. Disability rights, according to Jasbir Puar (2017), is a "capacitating frame" (xvii). The passage of the ADA delineated citizenship for disabled people, "based *not* on disability pride, interdependence, and collective care," but rather on neoliberal ideals of individualism, productivity, and personal responsibility (Elman 2014, 138). Logics of compulsory able-bodiedness and white supremacy are enshrined in the ADA, as employment in the labor market is privileged as the pathway for inclusion. The ADA's twenty-fifth anniversary blog post on the United States Department of Justice reveals this very fact, noting that "the true power and promise of the ADA lies in its ability to empower individuals with disabilities to dream bigger, and to enable them to pursue their own visions of the American dream." "Visions of the American Dream" evokes the possibility and promise of upward mobility through employment and assimilation. Despite the failure of the ADA to provide the conditions for a livable life for the majority of disabled people, celebratory claims of inclusion, empowerment, and pride, function within the framework of its vestiges. Further, as Puar (2017) notes, the ADA has done "less to incorporate people with disability into labor pools and more to cultivate a privileged class of disabled citizens" (70). It is important to emphasize that I believe #NoMoreCraptions performs important political work on a micro-level, but when conceptualized within the capacitating frame of disability rights, it becomes clear that it also forwards a post-ADA fantasy of disability inclusion that hinges on rights-based forms of protection.

Further, Rikki's brand partnerships, from Google, to Apple, to Facebook, speak to the fact that her self-brand is marshaled as a valuable symbol of corporate progress and expanded market share. As Nancy Doyle writes in a 2021 *Forbes* article about disability representation, diversity, specifically disability "inclusion" is good for business. The article emphasizes that the discretionary spending power of disabled people in the United States is around $500 billion dollars per annum, so if businesses were to "let their guard down" and become amenable to "changing the disability narrative" they would understand that they are "not doing someone a favor" but rather they are "benefitting themselves" (Doyle 2021). The crip-fluencer has become integral to corporate brands and businesses' ability to change the narrative. Here we see more clearly how disability is thus absorbed into the smooth machinations of neoliberal capitalism instead of operating as a disruptive political force.

#BeBeautifullyDifferent

On March 27, 2020, Charisse uploaded a YouTube video titled, *10 Years of Becoming Beautifully Different—Bullied Then Becoming an Inspiration*. The video introduced her hashtag #BeBeautifullyDifferent, which she now uses to tag all her content across her various social media platforms (Facebook, Instagram, and YouTube). *10 Years* strategically premiered a week after her debut on the Facebook Watch docu-series, "9 Months with Courteney Cox," a "self-shot" style show centered around couples who have "endured a variety of fertility struggles" and have found subsequent success—the goal being to "enlighten" the audience and introduce them to the "many faces of pregnancy." In the eighteen-minute video, Charisse reflects on the past ten years of her life through the lens of her YouTube career. The video begins in dramatic silence. In Charisse's characteristically lo-fi aesthetic, a slideshow appears with the following monologue written out in white on a starkly contrasting black background:

> June 13, 2012. Weeks after graduating high school, I uploaded a video titled "Charisse's Story—My Life Journey with Cerebral Palsy." I had spent weeks putting this video together, sharing so openly about my life story. I have never expected my story to be viewed over 200,000 times and teach strangers worldwide so many life lessons. I was a very shy girl trying to overcome a past full of bullying, social isolation, misjudgement, and self-acceptance struggles.

She writes that although she began to "make friends from all over the world," her journey was not "always bright." The summer after her junior year in high school, she experienced "cyberbullying," "trolls" who "made fun of her difference" and who took it so far as to "encourage" Charisse to end her own life. "I thought about quitting my videos," Charisse writes, "But I picked myself back up. I have decided I wasn't going to let anyone control my life anymore." In the next scene, Charisse is smiling and holding a plaque. The text that overlays the photograph reads, "A few months later I won the inspiration award from the City of Madison." *10 Years* continues in an upward trajectory—things just keep getting better for Charisse. Spliced in between footage of her old YouTube videos are photographs and screenshots of her various public engagements, awards, and news articles written about her channel.

The last scenes of the video take us up to present day. The camera tilts upward revealing first a white tulle skirt and a beaded corset. Then we see

From Disabled Girlhood 2.0 to the "Crip-fluencer" • 99

Figure 10. Charisse in her YouTube video, *10 Years of Becoming Beautifully Different—Bullied Then Becoming an Inspiration* (2020)

Charisse's face, smilingly softly and gazing to the right. She is wearing a tulle veil that cascades around her face and a rhinestone tiara that sits atop her head. The video then shifts to a clip of Charisse and her husband's first dance. Then, quickly, to an image of an ultrasound. The scenes that follow are of Charisse in the hospital, a newborn baby perched on her chest. A slide then reads, "10 years ago I never would have imagined facing a fear could lead to so many beautiful outcomes." The video ends with a still image of Charisse standing in the middle of the frame. She is wearing a coral dress and her leg brace is prominently displayed on her left leg. To the viewer, it looks as though she is walking away; a straight path forward is illuminated. Her image is flanked by the axiom "Different is beautiful." Above and below her image reads, "Throughout my childhood others made me believe that being different was a horrible thing. But as I got older I realized you have to be different to make a difference in this world." She frames her journey as epiphanic; through overcoming fear and accepting difference, Charisse ultimately concludes that it was her non-normative embodiment, all along, that has afforded her the insight to, as she articulates, "make a difference in this world."

#BeBeautifullyDifferent is the essence of Charisse's self-brand as a girl crip-fluencer. It is both a command and an affirmation and it evokes post-, or as Banet-Weiser (2018) would argue, popular feminist discourses of self-empowerment and confidence. It is no coincidence that the introduction of her hashtag with *10 Years* premiered so close to Charisse's debut on "9 Months with Courteney Cox." Trafficking in views and clicks, "9 Months with Courteney Cox," was destined to amplify Charisse's visibility online by extending her reach to new audiences and potential followers. *10 Years* serves as an introduction of sorts to Charisse's new followers, as well as presents a cohesive narrative that gives shape to Charisse's social media presence.

In *10 Years* Charisse weaves a powerful post-ADA narrative of overcoming. It encapsulates the fantasy and requirement that under the conditions of neoliberal capitalism, "we are not who we are, but what we make of ourselves" (Giddens 1991, 75). We could even argue that *10 Years* is a spectacular *rehabilitative* tale that provides a blueprint for putting disabled subjectivity to work. The success with which Charisse was able to move forward along the rails of normative life stages—high school, work, marriage, baby—is attributed to her personal decision to make herself visible, to put herself out there on YouTube and not "allow" anyone to control her life. The spectacular framing of heteronormative love and reproduction in *10 Years* also works to further sediment assimilationist modes of belonging and citizenship as a desirable measure of disability inclusion. In "taking back" her life, Charisse exercises her capacity to overcome. The conceptualization of overcoming that Charisse's story mobilizes is not the classic narrative of overcoming disability, necessarily, but rather, it mobilizes a different narrative of overcoming defined in terms of popular feminism's "dual dynamic of injury and capacity" (Banet-Weiser 2018). According to Banet-Weiser (2018), although popular feminisms have variegated modes of expression and goals, there is an overarching theme to this iteration of feminist ideology: what girls and women really need is self-confidence. Within the purview of popular feminism, women and girls are expected to "lean in and overcome imposter syndrome" and tap into their "inner selves" to simply "be more confident" as a method to overcome the structural barriers "that are keeping them down" (Banet-Weiser 2018, 172). Self-confidence, in an economy of visibility, "is that what is *seen*: it is articulated through the strong, earnest body" (Banet-Weiser 2018, 54). We see this in the last frame of the video, where Charisse is standing tall and proud with her leg brace in plain sight.

#BeBeautifullyDifferent commands the viewer to be more confident, self-assured, and resilient. Charisse's success—symbolized in *10 Years* both by her career and her family—gives shape to the aspirational myth that through confidence, hard work, and putting yourself out there, one can attain not only stability but self-actualization. Disability, for Charisse—finally figuring out that "to make a difference" one has to *be* different—becomes the source of her human capital. Through tapping into an "inner self" and making visible her authentic experience of disability as a method to enlighten others, Charisse becomes both a model and teacher for the construction of a post-ADA fantasy of disability inclusion. Her self-brand as a girl crip-fluencer recapitulates a cruelly optimistic post-ADA sensibility that promises with individual action and self-transformation disabled subjects can too put their disabled subjectivity to work and reap the rewards. Further, the narrative Charisse constructs and forwards tethers disability inclusion to white, heteronormative logics of reproductive futurity. We see this most clearly in her more recent brand partnerships with cleaning product companies and her streaming debut in "9 Months with Courteney Cox." Disability is domesticated and neutralized in the process of becoming Charisse's self-brand. It is not the condition of radical alterity, but it is positioned as character building exceptionalism.

However, I want to end by emphasizing the uneasy tension between crip and influencer. In offering the story of Rikki and Charisse and tracking their ascendence into economies of disability visibility as what I term girl crip-fluencers, I do not wish to paint a story of complete absorption or commodification by neoliberal capital. It is true that both have gained entrance into neoliberal capitalist consumer culture vis-à-vis the monetization of their disabled subjectivity, strengthening post-ADA fantasies of disability inclusion as they are tethered to economic productivity. It is also true that their YouTube channels have carved out an affective scene of belonging for other disabled people. Both things are true at the same time. With that being said, I want to leave you, dear reader, with Alex Turchey's response to Charisse's *10 Years*:

> I found this and I can not [sic] thank you enough. I am 17 and I have mild spastic diplegia cerebral palsy. I don't see many other teens with cerebral palsy. I've only ever spoken to one teen and one adult. I've been bullied, gone through 6 sets of casting, I get 16 botox shots every three months, dry needling for muscle spasms that last over a few weeks, and I finally got leg braces. [. . .] When I'm stuck in a wheelchair I get kicked and laughed at. When I was on crutches a girl kicked my crutches across the cafeteria so I couldn't get to them. Seeing you at my age and growing has given me hope. Thank you for being so brave and sharing your story.

Thanking Charisse for engendering feelings of hope, Alex Turchey's comment gestures toward the affective power of disability visibility. For Alex Turchey, Charisse's story provides a frame for imagining a better future in order to cope with an arduous present. The future that Charisse evokes for Alex Turchey is not necessarily a curative future—one without disability or impairment—but a crip future: one that is sometimes painful, sometimes mundane, and sometimes replete with disability insight.

Three

Domesticating Disability
Crip Girls and Their Dogs

"Instead of the kid with a disability, I want Meghan to be the kid with a dog."
—Sarah Cawley, Meghan's Mom (*Dogs* 2018)

"The Kid with a Dog," the first episode of Netflix's *Dogs*, spotlights white, eleven-year-old epileptic Corrine Gogolewski of West Chester, Ohio as she and her family prepare to welcome her new service dog, Rory, into the family. Released in November 2018 and produced and developed by documentarians Glen Zipper and Academy Award-nominated Amy Berg, *Dogs* is an anthology docu-series that explores the "deep emotional bonds" between humans and dogs (Turchiano 2018). Jen Chaney (2018) for *Vulture* describes the series as "so heartwarming, your heart will need a post-binge-watch ice bath to cool down." It is not surprising that the first episode of the "heartwarming" series centers itself around Rory and Corrine, as it is reflective of a recent cultural fascination with assistance animals—specifically service dogs—and their disabled handlers. Spectacularly sentimental stories abound in contemporary popular culture and academic discourse, celebrating the "life healing" capacity of service dogs (Helton 2009; Irvin 2014; Sharon 2016; Lopez Cardenas 2020). Within these feel-good stories, the service dog is overwhelmingly positioned as an "angel on a leash," a savior who offers the disabled handler—most often disabled children and veterans—with "a new lease on life" (Harris and Sholtis 2016; Lunsford 2021). According to the not-for-profit organization the American Kennel Club, the largest and most influential purebred dog registry in the United States, service dogs offer a "new future" for disabled children (Robins 2021).

As one would expect, in "The Kid with a Dog," Rory brings renewed hope that Corrine's mother, will, as she articulates, "have her little Corrine back." Indeed, at the end of the episode, viewers witness Rory's successful intervention into one of Corrine's uncontrollable meltdowns. In the scene, Corrine is lying on the couch crying and groaning, experiencing pain from her brain's non-stop seizure activity. Her mother explains earlier in the episode that Corrine often becomes aggressive—especially if her medication is "failing"—she bites, kicks, and yells. She "can't control it." But this time, Rory barks, trots up to her, and starts licking her face. Eventually both Corrine and Rory end up on the floor, paw in hand. The episode closes with Corrine staring into Rory's eyes, telling the viewer that "life with Rory is awesome." Rory restores "little Corrine," facilitating her return to the promises and possibilities that a more "normal" (read: less disabled) girlhood brings. Apropos to the discussion in the first chapter, Rory provides a "new future" for Corrine. "The Kid with a Dog" showcases not only Rory's exceptional rehabilitative value, or his remarkable capacity for healing Corrine, but also his success in healing the family—providing them, too, with a "new future."

It is this positioning—the "savior" service dog and the "saved," or rehabilitated, disabled girl handler—, its sentimental affectivity, and its relationship to ablenationalism that I was initially interested in exploring in this chapter. However, as I began researching and writing, I soon realized that the spectacularly sentimental, although overwhelmingly ubiquitous, is not the only operative representational genre of the service dog/disabled girl handler in the contemporary economy of disability visibility. In 2020, as the COVID-19 pandemic began to unfold, a critical mass of young people flocked to the short form video app, TikTok. It was there that I stumbled upon a vibrant and growing community of disabled girl handlers, showing off custom made service dog vests, recounting experiences of being denied entry to restaurants, and sharing clips of their service dogs "tasking"—assisting with meltdowns, mobility, and alerting for changes in blood sugar. Within "service dog tok," or the emergent subculture on TikTok comprised of users who upload videos about their everyday reality as disabled handlers living in partnership with service dogs, I found that the story that disabled girl handlers construct and broadcast about their relationship with their service dogs is quite different than the story constructed in popular culture and academic discourse. It is a story of a crip "becoming in kind," to use Harlan Weaver's (2021) concept that describes an enmeshment of identity and being, both human and non-human. Becoming in kind signals a deep togetherness through relationality, and it suggests a mutual process of "*becoming with*" (Haraway 2008). On service dog tok, viewers witness how the relationship between the service dog and the disabled girl handler is integral to the construction—or shaping of—disabled girl subjectivity. Rather than fold the disabled girl handler back into chrononormative imaginings of girlhood, on service dog tok the "new future" that the service dog offers is one that is decidedly crip.

In what follows, I advance two interconnected objectives by juxtaposing sentimental representations of the service dog/disabled girl handler dyad in popular media culture with representations that disabled girl handlers produce and upload themselves on service dog tok. My first objective of this chapter is to examine the work that sentimental representations of disabled girl handlers and their service dogs perform in the service of ablenationalism. To do so, I closely analyze the episode I began this chapter with, "The Kid with a Dog" and the viral story of a young, white disabled girl, Bella, and her service dog, George. As I stated above, the producers' choice to center the majority of the first episode of *Dogs* around the story of Rory and Corrine is unsurprising, as it reflects a larger cultural fascination with service animals, and particularly service dogs, in the United States in the late twenty-tens and early twenty-twenties (and the growth of the service dog community on TikTok is part of this). The episode's subplot follows the journey of Rory's littermate, Strax, and a second disabled girl handler, Meghan. The decision to focus the episode on not only one, but two white, disabled girl handlers is significant. I suggest that Corrine/Rory, Bella/George, and Meghan/Strax all circulate within an affective economy of "puppy love" that constructs and reflects an understanding of the contemporary service dog as an exceptional "good dog": an unmatched technology of rehabilitation at the intersices of "pet" and "laborer" that is the last resort for disabled girls' integration into the strictures of normative society. Perhaps unwittingly, these representations rely on an insidiously harmful rehabilitative logic that resecures compulsory able-bodiedness and chrononormative understandings of girlhood. I show how the affectivity of these representations take the "teeth" out of disability, so to speak, through forwarding a privatized understanding of care alongside a depoliticized understanding of disability, ultimately facilitating the uneven patterning of disabled girls marked for life.

In a similar maneuver to my investigation of the girl crip-fluencer, my second objective is to explore disabled girls' self-representational practices on TikTok, and more specifically, service dog tok. In effect, I extend the discussion that I began in the previous chapter, weaving together a larger story about disabled girls' participation in twenty-first century disability culture by illuminating their vital (yet woefully underacknowledged) roles as crip cultural producers. Taking two disabled girl handlers/creators as case studies, @rosie.the.sd and @muslimservicedogmom28, I show how their videos forge an alternative valuation of the service dog as a queer/crip companion who is integral to the disabled girl handlers' process of *becoming* disabled. This representation of the service dog/disabled girl handler dyad pushes back against the ablenationalist positioning of the service dog as an exceptional technology of rehabilitation and instead constructs a new cartography of interspecies "kinship beyond [the] heteronormative domesticity" of the nuclear family (Butler 2020, 688). Ultimately, I contend that through proclaiming their desire for and delight in their interdependent and (non-innocent) loving service dog companionships, disabled girl handlers on TikTok *crip* girlhood by upending the assumption that the desire for independence and autonomy is a "natural" part of growing up.

This chapter thinks with scholars writing at the intersection of disability studies and critical animal studies such as Kelly Oliver (2016), Sunaura Taylor (2017), Michael Lundblad (2020), and Chloë Taylor, Kelly Struthers Montford, and Stephanie Jenkins (2021), who have articulated with urgency the necessity of wrestling with the "animal question" in disability studies. Connections between disability and "the animal" have largely been undertheorized, which, in part, is due to the fraught relationship between disability studies and animal studies, inaugurated by Peter Singer's (2009) ableist (and I would add racist) claim that highly intelligent non-human animals are more deserving of rights than "severely" disabled humans. The drive for disability studies and disability activists to distance themselves from the question of the animal or from animality, writ large, makes sense, as there "has been an urgent need among dehumanized populations [. . .] to challenge animalization and claim humanity" (Taylor 2017, 20). Singer's (2009) claim is an example of how the boundary between human and non-human animal has historically operated as a tool to mark out certain populations (Black, Indigenous, disabled) as more bestial, as subhuman, as proximate to animal, or even, in Singer's opinion, as less than certain animals, thus justifying the violence and oppression of "rational man's" Others (Wynter 2003; Kim 2015; Boisseron 2018; Jackson 2020). For example, the paradigm of animality has long been wielded to position intellectually disabled people as subhuman, deserving of inhumane treatment because of their "animal-like nature," and therefore disposable (New York's Willowbrook School is but one example) (Taylor 2017, 106). In Singer's (2009) claim we see an echo of this history.

However, Zakiyyah Iman Jackson (2020) so persuasively reminds us that the "Human" has always been a violent category of exclusion. Rather than assimilationist bids for inclusion into the category, she argues that scholars must work to unsettle the category and its ontological integrity, and in doing so, question the grounds for its supremacy. Similarly, Sunaura Taylor (2017) asks, "How can we assert both our humanity and our animality?" (110). In that spirit, the second half of this chapter, especially, participates in this project of questioning and unsettling. Instead of proposing an assimilatory and inclusionist turn toward the human, I show how the service dog/disabled girl handler dyad provides an entry point for thinking about crip ways of being beyond the human. Moreover, thinking through disability and animality requires the recognition that ableism and speciesism,[1] or the belief that humans are superior to all other non-human animals (on the basis of intelligence, function, and rationality), are inherently intertwined. In the following sections, the discussion of the rehabilitative exceptionalism of the service dog and its capitulation to the "good dog" trope—defined as the dog who places humans' needs over their own innate "wild" instincts, specifically "in the service of his human family, the representatives of white Western civilization and of human culture"—provokes a consideration of the complicated ways in which the service dog is put to work in the service of securing the exclusionary category of the "Human," and in doing so, is also governed by ableist (and neoliberal) norms of function and productivity (Armbruster 2002, 358).

A "Hero Wearing Dog Tags": A Brief Note on the Service Dog

Representations of service dogs in popular media culture have hit a critical mass: from documentaries that showcase the painstaking process of training, such as *Prison Dogs*, a 2016 film about a service dog training program at Fishkill State Correctional Facility in New York state, to fictional representations in television, such as the 2019 *CW* crime drama, *In the Dark*, about Murphy Mason, a blind twenty-something who works at a training school for guide dogs as well as uses a guide dog named Pretzel.[2] This media saturation could be interpreted as signaling progress in the roll or march toward a more disability inclusive world. If understood as evidencing "some degree of societal will to facilitate fuller integration of people with disabilities in society," then representations of the service dog/disabled handler dyad that pepper the evening news, talk shows, and streaming docu-series implicitly attest to the value of these interspecies partnerships (MacPherson-Mayer and van Daalen-Smith 2020, 76). However, the stories about service dogs and their disabled handlers that often gain the most traction in the economy of disability visibility are the heart-wrenching and heartwarming, and most often these stories center the enduringly normative cast of sympathetic disabled characters: disabled children and veterans. Disability studies scholars have recently revealed that overwhelmingly within these popular media representations, the service dog is framed solely in terms of their utility, or as tools that enable the reintegration of the disabled person back into normative society, privileging the human perspective over the non-human animals' (MacPherson-Mayor and Daalen-Smith 2020). Furthermore, the ubiquity with which the service dog is framed as the "savior" of the disabled person insidiously reinforces an ableist, medicalized construction of disability as merely a target of "intervention and amelioration" and belies the nuanced experience of interdependency and relationality that many disabled handlers articulate in first person narratives about their relationships with their service animals (Mykhalovskiy et al. 2020, 27; Michalko 1999; Oliver 2016; Taylor 2017; Price 2017; Kuusisto, 2018). Although the following sections build on and deepen this critique, it is important to be clear here that I am not critiquing the use of service dogs, as they play a vital role in the material imagining and enacting of livable lives for disabled people. As much scholarship and first-person narratives have shown, the service dog/disabled handler partnership is one that can be enormously beneficial for both the disabled handler *and* the service dog (Michalko 1999; Oliver 2016; Taylor 2017; Price 2017; Kuusisto 2018).[3] With all that being said, before I move to more thoroughly explore the construction of sentimental representations of disabled girl handler/service dog dyads, it is of contextual importance to say a few words about the history of the service dog, its connection to wartime "innovation," as well as to the logic of rehabilitation. In the following section, I aim to highlight that what is interesting about the service dog—as opposed to other "tools" or inanimate technologies of rehabilitation, like the self-propelled wheelchair—is not just the service dog's animacy, but its fundamental inextricability from the variegated legacy of the dog itself, as a laborer in service of empire, family, and the human.

    Despite the novelty suggested by the recent fascination with service dogs, scholars argue that helping partnerships between dogs and disabled people have existed for centuries across the world (Price 2017). In the United States, the emergence of the "modern" service dog is tethered to a broader twentieth and twenty-first century history of war, disability, and rehabilitation. We see an allusion to this history, perhaps unintentionally, in "The Kid with a Dog" in the form of a graphic t-shirt worn by a service dog trainer. The t-shirt is emblazoned with the phrase "heroes wearing dog tags," which is a play on a colloquialism usually used in reference to human military service members, "heroes don't wear capes, they wear dog tags." Within the context of the episode, the phrase refers to the service dogs that are being trained, evoking a connection between the service dog and militarism.

Many scholars mark World War I as the beginning of the "modern" use of dogs trained to assist disabled people (Fishman 2003; Ascarelli 2010; Ostermeier 2010). In 1927, American philanthropist Dorothy Harrison Eustis, who was at the time breeding and training German Shepherd police dogs in Switzerland, wrote an article for *The Saturday Evening Post* detailing how Germany was training dogs to assist blind veterans: "because of their extraordinary intelligence and fidelity, Germany has chosen her own breed of the shepherd dog to help the rehabilitation of her war blind" (Eustis 1927). As the story goes, a twenty-year-old blind man from the United States, Morris Frank, read the article, sent Eustis a letter, and traveled to Switzerland to learn how to become a guide dog handler. A year later in 1928, Frank, his guide dog Buddy, and Eustis went on to establish the first guide dog school called The Seeing Eye in Nashville, Tennessee. A couple decades later, after the Second World War, guide dog schools rapidly proliferated in the United States. Many of them were launched by dog breeders who wanted to "take advantage of wartime emotions and of a new federal law, which appropriated funds to supply war blind veterans with dogs" (Ostermeier 2010).[4]

Prompted by an unusually high number of physically disabled soldiers returning home, World War I also marked a shift in attitudes and treatment of disabled veterans, transforming cultural understandings of disability (Stiker 1999). A consensus began to take shape where instead of viewing war injuries as "lingering memorials to the epic disaster of war" or the result of an "avoidable social calamity," disablement was instead perceived as "inevitable" or a natural consequence of an unavoidable event (James 2011, 138). This framing absolved the culpability of the state and transformed the body into an "object of repair," something that could be returned to a "prior, normal state" (Stiker 1999, 124). This is what many scholars of disability have characterized as the logic of rehabilitation. Not only does the logic of rehabilitation operate by transforming the injured body into an object of repair that can be normalized and restored, but it seeks to invisibilize the alterity that characterizes disabled embodiment. Made "ordinary again" successfully rehabilitated disabled bodies can be folded back into the nation and its attendant institutions. More than just a medicalized process, rehabilitation is a cultural logic that dominates how we still conceptualize disability (Stiker 1999; McRuer 2006; Elman 2014; Elman and McRuer 2020).

The seeing eye dog's history is strikingly parallel to another wartime technology of rehabilitation: the self-propelled wheelchair, developed in 1933 by

Everest & Jennings and first used by Canadian Lieutenant John Counsell, "a combat-injured paraplegic from an upper-class family" (Fritsch 2013, 137–38). Soon after acquiring the wheelchair, he lobbied the Canadian Department of Veterans Affairs to provide wheelchairs for paralyzed veterans. As "tool[s] of aggressive normalization," seeking to "repair" the body of disabled veterans, the seeing eye dog and the self-propelled wheelchair similarly facilitated disabled veterans' entrance into the workforce and allowed them to leave long-term care and medical institutions, restoring their once lost marketability (Gerber 2003; Stiker 1999).

Unlike the wheelchair, however, the characterization of the modern service dog as a "hero wearing dog tags" goes beyond this brief rehabilitative history and must be contextualized in relation to the broader legacy, role, and affectivity of the dog. In the United States, specifically, dogs are "widely loved," and by historic design are "understood to be loyal pets" embedded deeply within "affective structures of sentimentality and the heteronormative nuclear family" (Diamond-Lenow 2020, 10). In the early 19th century, pet dogs became understood as "love machines," capable of rousing strong, positive emotions, and were linked to a new "sensibility," one where love and kindness toward animals and pets was part and parcel of establishing white, "middle-class propriety" (Vänskä 2016, 79; Kete 1994). In tracing the genealogy of this conceptualization, Annamari Vänskä (2016) writes more specifically that in the 19th century, the practice of pet keeping that trickled down from the white upper classes to the middle classes "thoroughly sentimentalized the dog" and granted them a quasi-subjecthood as a sentient being deserving of care (79). The pet dog became an important tool of domesticity, a source and mediator of emotions like "love, loyalty, and care within the family," and transformed into a commodity (Vänskä 2016, 79). The practice of pet dog keeping was thoroughly intertwined with capitalism, as Vänskä (2016) notes, "already in 1860 dog biscuits were marketed to dog owners," thus purchasing things like dog treats and dog clothing became synonymous with establishing a communicative and emotional bond between oneself and one's pet (80).

Pet dog keeping was also conceptualized as a pedagogical tool to teach "compassion towards others and children" (Vänskä 2016, 79). In her discussion of John Locke's influential text *Some Thoughts Concerning Education*, Colleen Boggs (2013) contends that Locke, two centuries earlier, underscored the broader importance of animals to children's education. She writes that he afforded "special status to animals in the didactic enterprise of enabling children to develop their capacities: the affective relationship to animals forms the nexus between the body and mind that is requisite for liberal subject formation" (Boggs 2013, 138). For Locke, parents' treatment of children mirrored children's treatment of animals, and according to Boggs (2013), "what was at stake in these carefully calibrated relationships [was] children's initiation into proper modes of governance" (139). We could conceptualize pet dog keeping as a pedagogy of proper affectivity, then, as it appears to be an extension of Locke's belief that the liberal subject emerges through the process of learning and exercising compassion toward all "sensible" creatures (read: beings that have capacity for physical and emotional feeling, so excluded are Black people, Indigenous people, and people of color). Curiously, Vänskä (2016) argues that the civilizing logic that informed the newly established pet keeping industry in the 19th century dovetailed with that used in children's education. For both the pet dog and the child, the goal was the elimination of "animal-like" qualities through the control of sexuality and behavior.

In the shadow of this history is another one: the history of the violent ways in which the dog has been wielded to secure white domesticity—from the slave dog, to the police dog, to the military working dog (Wall 2016; Boisseron 2018; Diamond-Lenow 2020). Our "love" for the dog must also be understood in relation to these violent histories of racial terror, as the dog's historic role in securing the family, property, and empire is fundamentally linked to white supremacy and racial capitalism. Even the history of the "modern" service dog is explicitly linked to these violent histories, as Eustis was engaged in a project of training police dogs prior to seeing eye dogs. The construction of the service dog as a "hero wearing dog tags" and its circulation in popular media culture, then, must be carefully considered in relation to the project of white supremacy and racialized nationalism in the United States.

In the next section, I weave together the stories of Strax/Meghan, Rory/Corrine, and George/Bella to explore the rehabilitative exceptionalism of the modern service dog. Understood as "good dogs" exemplar, Strax, Rory, and George are lauded for their physical *and* affective labor. Not only do they successfully rehabilitate the disabled girl and facilitate her "return" to normative girlhood, but they play an integral role in re-securing the white, nuclear family from the disruption disability portends. To be clear, according to the 2011 revision to the ADA, a service animal is defined as a dog that is *trained to perform a task* for the benefit of an individual with a physical, sensory, intellectual, psychiatric, or other mental disability. Tasks are defined in terms of a *physical action*, such as picking up keys, guiding, hearing, or turning on lights. Emotional companionship or therapeutic support, according to the ADA, are *not acceptable tasks*.[5] Although, it is important to note here that disabled handlers and disability studies scholars such as Margaret Price (2017) and Kelly Oliver (2016) argue that, in practice, this parsing out of tasks and companionship is nearly impossible. So, as you may imagine, despite the ADA's codification of the service animal in contradistinction to the pet, these spectacularly sentimental representations circulate within an affective economy of "puppy love," wherein affects that "stick" to the pet dog are transposed onto the service dog. Ultimately, I find that these representations of the disabled girl handler figured in relation to the service dog, as a "good dog" exemplar, evince a weak form of inclusionism in service of ablenationalism that depoliticizes disability and insidiously re-secures the hegemony of the nuclear family as the ideal locus for care.

Cripping Sentimental Representations of Disabled Girl Handlers and Their Service Dogs

In 2015, multiple news outlets, from *The Daily Mail* ("Lean on Me: Girl, 11, with Genetic Condition which Left Her Unable to Walk Takes Her First Steps in Nine Years with the Help of Her Pet Great Dane George") to the medical talk show *The Doctors* ("Service Dog Changed Bella's Life"), ran stories about an "unlikely pair" with a "special bond": an eleven-year-old girl "with a rare genetic disorder" named Bella Burton and her Great Dane service dog, George (Bertsche 2015; ABC 13 Eyewitness News 2015). Bella, diagnosed at age two with Morquio syndrome[6]—a genetic condition that affects the bones, spine, and organs—first met George when she began volunteering at the Service Dog Project, an organization in Ipswich, Massachusetts that trains and donates Great Danes "for people with balance and mobility limitations" (Service Dog Project Instagram). News articles emphasize the unusual and serendipitous nature of her service dog pairing process. In her and George's case, the service dog picked the handler. As Bella states in multiple interviews, she volunteered at the Service Dog Project without the expectation of being paired with a service dog. She even surmises that most dogs did not like her because of her high-pitched voice. But, one day during a routine visit, Bella happened to go into George's kennel, and according to Bella, he did not want her to leave. He "blocked the doorway and tried to sit on [her] lap and tried to put his paw and head on [her] so she couldn't move" ("George (Great Dane)" 2016). Six months after they met, George allegedly facilitated the miraculous: Bella's renewed ability to hold her own weight and walk without crutches (Gordon 2015; "George (Great Dane)" 2016; Inside Edition Staff 2021).

A spectacularly sentimental representation of the disabled girl handler/service dog dyad, the viral story of Bella and George relies on and reproduces an insidiously harmful rehabilitative logic that positions the service dog as the last resort for the disabled girl's integration into the strictures of normative society. This positioning of the service dog in relation to the disabled girl handler works to reify a medicalized and individualized understanding of disability, cementing compulsory able-bodiedness, as well as chrononormative understandings of girlhood under the guise of loving companionship. In multiple news articles, the blatant abjectness that once constituted Bella's life with Morquio syndrome is written in dramatic contrast to her current life with George. Before George, Bella's existence is reduced to a tragic pathology: "suffering" from a "rare" degenerative condition whose prognosis is "hard to predict" (Gordon 2015; Pawlowski 2015). Articles note that her short life was punctuated by invasive and ineffectual surgeries—nine to be exact, including the "reconstruction of her hips and feet" (Pawlowski 2015). Her use of crutches as a mobility aid worried her mother, Rachel, as it appeared "Bella was losing muscle strength in her lower body, [. . .] swinging her legs rather than walking on them" (Pawlowski 2015). Thanks to George's help, instead of inevitably being "confined to a wheelchair," like most people with Morquio, she now can zoom around on a bike, swim, and most impressively, walk without assistance. According to Bella's mother, George has not only "sav[ed] [Bella] from much of the pain her condition could have caused her," but he has "rescued [Bella] from a life of immobility" ("The Rescuers" 2019). She is now "able to be a kid" ("The Rescuers" 2019).

George functions within this narrative as the rehabilitative linchpin to Bella's wondrous transformation from abjection to inspiration, figured as her happy "return" to childhood. In particular, the hyperbolic portrait painted of Bella before and after George—from swinging her body on crutches to walking unassisted—is an example of what Mykhalovskiy et al. (2020) call the "small miracles trope." Small miracles "combine the wonderous [sic] with the mundane" and naturalize a rehabilitative logic that position disabled bodies valuable insofar as they are always striving toward an able-bodied/minded ideal (Mykhalovskiy et al. 2020). I am not denying that it is quite remarkable that George's large body is the perfect height for the ideal harness placement for Bella, and it is true that this support eventuates Bella's ability to walk for short distances without any assistance. However, the celebratory narrative idealizes and reinforces the supremacy of bipedal ambulation. In an ableist culture, walking is positioned as a necessary precondition for a life and a future that is desirable. According to disability studies scholars Peers and Eales (2017) bipedal ambulation is socially mobilizing, as it is thoroughly caught up in ideas of neoliberal capitalist productivity and independence, and more broadly, chrononormative understandings of development.

Bella's happy return to childhood, and more specifically her happy return to an empowered girlhood, is evidenced in an extraordinarily idyllic scene from an episode of the Smithsonian Channel's television series, *Dogs with Extraordinary Jobs*. In the episode that features George and Bella, Bella is splashing around in a lake, somersaulting in the cerulean water. The scene quickly transitions to Bella zooming around on a bike with George running alongside her. Her mother Rachel laughs, and in implicit reference to Bella swimming and riding her bike says that Bella likes to "prove everyone wrong and do things that she was told she would never do" ("The Rescuers" 2019). The airy quality of the scene gestures toward the idealized, yet constrained freedom that defines normative ideas of childhood at the precipice of youth. As Slater (2012) argues, youth is often conceptualized as "a time of disruption, risk, and rebellion" that is understood in terms of transience (202). This temporal stage marks the transition from "childhood/development/dependence" to "adulthood/mastery/independence" (Apgar 2023, 53). For the disabled child, and the disabled girl more specifically, the disabled body presents a challenge to normative understandings of youth because of its perceived perpetual dependence. As I discussed in chapter 1, the disabled girl is always at risk of temporal failure, of a presumed inability to move through the transient stage of youth to a reproductive futurity that defines adult womanhood. However, for Bella, George is represented as (literally and figuratively) moving her past the "immobility" that the severeness of her disability confers, and in doing so, returns her to the linear rails of development: to a "girlness" and future womanhood that was once out of reach.

A few years after Bella and George's story went viral, the episode from the 2018 Netflix docu-series *Dogs* that I opened the chapter with, "The Kid with a Dog," catapulted another spectacularly sentimental story about service dogs and disabled girl handlers into the national imaginary. The episode spotlights the pairing process of two disabled girls and their service dogs and vaguely profiles the service dog breeding and training organization that the families utilize called 4 Paws for Ability out of Xenia, Ohio. As I mentioned in the introduction to this chapter, much of the episode centers eleven-year-old, epileptic Corrine Gogolewski and her journey being paired with Rory, a Goldendoodle who is trained as a seizure alert service dog. The episode also includes a parallel storyline that documents the pairing process between Rory's littermate, Strax, and six-year-old Meghan Cawley. Meghan was diagnosed with VACTERL[7] as an infant, a disability that is a cluster of impairments that affect her balance and ability to walk, which Strax is trained to assist her with. The episode's myopic framing of disability—as solely an object outside of one's "true self" that needs intervention—symbolically "embodies for others an affirmative answer to the unspoken question, 'Yes, but in the end, wouldn't you rather be more like me?'" (McRuer 2006, 10). The spectacular stories of Meghan and Corrine, like Bella, rely on and reproduce a rehabilitative logic that position striving toward able-bodiedness/mindedness (either figured as bipedal ambulation or, in Corrine's case, docility) as a precondition for a life, or girlhood present and adulthood future, that is desirable and "natural."

The viewers are first introduced to Meghan halfway through the episode at the 4 Paws for Ability training facility. The families receiving dogs are circled up, and Sarah, Meghan's mother, introduces Meghan and explains that she was born with VACTERL, so she can "get pretty unsteady on her feet a lot of times." As Meghan smiles and meets Strax for the first time, in a voice-over, Sarah solemnly wields the ubiquitous narrative, saturated with anxiety about the potential bad future waiting for the disabled girl: "You never expect your child to be born with special needs, but in a second, all of that changes." Meghan's "special needs," although constructed as less sinister than Corrine's epilepsy, are figured as nothing more than individual pathology and are presented as objects that exist outside of and in antagonistic relation to Meghan's "true" self and potential future. We see this play out in the next sequence of scenes that juxtapose Meghan dancing in a dance studio with her being weighed and x-rayed in a doctor's office. In the scenes where Meghan is dancing, Sarah explains that soon after Meghan learned how to walk, she started dancing. "She has this grace about her," Sarah says, "That's just the way she's built." The background music shifts from joyful to ominous, and we find out that Meghan has a "significant spinal deformity" and if she were to fall and hurt her neck, she could become paralyzed. She is then measured and weighed on camera, and her spinal deformity is visualized by a snake-shaped spinal x-ray—signifying the objectivity and knowability of Meghan's disability. The scene also works visually to distance Meghan from her disability: her disability is captured in the x-ray, while Meghan is sitting in a chair next to the x-ray. In stark contrast from the joy that her body brings her in the dancing scene, her disability as captured in the x-ray is threatening and perilous.

Like Meghan, Corrine's disability is constructed in antagonistic relation to her "true" self. Her epilepsy is hyperbolically constructed as a lurking corporeal boogeyman that is determined to snatch up "the real" Corrine at any moment. We see this most clearly in a scene where Corrine's mother, Beth, is sitting at the dining room table reading aloud from what appears to be a journal. In a pensive tone, she reads: "November 20, 2012. Corrine was overly aggressive the night before. She started crying really hard. She was hitting, biting, and pulling my hair. I felt horrible but I had to restrain her. The next day, they increased her meds, and it's made Corrine very irritable." She flips through pages upon pages of what the viewer can only assume are similarly distressing journal entries. Then, she lands on one that is quite the contrast: "December third to seventh, Corrine had an amazing week this week. She's happy, giggly, enthusiastic about reading and writing. She is the Corrine I haven't seen." Beth starts crying as she reads the next few sentences, "She is the Corrine I haven't seen in over a year, and I am so excited to have my little girl . . . I am so excited to have my little Corrine back." Beth ends with saying she understands Corrine will not "outgrow this"—and to the viewer it is unclear if she is referring to the seizures or to her meltdowns, although it would be impossible to disentangle—and, as Corrine gets older, it could "progressively get worse and worse." Understandably, the embodied reality (and unbearable pain) of Corrine's epilepsy is something that deeply worries Beth, as a seizure could lead to Corrine's death if she is left unassisted for too long. However, the episode disproportionately focuses on Corrine's out of control meltdowns and aggression as cause for her inability to live a "normal" life. Not only is Corrine's disability constructed in antagonistic relation to her "true" self, but her disabled bodymind is perceived as "dangerous" because it is "out of control" (Garland-Thomson 1997, 37). This is because the "threat of disability," as Liddiard and Slater (2018) argue, "endangers the carefully constructed myth of the 'able' body and self which is foundational to a neoliberal social order where multiple forces are in play to keep *all* bodies 'tidy,' manageable, and bound" (321). The "leakiness" of Corrine's epilepsy—her "out of control" meltdowns characterized by aggression and physical violence—is what must be contained for Corrine to progress forward to normative adulthood.

Rory is implicitly positioned as a technology of containment, as the arbiter of control over this out of control-ness: the "last resort" tasked with bringing "little Corrine back." Again, Liddiard and Slater (2018) provide a helpful frame for understanding the "border zone" of youth: a space wherein children are expected to be shaped from incomplete, irrational, and unproductive to complete, rational, and productive adults. Rory, then, operates as a tool of this shaping. For Meghan and Bella, the job that the service dog is expected to perform, most literally, is a straightening out of their non-normative choreographies of ambulation; they function as tools that shape and capacitate their mobility. And we see their success—from Bella being able to walk unassisted, to Meghan being able to walk and balance in a final scene that I will discuss in the next section. Rory too capacitates Corrine's mobility, facilitating the possibility of smoother movement through the world, containing through modulating Corrine's aggression. Like Strax and George, he, too, "returns" the possibility of a "normal" life, or girlhood, to Corrine. He facilitates her "return" to the docility of white girlhood, as well as holds the key to a future worth living for. Like in the case of Meghan and Bella, the "normal life" that Rory makes possible for Corrine is conceptualized in terms of a linear telos of development gestured toward in scenes that show her playfully engaging in soccer, dance, swimming, and school: signifiers of a middle class, white girlhood. Here it is important to note that throughout the episode, neither Meghan, nor Corrine are represented as totally helpless (and we see this in Bella's narrative, as well). Their parents emphasize their "natural" proclivity for independence and autonomy, which as Apgar (2023) notes, is an "ideal that defines the individual subject" in neoliberal society and is "central to American identity and the good life" (12). Their love for physical activity—Meghan's passion for dance and Corrine's competitive interest in soccer—is consistently foregrounded. Like Abbey Curran in chapter 1, they are imagined as disabled "future girls," lauded for their confidence, gumption, and willingness to "take charge of [their] life, seize chances, and achieve [their] goals" (Harris 2003, 1). Their partnership with their service dogs is constructed as the perfect antidote to aid in their naturalized desire to push their bodies past the corporeal limit that their disability accords, as well as affords them the status of exceptional proto-citizen subjects.

We see a glimmer of what this "normal" life looks at the end of the episode: Corrine is at school with Rory, walking through the halls side-by-side. She then goes to soccer practice with Rory, where he watches her on the sidelines. In a tense scene that functions as the climax of the episode, Corrine has one last meltdown where she is on the couch crying and yelling, unwilling to go to bed. Beth calmly asks Rory if he can help get Corrine to bed, and we see him trot over to Corrine and lick her face. The scene shifts and we see that Corrine has stopped crying and has moved onto the ground with Rory, holding his paw and staring into his eyes. The denouement is represented by Corrine's new bedtime routine. Rory, Beth, and Corrine are all in Corrine's bed together. Beth gets out of Corrine's bed and tucks in both Corrine and

Rory and prepares a mattress for the floor. In a voice-over, Corrine describes an interspecies intimacy that has developed between her and Rory: "Sometimes I wonder what Rory is thinking. And I think he loves me." The camera zooms out and we see that Beth is on the mattress on the floor next to Corrine, and we see her gaze over at Rory who is sleeping right next to Corrine. She says, "I will probably always sleep on Corrine's floor. I just think it's motherly instinct to never leave a child in this situation. But I do trust that he will alert us if anything strange is going on. It's like a tag team. It's not just on the weight of my shoulders anymore." The scene allows the viewer to breathe a sigh of relief. Hailed to protect Corrine, Rory functions as a pressure release valve, offloading from Beth some of the weight of Corrine's care. Here we see that Rory's role and value is not solely defined in relation to the physical labor he performs tasking for Corrine, but it is also figured in relation to the *affective labor* that he performs to keep the family together.

Ablenationalism's Love Machine

In 2015, George won the AKC Humane Fund Award for Canine Excellence in the service dog category. The awards "honor outstanding dogs that demonstrate the power and the importance of the human canine bond" ("George (Great Dane)" 2016). George received the award alongside four other dogs, one in the uniformed service K9 category, one in the exemplary companion category, one in search and rescue, and one in the therapy category. One could say that this award gestures toward the institutional recognition of the service dog as a "good dog" exemplar, or a dog that is imagined as willing to sacrifice it all for their human companion, demonstrating "loyalty to culture over nature" (Armbruster 2002, 354). A four-minute YouTube video on the AKC's channel captures the presentation of his award, and Bella and her parents are present to walk George across the stage, visually signaling his position as an integral member of the family. The caption of the video notes that George and Bella have an "inseparable bond" and that George will "do anything for Bella." It explains that "George has given Bella the strength and determination to walk and take part in activities she otherwise would not have been able to do. [. . .] He has helped her gain confidence, independence and happiness." More than simply animate equipment or a capacitating tool of mobility, the caption emphasizes his role as a cuddly companion—a "love machine"—that inspires strength, confidence, and happiness (Vänskä 2016).

As "love machines," Rory, George, and Strax generate good feelings. Unlike inanimate technologies of mobility that often evoke uncomfortable

Domesticating Disability • 119

Figure 11. The service dog George, Bella, and her parents at the AKC Humane Fund Awards for Canine Excellence from *George (Great Dane)-2015 AKC Humane Fund Awards for Canine Excellence* (2016)

feelings, such as the wheelchair or crutch, the animacy and affectivity of the service dog works to soften the effects (and affects) of embodied difference. Thus, the rehabilitative exceptionalism of the modern service dog must be understood as concomitantly derived from their successful role, or affective labor, as a "love machine." Bella and George's appearance on the medical talk show *The Doctors* serves as one example. When describing the story of their serendipitous pairing, Bella's mother, Rachel, notes that one of the Service Dog Project's mottos is "Drop the cane, get a Dane." After she says that, the audience raucously applauds and the hosts—the doctors—smile, clap, and voice their approval. "I like that," they affirmingly chorus. The positioning of the service dog as more desirable than inanimate mobility devices makes sense, as disabled people are often imagined as having an "uncomfortable dependence" on technological tools, evoking feelings of "uneasiness" (Peers and Eales 2017, 112). In each article and media appearance that circulate the story of Bella and George, the inanimate crutches that Bella once relied on are called forth in great contrast to George, who is lovingly (and somewhat cheekily) referred to as a "living, breathing, crutch." Right before Rachel mentions the motto, she gravely recounts that "once they put Bella on crutches, [they] kinda thought she would be on crutches for good and move on to a wheelchair with the progressive disorder." In this context, negative affects stick to crutches and the wheelchair as objects—as inanimate matter (Chen 2012)—that evoke ableist fears of dependence and anxieties about the inevitability of bodymind breakdown. The finality with which Rachel wields the wheelchair in Bella's story evokes the concept of "wheelchair bound" and the concomitant feelings of hopelessness and despair that the "loss" of walking portends for the ableist imagination. For Bella, "becoming with" the wheelchair (in crip/queer intimate relation), or at the very least, the recognition of the wheelchair as an object of care, in and of itself, is affectively foreclosed.

The affective power of the dog and the value imbued in their capacity for softening the uncomfortable feelings that disability evokes is similarly highlighted in the penultimate scene that features Meghan, Strax, and Sarah in "The Kid with a Dog." In the scene, the three of them are walking through the shopping mall, and Meghan is practicing tasking with Strax. Strax braces at Sarah's command as Meghan gets down off a stool. In a voice-over, Sarah explains that she wants to give Meghan "every opportunity possible to live her best independent life." Meghan is "going to be different," she elaborates, "She might walk differently and have a nurse following her around. [. . .] But if she's walking around with a dog, that's like instant cool for kids." Here Sarah gestures toward the idea that the aesthetic judgement of Strax as cool—and the value or cultural capital of that coolness—can, in some ways, soften the uneasy feelings that Meghan's non-normative embodiment evokes in her classmates. It is not only his physical labor—exemplified by bracing—that facilitates the "best independent life" that Sarah so desires for Meghan, but it is also his affective labor as a "love machine." In offering Meghan "instant cool," Strax animates positive affects that stick to the disabled girl handler/service dog dyad, potentially reshaping the encounter between the non-disabled other and Meghan.

The stakes of the service dog as it is enlisted as a "love machine" are laid bare within the comment sections of the YouTube videos that feature Bella and George's appearance on *The Doctors*. Multiple commentors state that Bella and George's story has inspired and moved them to tears. Scott Brandts, for example, writes "God, I absolutely love being brought to tears by stories like this. SHINE ON, LITTLE SUPERSTAR!!" Daisy Dejesus's comment, "Bella I'm super super happy for you and George," includes a heart eyes emoji and two paw print emojis at the end of the comment. Prerarana

Prathap writes "sooo cuteee . . . animals r really the best thing that happened to this planet. Love them." George and Bella, together, circulate as a cute object, eliciting pleasure from the viewers. Cuteness, as Sianne Ngai (2012) writes, is deeply tied to the child, and it "is not just an aestheticization but an eroticization of powerlessness, evoking tenderness for 'small things,' but also, sometimes, a desire to belittle or diminish them further" (3). Violence, as she makes clear, is "always implicit in our relation to the cute object" (Ngai 2012, 85). The girl and the dog, as a cute object provokes "warm and fuzzy feelings," but as I discussed in chapter 1, our affective relationship to the disabled girl is tenuous because of the impending reality of aging. We can understand George and Bella as a shared object of "puppy love," as the viewer's affectation toward the dyad is one that is transitory and always, already fleeting.

Relatedly, permeating the comment section is the construction of George as "hyper-able." He is upheld as a "near perfect organism" (Price 2017, 6), or as an "angel of god," as one commentor, Zakk Wylde writes. Viewers emphatically describe George as "such a good boy" with a "wonderful spirit." They characterize him as an "amazing helper and friend for Bella," and note his "selflessness" and "protectiveness." George's "goodness" per the comments is, in part, derived from his "natural" willingness to serve his human, Bella. Indeed, here we see how the affective grammar of the modern service dog is informed by exclusionary and ableist discourses of fitness, obedience, health, and excellence. What of the service dog that is too small, too slow, incontinent, not willing enough? As a "dog with an extraordinary job," as suggested by the titular name of the *Smithsonian* series that spotlights George, to be a good service dog is to conform to neoliberal human standards of productivity, personal responsibility, and self-sufficiency. To be a good service dog is to serve one's human, above all else.

Returning to Vänskä's (2016) historic investigation of the dog as a "love machine," she writes that when this mechanical metaphor was first utilized at the turn of the 19th century, it marshaled the dog as part and parcel of the industrial revolution's proto-techno-futurism. Specifically, she explains that the "mechanical quality of the pet symbolized the ways in which new technological advancements, humans, and nature, worked together to produce a better future" (Vänskä 2016, 81). Comments like Sean Obrien's about Bella and George's appearance on *The Doctors*, "STILL, SO MUCH GOOD IN THE WORLD," participate in this ongoing tethering of the dog to a conceptualization of a better future, one unrelentingly invested in a linear telos of progress. The service dog is celebrated as a new, "improved," and more effective technology of disability.

The conceptualization of a better future that the service dog points us toward as evidenced in these sentimental representations is not only one that re-secures compulsory able-bodiedness/mindedness and chrononormative understandings of girlhood, but it is one that offers up a privatized understanding of care, and as such participates in the larger political/affective defanging of disability politics under the auspices of ablenationalism. Returning to "The Kid with a Dog" one final time, I was particularly struck by a scene when all the dogs in Rory and Strax's graduating class get their photograph's taken with their new handler. In all the cases, the entire family makes an appearance to take a picture. Likewise, when Sarah is introducing Meghan during their pairing day, she says that they "lost their [family pet] Goldendoodle three years ago" and it is "special" that Strax, too, is a Goldendoodle. In Corrine's case, there is tension between her and her twin sister, Carly, because Carly was under the assumption that Rory was going to be the family pet. In one scene when we first are introduced to the work at 4 Paws for Ability, Jeremey, the training director says, "Talking to a lot of the families we work with, some of the parents have literally told me that this is their last chance for normalcy. They've tried everything else. And they hope the dog gives them their life back." Here it is interesting that Jeremey frames the service dog as the parents' last chance for normalcy. The service dog's job is again not solely defined in relation to the disabled girl handler, but also in relation to the family. In being "welcomed in" to the family as the "last chance for normalcy," the service dog's implicit role is to heal the broader family unit.

These sentimentalized representations fix the "white-normative space" of the family as the ideal locus of care, as it is the parents' and now service dog's job to provide care labor for the disabled girl (Weaver 2021, 137). As Chandan Reddy (1998) argues, in the United States, ideas of the home and family have historically been "defined over and against people of color" (Reddy 1998, 356). The service dog joins the ranks of other working dogs who have historically labored to secure the heteronormative, white, nuclear family, such as military working dogs and k9s, who have secured the family through perhaps more outwardly violent means. It is important to remember that service dogs cost on average around $25,000–$40,000 and are not economically viable for a large swath of disabled people (and the sentimental idea that the service dog just has a natural proclivity for helping their disabled human belies their rigorous training). Thus, the service dog as the "last chance for normalcy" isn't just an incredibly ableist idea, but it also puts forth a false "choice" of the service dog as a "technology that everyone is equally empowered to accept or reject" (Kafer 2019, 4). In our contemporary moment, accessible and good care is reduced to a waning dream that only the privileged can afford in the United States. The service dog has become ablenationalism's "love machine," a companion species whose uncritical celebration covers over the harm of the ever-expanding privatization and hyper-individualization of care labor for disabled people under neoliberal capitalism. Returning to the final scene with Meghan and Strax, as they walk away from the camera one last time, Sarah declares in a voice-over, "Instead of the kid with a disability, I want Meghan to be the kid with a dog." We see here that instead of provoking the viewer to consider disability as a "category to be contested and debated," this utterance fixes disability as an individualized problem to be managed by an individualized solution: a problem that must be worked on through the love of the dog and the family (Kafer 2013, 3).

Becoming Disabled, Becoming in Kind: Crip Girls and Their Dogs on Service Dog Tok

What stories do disabled girl handlers, themselves, tell about living in partnership with a service dog? I now move to disabled girl handler self-representations on the short form video app, TikTok. In particular, I look to the accounts of two creators: Claire (@rosie.the.sd) and Lexy (@muslimservicedogmom28). In broadcasting their everyday reality living in partnership with a service dog, disabled girl handlers like Claire and Lexy carve out space for themselves and their dogs on service dog tok, re-authoring the meaning of the service dog/disabled girl handler relationship. Their videos, ranging from showcasing their collection of service dog vests, to demonstrating their service dogs tasking, to "POV" (point of view) videos from the purported view of the service dog, overwrite the savior/saved dynamic, and instead construct the service dog/disabled girl dyad as an interdependent, (non-innocent) loving companionship. Within the economy of disability visibility, these self-representations circulate alongside the spectacularly sentimental and even on occasion leverage a similar affectivity (one cannot get away from the heartwarming, "good dog" trope). However, their videos forge an alternative valuation of the service dog as a queer/crip companion, and in effect, push back against the ablenationalist positioning of the service dog as an exceptional technology of rehabilitation. Claire's relationship with her service dog Rosie, and Lexy's with her service dog Lady, evinces a "kinship beyond heteronormativity" (Butler 2020, 688)—similarly documented by other disability studies scholars/handlers who are adults, such as Margaret Price (2017) writing about Ivy, Sunaura Taylor (2017) writing about Bailey,

Rod Michalko (1999) writing about Smokie, and poet, Stephen Kuusisto (2018) writing about Corky. On service dog tok, we see that for the disabled girl handler, their service dog is integral to their process of subjectivity construction and of claiming crip. Rather than a tool to aid in the disavowal of disability and return Claire and Lexy to the normative rails of time, Rosie and Lady, as queer/crip companions, facilitate the disabled girl handlers' growth "sideways" rather than up (Stockton 2009).

TikTok—like YouTube—has become a space of disabled girls' "participatory culture," where in producing, uploading, and interacting with videos and other users, disabled girls construct their subjectivities, perform their identities, and cultivate community through participating in "networked publics," or disability intimate publics of their own making (Jenkins 2006; boyd 2007; Boffone 2022). Launched in 2018 to a global market, TikTok is the sister app of Douyin, Chinese company ByteDance's short form video app.[8] The app saw a prolific growth in its user base during the 2020 global COVID-19 lockdowns, and as of 2021, has reached over 1 billion monthly active users. According to *The Economist*, in the first quarter of 2020, the app was downloaded an astounding 315 million times ("TikTok's Rapid Growth" 2021). As *The Guardian* puts it, TikTok was the "perfect medium for the splintered attention spans of lockdown" (Haigney 2020). Unlike "long form" video sharing platform YouTube, TikTok videos range from fifteen seconds up to ten minutes and video creation is largely based around snippets of audio, most often popular songs. Many characterize TikTok as the "most addicting scrolling experience on the internet" because of its sophisticated algorithm (Zeng et. al 2021, 3163). On the "For You Page" (FYP), the algorithm pumps out a precisely tailored, continuous loop of videos that users interface with (Zeng et. al 2021, 3163). Although users can follow others on TikTok, like "subscribing" to creators on YouTube or "following" accounts on Instagram, the continuous stream of content on the FYP is not limited to the content uploaded by the accounts that one follows. Despite its recent emergence, TikTok has become a bastion for youth culture, and, more specifically, girl culture.[9] Melanie Kennedy (2020) writes, "the iconography, rituals, spaces, and lifestyles of youth culture can be seen in TikTok's trends [. . .]; in the mis-en-scène of its videos (so often filmed in messy teenage bedrooms); and, in the demographics of the most followed TikTok stars" (with eighteen-year-old Charli d'Amelio leading at 112 million followers) (1070).

It is important to note that, like YouTube, TikTok has become part of the influencer economy. The advent of content monetization on TikTok, either via the TikTok creator fund, established in 2020, or through brand partnerships, means that the content that creators upload and the concomitant intimacy that they generate has become potentially remunerable[10] (Abidin 2021). Although this broader point about digital labor and remuneration is not the focus of this chapter or section, this dynamic runs in parallel with my discussion of YouTube and the crip-fluencer, as with TikTok there exists a similar tension between the platform as a vehicle for the creation of subjectivity and community and a vehicle that answers the neoliberal capitalist demand for visibility and the monetization of subjectivity.

At the time of writing, if one searches "service dog" on TikTok, one of the top videos featured is from creator and disabled girl handler, @rosie.the.sd. @rosie.the.sd is the account of Claire, a disabled, Asian American young woman and her service dog in training, Rosie, a Golden Retriever with a dyed rainbow tail. Claire's account is a collection of videos about her life with Rosie, ranging from comedic videos about Rosie's quirks to videos that document her process training Rosie, who is training to be a psychiatric and medical alert dog. Claire also posts educational videos that dispel myths and stereotypes about service dogs and handlers that have "invisible" or intermittently apparent disabilities. In a couple of particularly informative question and answer videos ("Why do I have a Service Dog?" and "All SDs are Valid!"), Claire explains that she has "depression, anxiety, borderline personality disorder, and anorexia," and "with those diagnoses comes with severe SH addiction (self-harm), SI (sacroiliac joint dysfunction), and a BFRB (body-focused repetitive behavior) called dermatillomania." She makes a point to remind viewers that "not all disabilities are visible" and that it is "important to remember that not every handler will be as open about their disability, so it is good to be cautious when asking questions like this."

Rather than a triumphant story of capacitation, Claire's most liked video foregrounds the vulnerable intimacy of dependency. In the video, Claire and Rosie are walking down an aisle in what appears to be a warehouse club, like Costco or Sam's Club. Claire begins to hyperventilate. Rosie reacts quickly to begin the process of de-escalation and starts to jump on Claire, prompting her to sit on the ground. As she does this, the caption on the video reads "Mom get down." The next caption reads "I do DPT (deep pressure therapy)," and we see Rosie putting her body on top of Claire's body. She begins to lick Claire's face as Claire cries and rocks back and forth. The caption then reads, "No crying. Kisses will make everything better." Claire starts to hit herself on the head, and Rosie responds by blocking, protecting Claire's head by placing her paws on Claire's shoulders. As this happens, the caption reads, "Oh no don't do that Mom." The video ends with Claire embracing Rosie. "It'll be

Figure 12. Claire and Rosie, her service dog, in her TikTok video, "She's my yellow . . ." (2021)

okay" flashes on the screen. Although the video is intended to be from Rosie's perspective (as she is the one narrating the situation at hand), the caption underneath the video, "She's my yellow [yellow heart emoji]," is written from Claire's perspective. The "yellow" is, of course, in reference to Rosie's breed, a Golden Retriever (or "Golden" as Claire colloquially says), but it is also a reference to the background audio, which is a slowed down snippet of Coldplay's song "Yellow." The audio performs a double function. First, the warped and drawn-out chorus mimics the slowing down or unraveling of time that panic attacks induce, making visible and visceral Claire's impairment(s) and her experience of crip time, or the "strange temporalities" of disability (Kafer 2013, 38). Second, the accompanying lyrics, "your skin, oh yeah, your skin and bones / turn into something beautiful / and you know, you know I love you so / you know I love you so," work to frame the Rosie/Claire dyad akin to a loving companionship, as the "love" that Coldplay sings about stands in for the love that Rosie and Claire have for each other.

Love is non-innocent, and as an affect is bound up in relations of race, gender, class, disability, sexuality, and empire. It can be wielded as a tool of violence and oppression. Donna Haraway (1997) contends that love is "often disturbing, given to betrayal, occasionally aggressive, and regularly not reciprocated in the ways lovers desire" (123). As I discussed at length, representations of love between disabled handlers and service dogs can uncritically reproduce the trope of the "good dog." It would be easy to characterize @rosie.the.sd's video as effusing the same sentimental affectivity that I took issue with in "The Kid with a Dog." One only needs to take a quick glance at the comment section to see that the love generated between Claire and Rosie evokes intense affective reactions—evidenced by countless viewers commenting that seeing the video made them cry. One could suggest that the video slides into the rehabilitative exceptionalism that quietly reproduces compulsory able-bodiedness, as Rosie's short circuiting of Claire's meltdown could be read as a heroic act that "returns" Claire to a prior (read: less disabled) state.

However, a comment that Claire pinned reveals the fact that, rather than a hyper-sentimentalized, "savior/saved" dynamic, her "loving" relationship with Rosie is characterized by caring for and being cared for; or, in other words it is built upon *mutual* acts of care. She writes:

> Note: this is a simulated episode. I am not comfortable posting a real one. We do this in public to train her for situations where she would need to perform these tasks. I also have a video about why her tail is

dyed (posted it on 7/25). Although I am apart [*sic*] of the LGBTQ+ community, it was not dyed to represent it. Rosie enjoys tasking for me—hence the wagging tail. Service dogs live a full and happy life. DPT stands for deep pressure therapy—kind of how a weighted blanket works. Rosie applies pressure to my body to lower my HR and calm me down.

If one imagines the service dog as solely a rehabilitative tool, it is easy to imagine how the service dog *cares for* the disabled girl handler. In this video, viewers witness Rosie use deep pressure therapy. Her narration "oh no don't do that mom," and "it will be okay," belie the easy parsing out of tasking and companionship, as it appears that it is also Rosie's presence that is a mode of support. The service dog can materially offer the possibility of care outside of the violent strictures of the state or the family, the two institutions that disabled people most often are forced to rely on for care, which often brings with them a lack of choice, self-determination, dignity, and even isolation and abuse. But how does the disabled girl handler care *for* the service dog?

Literary critic and animal studies scholar Rachel Adams (2020) argues that care is more than an ethical ideal; it is necessary, intimate labor, "manifested through practice" (Malatino 2020, 41). Care "is almost always characterized by asymmetries of power, ability, and resources" (Adams 2020, 295). In reminding the viewer that "service dogs live a full and happy life," Claire cements her commitment to caring *for* Rosie. When giving more context to viewers, not only does Claire carefully explain the labor that Rosie is performing, but it is clearly of utmost importance to Claire to note that Rosie "enjoys tasking." According to Sunaura Taylor (2017), "an ethic of care asks how we can learn to listen to animals, and how can we help and care for them without the paternalism and infantilization that allows for them to be seen as voiceless" (207). Claire interprets the enjoyment of tasking via tail wags. Rather than reproduce the narrative that dogs have some "natural" proclivity toward loving and helping humans, Claire foregrounds the importance of listening to Rosie, or of interspecies communication.

The dyeing of Rosie's tail rainbow colors is another poignant example of how Claire cares *for* Rosie. In one of her pinned videos (a video that stays at the top of a user's TikTok page, regardless of when it is posted in relation to other videos), Claire explains the reason for dyeing Rosie's tail and documents the process for viewers. Rosie is laying down on the bathroom floor near several paper bowls of dye. Her tail is resting on top of foil, presumably to protect the bathroom floor from dye. Claire begins with a disclaimer: "It is important to note that Rosie did not care at all about her tail being dyed. She was not stressed and you will see that she actually just slept through the whole entire thing." As Claire begins to smother the animal safe dye on Rosie's tail hair, the camera pans up and the viewer sees Rosie, who is indeed dead asleep on the bathroom floor. Claire goes on to explain that she dyes Rosie's tail to "keep her from being stepped on or stolen." "Dyed dogs," she elaborates, "have a much less chance of being targeted by dog thieves, since they have such a strong identifiable feature to them." Claire's "dognapping" concern stems from the fact that because service dogs are so highly trained, they are, as she contends, one of the top types of dogs targeted by dog thieves.[11] Dyeing Rosie's tail is care labor. It is also a recognition of Rosie's vulnerability and dependency. Again, here we see the overwrite of the service dog's rehabilitative exceptionalism, and instead in its wake blooms an interdependency that belies the neoliberal, ableist idealization of autonomy and independence. Claire's videos sonically and visually reveal different scales of dependency, often considered "private matters hidden within the family," provoking viewers to bear witness to the "reality that dependency is a part of all human" and non-human life (Apgar 2023, 13).

The rainbow tail not only helps to visually differentiate Rosie from other Goldens, who "all look the same," according to Claire, but it also could be read as playfully signaling the queer/crip nature of Rosie and Claire's partnership. The tail shapes how Claire and Rosie, together, are read by others. The tail, as a "vehicle for [. . .] strangeness," could be read as announcing Claire's queer/cripness, and in doing so operates to short circuit the demands of compulsory heterosexuality and compulsory able-bodiedness foisted upon Claire as she moves through the world (90). As Kathryn Bond Stockton (2009) persuasively argues, the dog in and of itself (not just dogs with rainbow tails) is a "child's companion in queerness," who can facilitate the child's growth "sideways" (90). In Rosie and Claire's case, the dog and the girl, together, move against the singular envisioning of the linear unfolding of girlhood to youth to womanhood (from dependence to independence, development to mastery) that is figured as vertical movement upward, as well as forward movement through time (Stockton 2009). On service dog tok, Rosie and Claire remain visibly out of time, lovingly embracing each other in the slow temporality of dependency. Rather than provide her with a "new future," Rosie sits patiently alongside Claire in the present.

Peppered throughout service dog tok are many other accounts that broadcast a similar queer/crip imagining of the service dog/disabled girl handler dyad. For example, let us look to @muslimservicedogmom28, the account

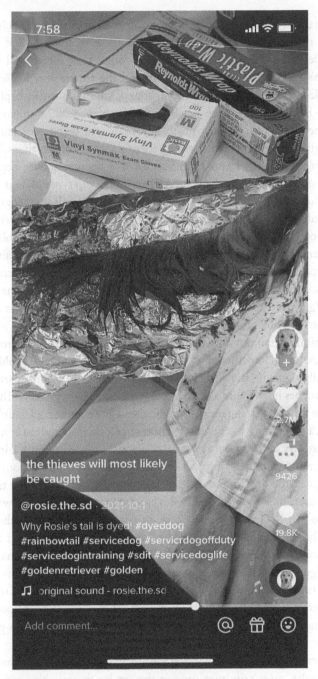

Figure 13. Rosie's tail being dyed in TikTok video, "Why Rosie's tail is Dyed! . . ." (2021)

Figure 14. Lexy and Lady, her service dog, in her TikTok video, "Pretty sure she's a lesbian also . . ." (2021)

of Lexy K, a nineteen year old, self-described Muslim, "mixed girl," and her service dog, a pit bull diabetic alert dog, Lady. Although much of her account is dedicated to her life with Lady and her experience as a Type 1 diabetic (like Claire, many of her educational videos serve as counter arguments to the ableist microaggression, "you don't look disabled"), Lexy also posts activist videos that advocate for the liberation of trans and queer people. Apart from her service dog content, some of her most watched videos are those that document her journey coming to identify as a "gay hijabi." Within her oeuvre of videos that specifically center Lady, Lexy, like Claire, conjures up an alternative envisioning of the service dog/disabled girl handler partnerhsip.

Several of Lexy's videos, including her most liked, are playful takes on Lady's sexuality, who, Lexy argues is also a lesbian. Posted during Pride month, her most liked and circulated video is one where Lexy is lip synching to a snippet of the song "Mood Swings" by A Boogie Wit Da Hoodie. Shot in what appears to be Lexy's bedroom, Lexy sits next to and embraces Lady, who is wearing a rainbow flag bandana. The text on the video reads, "Meet my service dog Lady who only humps and kisses girl dogs (when she's not working) . . . [rainbow flag] [hand over mouth emoji] [rainbow flag]." As the background audio streams, Lexy lip synchs along: "she's my bestie / yeah / never knew she was so nasty / yeah / and she is so sexy / kissing on bitches like a sex fiend." She alternates between kissing Lady on the head, petting her, and pointing at her, suggesting that the song describes Lady. The caption on the video reads, "Pretty sure she's lesbian also [crying laughing emoji] [rainbow flag]." The comment section is rambunctious; ohgodree writes in all caps: "LMAO TELL HER I SAID HAPPY PRIDE." Jokingly, one commenter writes, "not you outing her!! [blushing emoji] [blushing emoji] #cancelled," to which Lexy responds, "[crying face emoji] [crying face emoji] she outed herself awhile ago at the dog park." "Is she a hey mamas?" xnicedogx asks, referring to a lesbian archetype that circulated widely on TikTok in 2021—characterized, according to Shelli Nicole of *Autostraddle*, as a "culturally appropriating (usually non-Black) wannabe fuck boi with access to wifi who was probably born after 1998." Several other commentors as well as Lexy concur with xnicedogx's characterization of Lady.

Although one will never know truly how Lady identifies, the characterization of her as a "hey mamas" lesbian is figured not only through her same sex behavior at the dog park, but it is figured in relation to Lexy, and through her "breed" as a pit bull. Pit bull is not a breed per se, but it is an "idea"—signifying a short-haired dog who is "squat, muscular, with forward flopping ears" (Weaver 2021, 3). Categorically the pit bull's reputation is one of a "bad dog." In the 1980s and 90s, representations of pit bulls in the media, for example, advanced the image of the pit bull as prone to attack, innately aggressive, and in possession of a "will to kill" (and also these representational practices were tethered to attempts to ban pit bull-type breeds in the form of breed specific legislation, some of which is still being put through today) (Weaver 2021, 6). In the 2000s and 2010s, however, perceptions of pit bull-type dogs began to shift from "nature" to "nurture": from the idea that pit bull-type dogs are innately aggressive, to the idea that their behavior is a matter of how one raises the dog. Despite shifts in perception—largely indebted to animal rescue advocates who campaigned for greater acceptance and understanding of pit bull-type dogs—the pit bull still has a reputation that precedes the "breed." Pit bull politics is intimately intertwined with the politics of race and gender. For example, when commentors call Lady a "hey mamas lesbian," we see how she is encountered and understood via a racialized framework of human sexuality (and this is not to say that she "has" a race, or is a white dog appropriating [Black] stud culture, but rather that she is encountered via a racialized and anthropomorphic way of thinking).

More than just a cheeky projection of her own lesbian identity, Lexy's videos about Lady's sexuality evince an enmeshment of human and non-human animal identity and being—what Weaver (2021) terms "becoming in kind" (101). Weaver's (2021) theorization of "becoming in kind" comes out of his experience adopting and living with his pit bull-type dog, Haley. During his time with Haley, Weaver (2021) transitioned from "presenting feminine to masculine" (101). He writes,

> Haley's presence deeply shaped my world. When my appearance was at its most liminal, when I felt vulnerable as a visibly transgender person, she ensured my safety. Concurrently, my whiteness, queer identity, and middle-class status encouraged other humans to read Haley as less threatening in my presence. Each of this shaped who the other was. (Weaver 2021, 101)

According to Weaver (2021), becoming in kind offers an ontological frame for thinking through the connections between human specific categories—race, gender, class, sexuality, and I would add, *disability*—and species distinctions. Pairing becoming with kind "connect[s] the ontological stakes of jointly crafted ways of being and unexpected connectivities with identity categories of larger social worlds" (Weaver 2021, 102). Becoming in kind speaks to a togetherness—a we.

In Lexy's videos, viewers witness how gender, race, class, sexuality, disability, and religion shape Lady's experience of breed, species, and *role* as a service dog. And, likewise, Lady's breed, species, and role shape the experience and expression of Lexy's gender, race, class, sexuality, disability, and religion. As one example, in one particularly sardonic video, Lexy remarks that she did not think that she would "find anyone to match [her] hatred for men . . ." until she met her "service dog who is a lesbian and also isn't a fan of men." Her and Lady, together, like Claire and Rosie, constitute a queer partnership: a "strange relation" manifest (Stockton 2009, 15). Lady's queerness is positioned here as an integral part of Lexy's development and experience of her own queerness; Lady's queerness as it exists in relation to Lexy's becomes a vehicle through which Lexy constructs her lesbian subjectivity. From this we could also infer that Lexy's desire to exist outside of a heteronormative imaginary is, in some ways, made manifest through her partnership with Lady.

Many of Lexy's videos document how Lady's breed, as a pit bull-type dog and the invisibility of Lexy's disabilities (in combination with her age, race, religion, gender, and sexuality) shape their intelligibility as a disabled girl handler and a service dog dyad. In one video she calls Lady, who is a diabetic alert dog, her best friend and "lifesaver," having "saved a bitch without a functioning pancreas like 100+ times" as the text on the video reads. Despite her proficiency as a service dog, Lady's pit bull-ness occasionally calls her status into question, as she does not look like the ideal service dog, as pit bull-type dogs are still largely understood as "bad dogs," as unruly, dangerous, or disobedient. Lady's pit bull-ness, however, could occasionally be protective for Lexy, as a queer, young woman who is Muslim and wears a hijab (like how Harlan Weaver discussed vulnerability, safety and his relationship with Haley), aiding sometimes in safer movement through a queerphobic and Islamophobic world. In one particularly somber video that includes clips of Lady doing innocuous things like eating ice cream, the following text appears: "Mom, why do you advocate so hard for my breed and breeds like mine and strive to make sure we don't mess up in front of others as a SD team?" The video transitions to Lexy holding Lady and lip synching to the background audio: "Waking up but wishing that you don't / It's something that I pray you'll never know." The accompanying caption under the video attests to Lexy's commitment to caring for Lady: "yes, I know they make mistakes but because of her breed the first she slips up in a large public place is where she gets verbally attacked its [*sic*] my job to protect her [red heart emoji]." As Price (2017) argues, these attempts to police service dogs inevitably bleed into an attempt to police disabled humans—as potential malinger-

Figure 15. Lexy and Lady in her TikTok video, "#greenscreen #greenscreenvideo yes I know . . ." (2021)

ers. But, also, criteria used to police boundaries between legitimate/illegitimate such as functionality and intelligence, result in the "'the nonproductive type of line-drawing' that inevitably seems to end in declaring a hierarchy of ways to exist" (Price 2017, 7).

In another video about how Lady's breed informs how others interpellate her (or, in this case, do not) as a service dog, Lexy reflects on the "invisibility" of her own disabilities. In the first part of the video, the text reads, "When someone tells me my new service dog is fake because of her breed and that im [*sic*] not disabled," and then it transitions to a "gotcha" moment, with the text reading: "then they find out I have Type 1 diabetes, two other autoimmune disorders and various mental illnesses and that she was trained by a renowned service dog organization." In this case, we see how Lady and Lexy, together, via their visible identities are regularly rendered suspicious, as bodies out of place. This is similar to how, Taylor Johnson (2021), a Black woman who is diabetic, writes about her experience as a service dog handler: it is her "responsibility to ensure that [her dog] Claire is always groomed and is as unobtrusive as possible" because if she doesn't, then she is more often denied access to spaces (198). And sometimes even when she is accommodated, it is often at the expense of her "privacy and dignity," as she often must exaggerate her pain to justify her need for a service dog (Johnson 2021, 198). She goes on to write that especially in the racialized context of diabetes, her experience makes clear that ableism, racism, and capitalism dictate not only how we experience heath, but to whom, as a society we deem deserving of support, and of quality support. Lexy's videos that discuss her and Lady's experiences being excluded from spaces and being questioned about her disability or Lady's qualifications, in effect, illustrate and broadcast a politicization of disability as it is linked to other systems of oppression. Disability, as it is experienced in and through her relationship with Lady, is not a private, individual matter, nor is it a "single issue."

Ultimately, against the savior/saved dynamic so overwhelmingly present in popular culture and academic discourse, accounts like @rosie.the.sd and @muslimservicedogmom28 proliferate TikTok with stories that define the disabled girl handler/service dog dyad as queer, as a "social and cultural formation of 'improper affiliation'" to use the words of Mel Chen (2012, 14), and as crip. The videos lay bare the mutual dependencies and vulnerabilities that shape the relationship between the service dog and the disabled girl handler and showcase what a dynamic and intimate ethical obligation to interdependence looks like. The service dog, rather than uncritically celebrated for its rehabilitative exceptionalism—a "good dog" exemplar—is instead recognized

Figure 16. Lady, Lexy's service dog, in her TikTok video, "we had to put my other . . ." (2021)

as a being that needs and deserves to be listened to, that needs and deserves to be cared *for*. Ultimately, the relation between the disabled girl handler and service dog as evidenced in Lexy's and Claire's videos is not one that folds the disabled girl back into normative strictures of girlhood; the service dog does not help the disabled girl grow "up." But, rather, the videos on service dog tok evidence a partnership wherein the viewer witnesses the fluid interaction between the disabled girl and the service dog, a partnership that blooms new possibilities for existing and surviving in an ableist and heteronormative world.

Four

The Crip Afterlife of Jerika Bolen

"I used my voice."
—Jerika Bolen (2016)

Jerika Bolen, a Black, disabled, gay[1] girl from Appleton, Wisconsin, incited a flurry of news headlines during the summer of 2016 when, with the consent of her mother, she made the decision to cease her ventilator treatments, enter into hospice, and die. Diagnosed with spinal muscular atrophy type 2 (SMA type 2)[2] as a young child, by age fourteen Jerika was reported to have undergone around thirty-eight surgeries. According to interviews with various news media outlets, her chronic pain, consistently at a seven or more on a scale of ten, is what precipitated her decision to die. A couple of months after turning fourteen, Jerika "sat herself down" and asked herself, "Jerika, am I here for me or my family? I can't even do anything besides lie in bed because I am so sore" (Premack 2016). She concluded that the afterlife would provide her with more freedom than her earthly life: "I have been realizing I'm going to get to walk and not have this pain anymore and not have to, like, live this really crappy life. [. . .] I'm going to be free" (Premack 2016). Before she entered hospice, Jerika had a couple of "final wishes," one being a prom dubbed "J's Last Dance." The prom was financed through GoFundMe with over $36,000 in donations. On July 22, over a thousand people from all over the United States gathered in Appleton, Wisconsin to celebrate "J's Last Dance." A couple months later, in September, Jerika entered into hospice, and she died soon thereafter, on September 22, 2016.

Jerika's story became a global sensation, and her decision ignited debates about the ethics of assisted dying for people with non-terminal disabilities, the value of chronically pained and disabled lives, and the decision-making capacities of fourteen-year-old disabled girls. This chapter explores these debates and makes the case that Jerika is an exceptional disabled girl subject. More than just the spectacular star of a series of heart-wrenching human-interest stories, Jerika performs vital work that greases the wheels of the US project of ablenationalism. Throughout *Cripping Girlhood*, I have tracked the process by which newly visible, exceptional disabled girl subjects are called forward, recognized, and offered incorporation into the national imaginary. Beyond tracking the specific machinations that engender Jerika's spectacularization, this chapter explores what is at stake when we consider that the visibility and recognition of Jerika as an exceptional disabled girl subject is always, already tethered to her death. I ask two questions with the understanding that the answers are in fundamental tension: Under the auspices of ablenationalism, what kinds of ideological work do representations of Jerika's pain and disability, decision and death perform? And what does it mean to seriously consider Jerika's desire and enactment of her own death an act of *cripping* girlhood?

The event of Jerika's death animated a debate whose contours will be familiar to many of us in disability studies. On one side, we have mainstream media outlets and the general public, overwhelmingly supportive of Jerika's decision. In this narrative Jerika is lauded for her enlightened choice to die; she is wise, brave, and inspiring. Her disability and pain are framed as exceptionally tragic, and her choice to die is framed as common sense under such devastating conditions. Their position is exemplified in headlines such as "'I'm Going to Be Free': Terminally Ill Wisconsin Teen Schedules Her Death and One 'Last Dance'" (Premack 2016); "Friends Say Jerika Taught Life Lessons" (Collar 2016g); and "Farewell Jerika, 'She Was Absolutely Beautiful'" (Collar 2016h). The headlines suggest that Jerika's death, as it brings freedom from chronic pain and disability, is at once tragic and aspirational. Jerika's mother, Jen Bolen, also plays an outsized role within the narrative spun on this side of the debate, represented as devoted and selfless for supporting her daughter's decision and facilitating its fruition. Before I go on, it is important to note here that Jen is white and was the only parent caring for Jerika. Her single motherhood was a point of discussion in the mainstream media's narrative, mostly in terms of the difficulty single mothers encounter raising and caring for a disabled child without a partner's assistance. However, Jerika's race was never a point of discussion. Her Blackness was unremarked upon.

Disability rights organizations and the disability community constitute the other side of the debate, voicing concern over what they believed to be an egregious example of systemic ableism's deadly effects. Four organizations—

Not Dead Yet, Disabled Parents Rights, the Autistic Self Advocacy Network, and NMD United—sent a letter to the Wisconsin Department of Children and Families asking for intervention into Jerika's case. One part of the joint letter, a searing indictment of the ableist structures of power that appeared to be engineering Jerika's death, reads, "Ms. Bolen is clearly suicidal. This teenager deserves intervention rather than assistance to end her life" (Collar 2016f). Then public policy director for Disability Rights Wisconsin, Lisa Pugh, incisively points out that it appears Jerika's care team "made their decision based on ableist assumptions about quality of life" (Collar 2016f). Jerika's young age is also rendered suspect by the organizations. Because she was only fourteen years old, they question her capacity to make informed decisions about her life and death. For example, Carrie Ann Lucas, executive director of the Colorado-based Disabled Parents Rights, pleaded, "A child doesn't have the capacity to make those types of decisions, and under the eyes of the law, this is a child" (Collar 2016e). The organizations went so far as to file child protection referrals, citing child neglect on the part of Jerika's mother, Jen (Collar 2016f).[3]

People in the disability community, too, mobilized against the dominant narrative, one that they perceived to be a tacit endorsement of premature death for Jerika.[4] Their tactic, though, was to personally reach out to Jerika, rather than appeal to institutional gatekeepers like child protective services, who have historically enacted violence on disabled, Indigenous, Black, and brown mothers and children.[5] The founder of the disability self-advocacy and empowerment organization/blog, Ramp Your Voice!, Vilissa Thompson, launched a letter-writing campaign called "Letters for Jerika." The campaign solicited letters (both digital and physical) and social media posts from other disabled people—specifically Black disabled people—for Jerika. In effect, Thompson assembled a community of Black disabled people to first, affirm the inherent value of Jerika's Black, disabled, chronically pained life and future; and second, more broadly combat the systemic devaluation of Black disabled girls' lives. Thompson (2016) explains in her mission statement for the campaign:

> For me, Jerika's story struck a significant chord because she's a Black disabled girl, and I am a Black disabled woman. [. . .] One thing that popped into my head was whether Jerika knew of any disabled adults in general, disabled adults with her particular disability, and specifically Black disabled people like me. When it comes to the last group, does she know that she has a village of Black disabled women, particu-

larly, she could get to know? Has she seen empowering and positive examples of adult Black disabled women who have skyrocketed past their teen years, proof that struggles she's facing in adolescence won't last forever? [. . .] Has she been given access to our voices, that states [sic] that Black lives are worth living?

Thompson makes clear that the letters are not meant to "condemn or shame" Jerika, but rather they are an attempt to make it known to Jerika that she has a community, one that she may not have realized exists. In contradistinction to both the well wishes and support offered by the mainstream media *and* the condemnation and appeal to historically violent institutions offered by disability rights organizations, Thompson and her campaign offer something quite different. An act of crip solidarity and care work,[6] "Letters for Jerika" envisions a crip future otherwise: one wherein Jerika feels the desire to continue growing older. The campaign operates from a disability justice framework, or a perspective that recognizes that ableism is inextricable from white supremacy, heterosexism, classism, and ageism (Lamm 2015; Mingus 2017; Piepzna-Samaransinha 2018). It decenters the role of the state and instead calls upon the disability community to intervene in a moment of crisis.

My intention is not to come down one way or another about Jerika's decision itself; rather, this chapter is an attempt to make sense of the national captivation and affective attachment to the event of her death. One can theorize Jerika's death as premature; her desire accelerated by the mundane and normalized everyday violence of ableism, racism, and sexism; her wish sanctioned and upheld by the prevailing eugenically inflected, racist and ableist institutions and logics that deem death a better option than disability. One can also theorize Jerika's death as the fulfillment of her desire; an event that honored her voice, when all too often the voices and desires of disabled, Black, queer girls are pathologized or quelled. As she articulates in a video interview about her decision, "I used my voice that I have and said, 'this is enough pain. I don't need this anymore. It's not fair'" (Collar 2016a). This chapter holds both theorizations in tension.

To track the reverberating discourses and affective mechanisms that engender Jerika's spectacularization and her ascendence into the economy of disability visibility, I crip representations of Jerika's pain, suffering, and death, or uncover how normative discourses of pain, disability, girlhood, heteronormativity, and Blackness converge and recapacitate Jerika into an exceptional disabled girl subject. To do this work, I traverse between three different but interconnected spaces online that circulate Jerika's story in perpetuity. My first site of analysis, the *Post-Crescent*, is a daily newspaper based in Jerika's hometown, Appleton, Wisconsin. The leading architect of the mainstream media's narrative, the *Post-Crescent*, published a series of over twenty articles documenting Jerika's last summer. I show how the newspaper advances a common sense understanding of the relationship between Jerika's disability, pain, suffering, and the desire to die. In this narrative that eventually circulates beyond the purview of the local community, Jerika's decision is represented as both reasonable, as her pain is too much to bear, and epiphanic. She is heralded as a pedagogue of death, teaching her able-bodied and unpained audience that dying is a good decision weighted against future loss.

Next, I move to my second site of analysis, the GoFundMe campaign that Jerika's mother, Jen Bolen, organized to generate capital for Jerika's "final wishes" before her death: a "last dance" and a visit with friends at a SMA fundraising race. I analyze the public mourning of Jerika to show how "J's Last Dance" works affectively to produce Jerika as an exceptional disabled girl subject vis-à-vis her relationship to her mother, Jen. Making the decision to die is constructed within the comments on GoFundMe as common sense and as an act of love: one that relieves her mother of the burden of care. For Jerika, to be a pedagogue of death is to be a loving daughter.

In my concluding site of analysis, the media representations of Jerika's "last dance," I highlight the necropolitical stakes of Jerika's spectacularization. In the celebratory narratives and visual artifacts that accompany the story of the dance, Jerika circulates as a foil for the unruly Black girl. Unlike Jerika, Black girls who are not intelligible as disabled, those whose disability is non-apparent or intermittently apparent, those whose bodyminds fall away from the normative, neurotypical standard and are interpellated as disruptive or unruly, or those whose debilitation is not recognized as producing a disabled subjecthood, remain outside of the available paradigms for inclusion that a post-ADA disability rights imaginary proffers. As one of the privileged disabled girl subjects of ablenationalism, Jerika's value is accrued through her capacity to generate a vision of a benevolent future, one that is built upon individual acts of able-bodied rehabilitation: from donations on GoFundMe to utterances of support in death. I show how the future that the project of US ablenationalism wants us to buy into privileges disabled people walking hand in hand with the police to their premature death, not a collective dismantling of anti-Black, ableist systems and imaginaries. Ultimately, these sites work together, showing us how the figure of Jerika is mobilized as a pedagogue of death, teaching her audience that good dying is a practice of good citizenship. As she circulates, she becomes a container in which national anxieties about bodily sovereignty, pain, disability, death, and mourning are affectively managed and spectacularly resolved. I briefly end with tending to the crip afterlife of Jerika Bolen, asking what would it mean for us to read Jerika's decision as an enactment of her desire, or as an act of cripping girlhood.

Methodological Interlude: On Re-presenting Jerika Bolen

In the annals of history, much Black girl death—by way of spectacular and mundane state violence—is forgotten, erased, or perversely justified. Take a recent example, the death of sixteen-year-old Ma'Khia Bryant. On April 20, 2021, Ma'Khia was fatally shot outside of her foster home in Columbus, Ohio by white police officer, Nicholas Reardon. Officer Reardon responded to a 911 call from Ma'Khia's younger sister, Ja'Niah Bryant. Ja'Niah called 911 and told "police that she and her older sister were being threatened by two young women who used to live at the house" (Bogel-Burroughs et al. 2021). Officer Reardon witnessed Ma'Khia wielding a steak knife; allegedly she was "threatening" another young woman. He then made the decision to shoot her four times, "in an attempt to save the life of the other young woman" (Bogel-Burroughs 2022). Soon after, many who watched the body-cam footage were quick to take to social media, calling Ma'Khia the "aggressor": the "fat," "maniac," "knife-wielding attacker" (Cineas 2021). Ma'Khia could never be the "perfect victim," Fabiola Cineas (2021) writes, and "the cries for justice that applied to George Floyd did not ring out loudly" for Ma'Khia. In 2022, a grand jury voted to clear Officer Reardon of any criminal wrongdoing.

One could argue that Jerika's death, too, was perversely justified. However, it was not erased, nor was Jerika figured an ungrievable subject like Ma'Khia. Notwithstanding, I tread lightly here. All too often Black girls and children, both dead and alive, are called forth in research, used as objects in the service of a scholar's argument, rather than as subjects who have a voice. Although I am critiquing representations of Jerika and the afterlife they enliven, I too am participating in the extractive and reductive project of representing: of re-presenting Black disabled girl death and pain.[7] How do I do justice to Jerika Bolen and the largeness of her Black crip, queer, girlhood? How do I read and construct an archive of Jerika Bolen that resists reenacting the anti-Black violence that I am critiquing: the repetitive yoking of Jerika to Black girl death "over and over again" (McKittrick 2011, 945)? In an attempt to construct an archive with care, I write the ordinary, center Jerika's voice whenever possible, and remain ambivalent. I lend attention to minor details of Jerika's life: her companion animal, her love of *The Sims*, her favorite colors. This chapter also includes many quotes, wherever possible, from Jerika, herself, centering her voice and desires—especially when it gets uncomfortable. My admitted ambivalence about Jerika's decision is also a practice of tending to her memory with care, as I want to firmly push back against the racist, ableist, ageist, and sexist notion that she did not have the capacity to make decisions about her own bodymind. I am not suggesting here that Jerika arrived at her decision as a matter of free will, but I do not wish to paint Jerika as somehow less capable or qualified to make a decision because of her young age, for example, as the disability rights organizations alleged.

Although this chapter is about Jerika's death, my hope is to affirm the enduring value of Jerika's life; her Black, crip queer girlness. Black studies scholar Christina Sharpe's (2016) query has been in the forefront of my mind as I write this chapter, as I attempt to discuss Jerika Bolen with care: "What happens when we look at and listen to [. . .] Black girls across time? What is made in our encounters with them? This looking makes ethical demands on the viewer; demands to imagine otherwise" (51). I invite you, too, reader, as you learn about the life and death of Jerika Bolen to imagine otherwise. What can Jerika Bolen tell us about disability liberation?

On Pain

Despite Elaine Scarry's (1985) famous (and disputed[8]) claim about embodied pain's "unsharability," in that it both shatters language and resists communication, the pain of others is consistently evoked in public discourse (4).[9] Particular stories of pain, more than others, are consistently called forth and circulate in the public's imaginary. Stories of pain and the concomitant "suffering" bodymind subject circulate unevenly—as cautionary tales, as sources of entertainment, as inspirational fodder. What we must remember is that the stories that are told and the forms of pain and suffering that are told in these stories work as "crucial mechanisms for the distribution of power" (Ahmed 2004, 32). Attending to the specificity of whose stories of pain and suffering become legible (in Jerika's case, hypervisible) and valuable within public discourse affords a broader opportunity to understand more fully whose disabled and pained bodyminds come to "matter" in our contemporary moment and under what conditions of existence, or, as I argue in this chapter, non-existence (Butler 2009).

A particular construction of Jerika's story of pain and suffering was called forth in the public imaginary. Suffused with celebratory and sentimental affects, it is a heroic narrative wherein she defeats pain through death. This narrative was circulated, shared, "liked," "commented" on, and even invested in on GoFundMe. And it continues to live on in perpetuity. Fragments of the story circulate online as "virtual fossils," serving to animate a crip afterlife (Kuntsman 2012). I suggest, however, the case of Jerika Bolen illuminates, produces, and circulates competing interpretations and claims to pain. Jerika reportedly argues that her SMA type 2, having manifested in an embodied, unmanageable chronic pain drives her to make the decision to die. Disability Rights organizations argue that Jerika's desire to die could be explained by her untreated "emotional" pain: her desire to not live on being a consequence of depression. Thompson's "Letters for Jerika" campaign acknowledges the multifaceted nature of Jerika's pain and offers her space to "feel vindicated and empowered through [the] toughest of days." And in both the *Post-Crescent* and GoFundMe narrative, Jen articulates her own relationship to pain, most acutely, her own psychic pain, or the pain in anticipation of losing her daughter. One consequence, then, of the overwhelming blanketing of one narrative, or of one celebratory story of pain and death, is that it evacuates the nuance of Jerika's case and reinforces normative understandings of pain.

In recent years, feminist disability studies scholars have taken up the question of pain in all its complexity. Scholars have revealed how, like disability, pain is most commonly conceptualized through a medical or individual paradigm. This paradigm or model frames the pained bodymind as abnormal and unhealthy, and frames pain, itself, as inherently problematic and as a failure of health (Wendell 2001; Campbell 2009; Patsavas 2014; Price 2015; Sheppard 2018; Sheppard 2020). Within this model, pain is regarded as an individual problem to be eradicated through biomedical intervention. If not eradicated, then pain is to be constantly managed, as neoliberal discourses of personal responsibility compel the expectation that the pained person will exercise vigilance and persistence in seeking out effective treatments. And if treatments fail, the pained person is at fault (and is marked a "failure"), rather than the treatments themselves. The pressure to "perform" health traps the chronically pained into an endless cycle of finding cures (Patsavas 2014; Sheppard 2020). According to feminist disability studies scholar Alyson Patsavas (2014), representations of pain in popular culture ubiquitously send the message that "chronic pain is a worse fate than death" (203). We see this line of thought clearly in the *Post-Crescent*'s coverage of Jerika's decision. Patsavas (2014) goes on to argue that the cementing of pain, disability, and the desire to die in popular discourse perpetuates a singular understanding of pain: as a devastating tragedy that must be avoided at all costs. If pain is only understood through this singular lens of tragedy, suffering, and inevitability, other ways of "knowing" pain and understanding pain in relation to disability are evacuated (Patsavas 2014). Further, knowledge about pain is most often only legitimated through and by medical practitioners or the broader medical-industrial-complex. To combat this systemic devaluation of knowledge, Patsavas calls for recovering a cripistemology of pain, or a "process of knowledge production that situates pain within discursive systems of power and privilege" (Patsavas 2014, 205). A cripistemology of pain is produced from the standpoint (or sit-point) of disabled or pained subjects, themselves, and is committed to revealing the ableist assumptions and values that undergird the conceptualization of pain, recognizing that knowledge claims are always, already partial.

The oversimplification of pain in popular discourse also works to obscure the uneven distribution of pain, or how structural conditions and systems of oppression create the material conditions that beget pain for certain bodyminds more than others. Conceptualizing the politics of pain from a materialist, feminist disability studies perspective reminds us to consider how like "becoming disabled," becoming a pained subject "is produced within the actual material violence of transnational capitalism" (Erevelles 2011, 38). For example, people who labor for long hours for low pay under precarious (and sometimes toxic) conditions in the United States, such as custodial workers, fast food workers, day laborers, domestic workers—the majority of whom are marginalized, poor, Black, brown, queer, or undocumented—are more apt to experience pain than, let's say, white collar workers who work from the comfort of an air-conditioned office or home. The COVID-19 pandemic threw this dynamic into sharp relief when "essential workers," many of whom were low paid service workers, were required to repeatedly come into contact with a deadly and potentially painful virus, while white collar workers were given the luxury to protect themselves and stay home. This also brings to the fore a necessary conversation about access and care. Patsavas (2014) recounts how she was deemed an "uncooperative" patient after refusing experimental treatment for pain and was abruptly shut out of other treatment options. She writes "faced with suddenly inaccessible care—a consequence of growing cultural anxieties of opiate abuse and the doctor's resulting reluctance to prescribe medication—my ability to imagine a livable life became precarious" (Patsavas 2014, 204). The oversimplification of pain papers over an examination of the asymmetrical distribution of pain and the material, social, and political conditions that engender the experience of pain. In framing a painful life as not worth living, cultural discourses of pain slot certain bodyminds more than others into an abjected zone of non-life.

Feminist disability studies scholars have also recently paid closer attention to psychological pain—a cogent recognition of the imbrication of body and mind (bodymind). Merri Lisa Johnson (2021) makes intelligible the "emotional pain" of borderline personality disorder, and although she argues that it might be "different [from] the sharp stabbing knife-like [. . .] pain of endo" for example, emotional pain must be recognized as occurring in the body (638). Margaret Price (2015) too has directed attention to mental disability in relation to the phenomenological or sensory experience of unbearable pain, or the pain that "impels one to self-injure or consider attempting suicide" (276). Could we classify Jerika's pain, as it is represented, as unbearable? Price (2015) goes on to argue for the importance of crip theorists to critically reflect on disability's "turn to desire" and think through the fact that this emphasis on desire could unhelpfully obscure a deep consideration of "what to do with" the undesirability of disability, or the negativity of impairment/pain. As Liz Crow (1996) has persuasively remarked, some forms of bodymind suffering, pain, and impairment are "not imposed [. . .] by social/political contexts," and it is "vital not to assume that [disabled and/or pained people are] experiencing a kind of false consciousness" (qtd. in Price 2015, 275). Proposing an ethics of care that includes witnessing and desiring to help alleviate pain ("rather than denial and eradication of pain"), Price (2015) asks us to move away from "judgements of desirability" (279). Discussions of pain, too, must be handled with care. As I emphasized in the introduction to this chapter, my intention is not to come down one way or another about Jerika's decision. My intention is to explore what the circulation and consumption of racialized disabled girl pain, suffering, and death can tell us about the work disabled girlhood performs in the service of ablenationalism. With that said, I recognize Jerika's pain as *real* and attempt to handle her story with care.

Cripping Jerika's "Heartbreaking Decision to Die"

"Appleton Teen Makes Heartbreaking Decision to Die," the first article about Jerika published by the *Post-Crescent*, builds out the mainstream media's framing of Jerika's case. A prototypical human-interest story saturated with emotional appeal, the article Jim Collar (2016a) writes spins a tale of grief, selflessness, devotion, and ultimately peace. The article advances a common sense understanding of the relationship between Jerika's disability, pain, suffering, and the desire to die. Or, in other words, Collar (2016a) relies on and reproduces ableist understandings of chronic pain and disability as a fate worse than Jerika's immanent death (or rather, as Jerika's fate that always, already condemned her to death). Although tragic, Jerika's decision to die is represented as an exceptional act of free will and agency over her body. In the narrative that eventually circulates outside the purview of this local newspaper, living on for Jerika is naturalized as the choice that is inconceivable—not only because of commonly held ideas about the ontological impossibility of chronic pain, but also because of normative understandings of girlhood as a developmental stage of leisure, health, and future possibility.

To set the stage for Jerika's decision, Collar rewinds back to the beginning of Jerika's life. Born and raised in Appleton, Wisconsin, Jerika was diagnosed with SMA type 2 at eight months old, which he describes as an "incurable genetic disease" that "destroys nerve cells in the brain stem and spinal cord that control voluntary muscle activity, and the lack of movement causes the muscles to waste away" (Collar 2016a). Initially, Jerika's prognosis was grim. Healthcare professionals predicted that Jerika would most likely not live past the age of two years old. As Collar (2016a) writes,

> Jen was encouraged by doctors to prepare for the end almost from the beginning—but 13 years ago she wanted no part of defeatist talk. [. . .] A devastating diagnosis, however, served as a call to action, and Jen bolstered herself to do anything for Jerika to not only survive but to live to her fullest while praying for scientists to make breakthroughs.

Jerika reportedly lost much of her physical strength as a baby and began to use a wheelchair at age two. Despite periods of plateau between her muscle loss, "the loss always returned, and the pain has always built up" (Collar 2016a). Collar reports that at one point in the past, Jerika was able to raise her arms over her head. However, by the age of fourteen, Jerika was only able to use the joystick on her powerchair, a computer mouse, and her phone, as her strength was "limited to her hands" (Collar 2016a).

Collar viscerally describes Jerika's chronic pain as unrelenting, oscillating between persistent aching and sudden sharp pains. For example, she has "nerve spasms" and because she has never been able to walk, her bones are "weak," and her pain—mostly felt in her hips and back—is "a seven on the scale of one to ten on her best days" (Collar 2016a). When Jerika's pain is an eight or above, she takes "heavy doses" of painkillers (Collar 2016a). Although they purportedly "wreak havoc on her already battered body," the painkillers are the only way to provide comfort (Collar 2016b). In 2015, just one year prior to her story gaining international attention and two years after her spine was fused, the heads of her femurs were removed to "bring comfort to her aching hips" (Collar 2016a). By fourteen, Jerika allegedly had been in and out of the operating room thirty times. This fixation on the corporeal—the nerve spasms, muscle loss, aching hips—locates chronic pain and disability as indisputable objective "facts" of the body. Evacuated from the narrative is the possibility of conceptualizing chronic pain and disability outside of a medical framing that positions a pained and disabled bodymind as defective, in need of treatment, and best understood and addressed by the purview of medical professionals.

In this article and others, medical professionals positioned as experts on Jerika's case attest to the fact that Jerika's chronic pain is beyond effective management, rendering her decision to die common sense. Kari Stampfli, Jerika's nurse and director of the pediatric palliative care program for UW Health in Madison, notes, "There is no doubt [Jerika's care team and Jen] turned over every stone and tried every treatment to make things better for her, but we really haven't been able to help her pain" (Collar 2016a). Stampfli continues and "dismiss[es] all the notions of those who'd question Jerika's decision" (Collar 2016a). She argues that "for kids with spinal muscular atrophy, 'the standard of care is often comfort measures from the beginning'" (Collar 2016a). So, like with any course of treatment she reasons, "there's always the option to stop if it isn't offering the quality of life that was hoped" (Collar 2016a). Because Jerika is unable to strive for cure, or at the very least effective management of her chronic pain, Stampfli understands Jerika's decision as something that is not up for debate. Her knowledge as a medical professional is presented as "Truth," as Jerika's case is rendered best understood within the purview of professional medical knowledge (recall Jen "praying" for scientists to make "breakthroughs"). As she reasons, the standard of care is "comfort measures" from the beginning, so stopping "treatment" or ceasing the use of the ventilator, which facilitates death, is presented as the logical next step in Jerika's care plan. Although presented by Stampfli as an indisputable and face-value measure of the worth or value of Jerika's life, "quality" of life—as feminist disability studies scholar Alison Kafer (2013) reminds us—is not an objective fact or inherent truth (63). What a "quality" life looks like and feels like is up for debate; it can be affected by lack of access to resources, knowledge, and/or appropriate care.

Embedded throughout the *Post-Crescent* is a medicalized and individualized framing of chronic pain and disability that offers only one way forward for Jerika, one toward the "gains and benefits that cure may bring" (Kim 2017, 6). As Kafer (2013) and Kim (2017) both argue, in our ableist imaginary, disabled bodyminds become valuable when they are actively moving toward cure, or when they are "cured," brought back to a fictitious state of bodymind wholeness. Once "normalized" and rehabilitated, disabled bodyminds are afforded a "starring role" in our ableist imaginary: "the sign of progress, the proof of development, the triumph over the mind or body" (Kafer 2013, 28). Jerika, however, is relegated to the status of "incurable." She is unable to be rehabilitated, as her pain is "untreatable" and her SMA type 2 is represented as rapidly degenerative. When bodyminds, such as Jerika's, are "pronounced uncurable" Kim (2017) argues, "they are read as being in a condition of 'nonlife'—without a future and denied meaning in the present" (7). It follows then, that ideas about normative time and futurity, specifically Jerika's lack of an imaginable future, are evoked throughout the *Post-Crescent* as evidence in support of her decision to die.

Formulations of time are ubiquitously used to govern, describe, and make sense of disability (Jain 2007; Kafer 2013; Samuels 2017; Clare 2017; Samuels and Freeman 2021). Replete in the *Post-Crescent* are references to temporal aspects of Jerika's pain and disability, the most obvious being chronic, which functions as a linchpin in the mainstream narrative.[10] It defines the duration of Jerika's pain "in and through time" (Kafer 2013, 25). Projecting particular ideas about Jerika's future onto her present bodymind, chronic signals a future without relief; a painful future; a future that no one would want; a future of no future. As a Black, disabled, gay, fourteen-year-old, chronically pained girl, Jerika is not a "time-rich" youthful subject like the young pageant queens from the first chapter's discussion of *Miss You Can Do It*. Rather, in contradistinction, Jerika's SMA type 2, chronic pain, and queerness, specifically, position her life outside of a chrononormative imaginary (Freeman 2010). That is to say, Jerika's life and experience of time twists a linear imagining of time and futurity. Throughout the pages of the *Post-Crescent* she comes to represent a crisis of the future.

In an article published after Jerika's death—one of the final articles in the *Post-Crescent* series—Collar (2016g) deduces that, ultimately, Jerika's decision was made against a life of "further loss." Collar (2016g) specifies, "Her pain was the lone factor in her decision to head to hospice care. [. . .] She said she knew that to go on would mean further loss—perhaps her voice and her hands—and knew it wasn't a life she wanted." Further loss, in a literal interpretation, refers to the material functionality of Jerika's body—specifically here referencing her voice and hands. With no hope of forward motion (e.g., treatments, therapies, surgeries) toward cure or rehabilitation, this gradual change in capacity is framed as inherently tragic. The audience is already privy to the fact that Jerika is assisted by "home nurses for up to eighteen hours a day," uses a ventilator for twelve hours a day, and has limited mobility, so she uses a powerchair (Collar 2016a). This further change in capacity is framed as the ultimate loss because compulsory able-bodied/minded logics uphold communication through speaking, or "compulsory fluency," normative and desirable, as conceptions of white, Western personhood are "tied to individual ability to speak for one's self" (Duque and Lashewicz 2018, n.p.). Likewise, the loss of Jerika's hands stands in for complete loss of mobility, independence, and productivity. This "regression" toward a more dependent relationship with others—her mother, her home nurses—ideologically butts up against the temporalities of neoliberal capitalism, which include "productivity, capacity, self-sufficiency, independence, and achievement" (Kafer 2021, 416). "Further loss," then, could also be interpreted in a more abstract sense, referring to the loss of a normative adulthood or womanhood, defined through neoliberal ideals of autonomy and productivity and heteronormative, gendered expectations of reproductivity. In effect, Jerika's chronic pain and SMA type 2 disrupt chrononormative understandings of time that presume that properly temporalized bodyminds move forward along a linear telos of events: birth, schooling, labor, marriage, reproduction, and death.

In contradistinction to the expected forward movement along the "smooth rails of normative life stages," Jerika's life is variously represented throughout the pages of the *Post-Crescent* as static, with the ever looming potential to backslide into total regression (Samuels and Freeman 2021). In "Appleton Teen Makes Heartbreaking Decision to Die" Jerika is stuck in an endless loop of homework, laying down in bed, and playing the life simulator game *The Sims*. We could conceptualize this endless loop as a strange temporality, or space of queer/crip liminality, wherein within the repeated looping of homework and bed, Jerika carves out space for a different experience of time and existence in the virtual worlds she builds on *The Sims*. However, Collar (2016a) suggests a different reading. He writes that in playing *The Sims*, Jerika is able to imagine "a more typical existence," which we have to imagine is defined through ideas about heteronormative (or homonormative) domesticity, romance, and reproductivity, as gameplay on *The Sims* occurs in-part through embracing white, suburban consumptive practices. Collar implies that through *The Sims*, Jerika can attain the "American Dream"—a house, family, and a white picket fence—a hetero-gendered (and settler colonial) reproductive futurity that is implicitly assumed to be otherwise foreclosed due to her chronic pain and disability.

The static framing of Jerika's life and threat of regression also works to uphold a hyper-sentimentalization of a non-disabled childhood, which in this narrative is defined through the ability to pass through normative developmental "stages" (crawling, walking, riding a bike). Jerika's childhood is represented through stories of ineffective treatments, degenerating function, and use of a ventilator twelve hours a day. It is emphasized that Jerika was never able to walk or ride a bike and she stopped attending in-person school after the seventh grade (Collar 2016a). The juxtaposition of a hyper-sentimentalized able-bodied/minded childhood to Jerika's pained and disabled childhood is stark, and it functions in two ways. The stark contrast, first, produces the second childhood—the disabled and pained childhood—as fundamentally not a childhood. Jerika's "maturity" and "wise" disposition are consistently evoked in the narrative, suggesting that her chronic pain and disability have forced her to "grow up too fast." This relies on and reproduces an idealized construction of childhood that posits childhood as a time of innocence, leisure, and health. This idealized childhood is clearly not available to racialized, disabled, poor, queer, and trans children, as their abjection is constituted in relation to "the always already white Child [who] is also always already healthy and nondisabled" (Kafer 2013, 32). The mainstream narrative then also works implicitly to sediment exclusionary conceptualizations of childhood, suggesting that a disabled or pained childhood is an ontological impossibility. The stark juxtaposition between childhoods also subtly asks the reader, "hasn't she already been through enough?" This suggestion is more insidious, and it is haunted by the eugenically inflected cultural anxieties manifest from imagining potential futures that are Black, disabled and chronically pained, as the bodyminds that inhabit these futures are assumed to be dependent, unproductive, and a drain on the nation-state's resources.

Not only is Jerika's decision rendered common sense by the *Post-Crescent* because of normative ideas of pain and futurity, but it is also rendered epiphanic. Within the mainstream narrative, the "mature" and "wise" figure of Jerika transforms into a pedagogue of death and dying. We see this most clearly in "Lessons Plentiful as Teen Prepares to Die," an ode to Jerika's uncanny wisdom and capacity to teach others, wherein Collar (2016b) extols Jerika's lack of bitterness and self-pity, as well as her remarkable ability to casually discuss her impending death. Again, Jerika's nurse, Kari Stampfli is interviewed, and she adds that despite the excruciating pain Jerika experiences, her bright smile and sanguine disposition light up a room (2016b). Jerika's chronic pain and SMA type 2, in Collar's (2016b) calculus, have engendered insight that prompts a reevaluation of the ephemeral nature of living, and he writes, "she's as strong as they come. I'm stronger, and I think a bit wiser, for knowing her." The key to living well, as Collar has learned from Jerika, is to savor and hold dear the fleeting and banal moments and to remain positive, happy, and strong. Jerika's decision to die is positioned as a strong and definitive refusal to succumb to her pain and disability any longer—as it is made against a future of further loss, more pain, and less function. Her positive internalization of her experience and decision is transfigured into a valuable lesson—a blueprint for mindful living and, most persuasively, good dying. As a pedagogue of death, Jerika is framed as judiciously exercising her own free will to transcend her pain and withering body. In turn, she teaches the readers of the *Post-Crescent* that they, too, have the capacity to exercise control over their own corporeality, and more abstractly, the existential terms of their own living and dying.

...

Despite the insistence that Jerika's case is straightforward, there are a number of elisions in the *Post-Crescent* articles documenting her final summer. These omissions in the narrative evacuate a more ambivalent framing of Jerika's decision and abet the overwhelming assumption that is reflected and is produced in the mainstream narrative—that a life in unabating chronic pain is not a life that is worth living. For example, the reader is never quite clear about what, exactly, engenders Jerika's chronic pain, and when discussing her desire to die, there is a consistent conflation of her disability SMA type 2 and her chronic pain. Is the pain directly related to her disability, SMA type 2? Which, as Not Dead Yet, in their "Statement on Mourning the Death of Jerika Bolen," clarify "contrary to media misinformation, pain is not characteristic of SMA Type II." Or, was Jerika's unmanageable pain a consequence of racist, sexist, ableist, and ageist ideas about pain and pain management? Were her experiences minimized or dismissed until it was too late? Here it is important to underscore the fact that discourses of disability, pain, race, gender, and age are co-constitutive and inform the routine minimization, disbelief, and dismissal of Black, disabled girls' pain. Historically Black bodyminds, and specifically Black women's and girls' bodyminds, have been deemed "less susceptible to pain, more susceptible to disease, and inherently in need of white care and control" (Boster qtd. in Schalk and Kim 2020, 40). Cultural discourses of dependency, criminality, and stupidity also routinely pathologize Black women and girls, insidiously facilitating and justifying the expendability of racialized life (Kim 2017). This pathologization engenders a Gordian knot of Black women's and girls' pain: it is simultaneously erased as it is cultivated by the state-sanctioned and extralegal violence of racial capitalism. As Thompson wonders in the "Letters for Jerika Campaign," did

Jerika have access to the voices of Black disabled women, specifically voices that push back against these persistent and invisible discourses that seek to delimit the life chances of Black disabled women and girls?

It has been well documented, too, that young women's experiences of pain are routinely dismissed, as age plays an insidious role in whose pain is taken seriously by medical professionals (Hoffmann and Tarzian 2001; Patsavas 2014; Przybylo and Fahs 2018; Sheppard 2018). In our cultural imaginary, young bodies are figured as spry and resilient. Normative ideas about youngness butt up against our conceptualizations of whose bodyminds are subject to chronic pain, constructing young, pained subjects as "ontological impossibilities," as pain and youngness are considered a mutual impossibility (Campbell 2009). Young people's capacity to generate accurate knowledge about their own bodyminds is also habitually questioned by adults. As I have discussed throughout the pages of *Cripping Girlhood*, knowledge about disabled girls and girlhoods, specifically, is most often generated by others *about* disabled girls. Susan Wendell (1996) speaks about "epistemic invalidation," or the experience of perpetual disbelief that chronically ill, pained, and disabled people must contend with. Rarely are disabled girl epistemologies, or more specifically, Black disabled girl cripistemologies—ways of knowing generated from the standpoint of Black, disabled girls, themselves—valued. It is possible, then, that Jerika's medical team could have dismissed or invalidated her experience of chronic pain as one that was "overexaggerated"—until it was too late. Even more insidiously, I am left wondering if Jerika's 30–38 surgeries were somehow related to her unrelenting pain. Perhaps they were enactments of curative violence: harm inflicted via the fixation on cure as the only way forward (Kim 2017).

Anticipatory Mourning, Neoliberalism, and Affective Attachments on GoFundMe

The public's fascination with Jerika and her story extended well beyond the purview of the *Post-Crescent* series. The success of "J's Last Dance," the GoFundMe campaign that Jerika's mother organized to fundraise for a prom—Jerika's "final wish" before her death—further attests to the public's deep investment in Jerika and the event of her death.[11] The campaign was extensively engaged with. It was "shared" over 4,400 times, indicating a vast circulation and reach online. Over 345 comments were left, and although a few commentors protested Jerika's decision and expressed profound discomfort at the overwhelming consensus in support of it, the majority lauded

Jerika for her bravery and strength in making the decision and offered condolences and support for Jen. What is most telling is the massive amount of money the campaign generated. Within the course of two months that the campaign was active, it far surpassed the stated goal of $25,000. Around 830 people donated a total of $36,000, signaling the public's literal investment in Jerika, her story, and her inevitable death. As I will show in this section, the campaign, more than just a mechanism to raise funds for "J's Last Dance," operates as a space of anticipatory mourning, where the commentors, alongside Jen participate in publicly mourning the "not yet" but inevitability of Jerika's death. The commentors' responses to the campaign reveal two things. First, they showcase how neoliberal discourses of bodily sovereignty, privatization, and individualism shape Jerika's value as an exceptional disabled girl: a privileged subject of the US project of ablenationalism. Second, the comments help to reveal more clearly why her role as a pedagogue of death is so valued in the contemporary moment. As accessible and good healthcare in the United States becomes more of a waning dream than a reality, there is increased pressure for those who reside in the United States to manage our own deaths. Jerika affectively orients her audience toward this goal: toward good dying and good death as a practice of good citizenship.

In the campaign description of "J's Last Dance," Jen lays out the familiar terms of Jerika's case to the campaign's audience. Included is a strikingly intimate photograph of Jerika and her dog, JuJuBee, her dutiful companion. In the photograph, Jerika is lying down in bed cuddling with JuJuBee. She is wearing thick rimmed black glasses and is smiling wide at the camera. Resting behind her head, there looks to be a feeding bag. Jerika's serene, wide smile contrasts with the narrative of pain and suffering that is evoked in the campaign description. The affective register of Jen's campaign description closely follows that found in the *Post-Crescent* narrative. Jerika is constructed as an exceptional disabled girl figure; she has endured more than most adults, but still her happiness persists. Even more specifically, she is positioned as a "gift" to Jen's life. What is most evocative in the campaign description is Jen's articulation of her relationship with Jerika. Their mother daughter bond is represented as unparalleled, wrought out of struggle and self-sacrifice. The narrative works to construct Jen as a "good mother," one who is willing to do anything for her child. Jen immediately positions the reader as an intimate witness of a mother's grief through addressing the campaign to "friends and family." The reader is soon captivated by Jen's visceral recounting of "D-day," thus not only witnessing a mother's grief but also her own experience of pain. In military parlance, D-Day is the day on which combat is initiated, and in

Figure 17. "J's Last Dance," Jen Bolen's GoFundMe campaign

Jen's narrative, it is the day on which Jerika was diagnosed with SMA type 2. She writes that from the moment Jerika was diagnosed, she fought for her, "refusing" to listen to the neurologist's limited prognosis and instead sought out a specialist. Again, like within the pages of the *Post-Crescent*, Jerika's disability is constructed as a "fatal disease"—the enemy other—that is "relentless" and so "incredibly" painful that young Jerika's choice to die is rendered both tragic and common sense. However, in the campaign narrative, Jen persuasively stakes her own claim to pain and suffering. Jen carefully defends her support of Jerika's decision by explaining that "like any parent" she promised Jerika that when her pain became too much, "she would be behind her no matter what." She, too, is poised to lose against the "unwinnable fight" that is Jerika's SMA type 2.

"J's Last Dance" evinces a networked sociality of pain, as Jerika's corporeal pain and Jen's psychic pain of losing her daughter attaches them to a world of other bodies.[12] The campaign invites others to witness Jen and Jerika's pain, Jen's grief, and participate in a collective digital, anticipatory mourning (the "not yet" but inevitability of Jerika's death). In psychological and anthropological literature, grief is theorized as "central to sociality," it is an "affective domain and set of practices in which our attachments to, care for, and investment in others is revealed in life's breach" (Wool 2020, n.p.). Mourning, according to Sigmund Freud (1918) is "regularly the reaction to the loss of a loved person" (243). Different from melancholia, in which the loved object is incorporated into the self and the object loss remains unclear, thus the attachment to grief holds, mourning is when the lost object is separated from the self and let go (Freud 1922).[13] In some ways, the campaign facilitates a symbolic letting go of Jerika—it makes possible a grand send off in the form of a last dance. In disability studies, however, mourning is often critiqued as the normative frame for conceptualizing the non-disabled bodymind or future that a disabled person is imagined as having "lost" and must let go of (Kafer 2013; Clare 2017). In Jerika's case, we see this in the GoFundMe narrative: Jen implicitly mourns the able-bodied childhood (signified through crawling, walking, riding a bike) that Jerika never had, thus reifying normative attachments to a "previous" able-bodied and pain-free state of being that never actually existed, but that is longed for or desired. Not only does Jen mourn Jerika's non-disabled childhood in the GoFundMe narrative, but the campaign, itself, becomes a vehicle through which the performance of mourning is enacted.

The campaign also functions as a technology of intimacy—similar to disability vlogs in chapter 2—inviting users to connect with Jen, Jerika, and other users.[14] We can understand "J's Last Dance" as adjacent in structure to "virtual crypts," such as Facebook pages of the deceased. These living memorials exist online in perpetuity and offer a public space for people to reflect and share their pain and grief through commenting or "conversing" with the dead, as well as participate in a process of ongoing memorialization through sharing stories of the deceased.[15] In this way, the digital architecture of GoFundMe itself—the option for the campaign organizer to post a picture, a narrative, as well as "updates" on the campaign and the ability for the audience/investor to interact through commenting and sharing the campaign with their social networks—makes possible perpetual circulation of spectacular stories of pain, suffering, and death, such as Jerika's.

As a crowdfunding campaign, however, "J's Last Dance" differs from other sites of virtual memorialization in that its purported goal is to generate capital. It is a space where we can clearly see the ways in which the convoluted assemblage and exchange of affect, capital, and technology is at once the spectacular and mundane embodiment of our neoliberal imaginary. Harnessing the power of "micropatronage," or the power of many small donations, GoFundMe—like similar crowdfunding platforms—alleges that with one click of a button, anyone can raise money for a cause that they believe in. GoFundMe is the number one fundraising platform on the internet and, according to the website, since its inception has raised over ten billion dollars for various campaigns. GoFundMe is a scene of "cruelly optimistic" attachment (Berlant 2011). Many campaigns do not meet their fundraising goal, but, even so, GoFundMe charges a transaction fee for each donation. By way of these fees, the platform itself profits off the precarity of its users. Insidiously, GoFundMe further consolidates wealth through funneling these associated fees to corporate owners. However, it is a space of hope and optimism, as it offers the potential promise of funding. It is no surprise that the medical fundraising category is the largest on the site (at $650 million a year as of 2021). The lack of universal healthcare and crumbling social safety net in the United States in combination with the neoliberal hyperfocus on the wellbeing of the individual rather than (and at the expense of) the collective is one way to interpret GoFundMe's success (and ubiquity). Scholars argue that the growing practice of crowdfunding for medical care, although a response to the dysfunctional medical system in the United States, in fact further individualizes the "burdens of a malfunctioning healthcare system" and reproduces inequalities through a life-or-death popularity contest (Berliner and Kenworthy qtd. in Barcelos 2019, 1395). Although "J's Last Dance" was not a medical fundraiser, Jen used that category to classify the campaign. While I cannot speak to Jen's motivations for using that classification category, it strategically provides a framework for understanding and engaging with the campaign and traffics in attendant affects (urgency, grief, hope, strength, love).

Key to a successful GoFundMe campaign is the construction and circulation of an effective *affective* narrative. Campaigns that evoke empathy, for example, are primed to compel, or move, readers to invest. Campaign organizers must labor to brand their campaign in an intensely affective way as to entice an audience to invest in their "cause" as well as to facilitate the circulation or potential virality of the campaign. On their website GoFundMe lists off some key tips for a successful campaign: use a title to tell a sharable story ("make it short, descriptive, inspiring, and easy to find"), describe a unique, compelling story (using details that "will inspire empathy and compel readers to care enough to make a donation"), upload a photograph ("high-quality images can instantly evoke empathy"), build a community, and get press coverage. One could argue that Jen mobilized all aforementioned strategies in constructing "J's Last Dance."

The campaign was clearly effectively *affective*. Countless GoFundMe commentors describe being moved by Jerika's bravery and commend her for making the courageous, albeit difficult, choice to die. Amelia Durand refers to Jerika as a "lionheart" and earnestly writes, "Inspired by your courageous heart, your selfless kindness and emotional care taking of your loved ones, and your strength in self determination [*sic*], Jerika, you absolute wonder." Durand is one of many commentors who specifically articulate feeling "inspired" after encountering Jerika and her story. In effusively applauding Jerika's courage and self-determination the comment reinforces the mainstream narrative's understanding that choosing death over disability and chronic pain is a valuable and agentic act of bodily self-sovereignty, i.e., taking "control" of life by way of death. However, what is most curious to me about Durand's comment is their mention of "emotional care taking." Does Durand mean that they feel inspired after witnessing the care labor that Jerika performs for her mother, or the labor that Jerika performs in anticipating and managing her mother's emotional state? In one video interview, Jerika plainly states that she understands that her decision will hurt her mother, and that she wants to be sure that someone is there to make sure that her mother sleeps and eats after she passes (Collar 2016a). As a reader, we cannot be sure that this is the care that Durand is referring to, but one way to interpret care is with this frame in mind.

Another way to interpret what Durand is referring to as care, however, rests on the idea of disability as a burden of care. Because caregiving in our contemporary neoliberal imaginary is so often gendered and understood as the burden or responsibility of the nuclear family, or within the private sphere, another way that Jerika's decision can be interpreted is one that manifests from the desire to relieve her mother from the burden of caring for her. Her concern for her mother's well-being trumps her desire to continue living on. It is important here to note that the *Post-Crescent* series includes many photographs with Jerika and her personal care attendants. Several articles include soundbites from the care attendants, many of whom express the fact that they have cultivated deep relationships with Jerika, as they care for her up to eighteen hours a day. The commentors on the GoFundMe however only reference Jerika's "heartbreaking" decision in relation to her mother, further individualizing Jerika's case and redefining it as an exceptional familial tragedy.

This affective framing of Jerika's case, as a matter between a grieving mother and her child, further positions Jerika's decision as something that is not up for debate. A discussion about the quality of Jerika's care or her access to different support systems, for example, within this privatized, individualized interpretation is conceived of as an attack on the family or Jen as a good mother, which obfuscates a vital consideration of how systems of power shape the terms of Jerika's care, life, and death. Commentors on the GoFundMe, though well-meaning in their earnest attempt to pre-emptively commemorate Jerika, in effect facilitate the depoliticization of Jerika's decision. Not only is it common sense, but it is cast as a "private problem concerning the family that has no place in the public sphere" (Kafer 2013, 62). The commentors' affective attachment to the figure of Jerika, as an exceptional disabled girl—one who inspires by way of her bravery, selflessness, and confidence—refract any questions, debates, or ambivalent feelings about the case, and reroutes them as personal attacks against or "judgements" about Jerika and her mother.

The celebration of Jerika's decision to die, couched in discourses of freedom, agency, and selflessness evinces the fact that death has become transfigured into yet another scene through which we are compelled to develop and exercise good neoliberal subjectivity. As disability studies scholar Margrit Shildrick (2015) argues, the "neoliberal mantra of self-responsibilization" facilitates conceptualizing death—both assisted and not—as another area for us all to perform "our capacities for self-development" (3). This expectation to manage our own death as a matter of self-development is intensified in the context of the contemporary United States, where over 30 million people are uninsured,[16] the exorbitant cost of care for those who are insured has become somewhat of a national joke (for one example, see NPR's special series, "Bill of the Month"),[17] and caregiving for disabled, ill and elderly people has increasingly become the unpaid labor of the family and/or inaccessible.[18] Kateřina Kolářová (2015) further develops this idea of good death as an exercise of good neoliberal subjectivity in specific reference to what she characterizes as a period of affective vulnerability and "anxious recognition for the global North with respect to its own biological precarity" (396). Under the governance of neoliberal biopolitics, we all come to know our embodied selves through understanding that they "contain a matrix of referenced pathologies deviating from a narrow (and, ultimately, fictitious) norm of health" (Mitchell and Snyder 2015, 39). The debilitated body, in Kolářová's (2015) argument, has transformed into the locus from which this precarity can be "magically and spectacularly resolved" (399). Therefore, in many ways, Jerika, like the other exceptional disabled girls in *Cripping Girlhood* becomes valuable vis-à-vis her cripistemological knowledge and embodied experience of disability. She is "welcomed home" into the national imaginary through her capacity to teach the able-bodied other about how to manage their own *potential* and *inevitable* incapacity, or "the new normal," as Mitchell and Snyder (2015) have persuasively argued. Even more specifically, Jerika teaches her audience what good dying in neoliberal times looks like. A good death, then, comes to be defined as an agentic act of un-burdening: of familial love. And in Jerika's case, it is collectively celebrated and mourned vis-à-vis individualized feel-good acts—donations and utterances of support on GoFundMe. The affective attachment to a good death, however, shores up ableist ideologies that further justify the disposability of disabled and pained bodies.

As a pedagogue of death, Jerika becomes a repository for anxieties about disability, caregiving, and bodily precarity, under the hermetically sealed veneer of powerful feelings. Ultimately, within the comment section, to die and to *let* die become resignified as acts of true love, further cementing Jerika's case outside the realm of the political. This affective resignification is most clear in the longest comment posted to the GoFundMe, wherein Michael Zhuang explicitly references Jen's selflessness and connects her willingness to "let her daughter go" to love. Multiple utterances of love are sprinkled throughout Zhuang's comment. Jerika is positioned as a "lovable" person; Jerika and Jen's love for each other is "deep," wrought out of adversity; and Zhuang is moved by and hopes for a "fraction" of Jerika and Jen's love. Ahmed (2010) posits that to love might be experienced as a happiness duty: to love "another is to want that person's happiness" (92). Reading Zhuang's comment through this conceptualization of love, for Jen to desire and enact happiness for Jerika, or to love Jerika, is to "let Jerika go," as Zhuang explicitly writes. And, for Jerika to desire and enact happiness for her mother, or to love her mother, is to make the decision to die. That is to say, Jerika's chronic pain and SMA type 2 as they are constructed throughout the mainstream narrative are imagined as engendering an unhappy (painful) life, a future of no future, or a future at least not worth living for. To "free" Jerika of her "broken body," as Jen writes in the GoFundMe narrative, is to "free" Jerika of this unhappy (painful) life and future. This facilitation of freedom from unhappiness is read as the ultimate sign of a mother's love. Likewise, for Jerika, the decision to die could also be read as desiring and enacting happiness for her mother. To love her mother is to facilitate her freedom from an unhappy and painful life, as Jerika's pain has become her mother's pain. Both to die and to let die are represented as selfless acts, as both decisions are framed in terms of the fundamental desire for happiness for the other.

Within the comment Zhuang also repositions Jerika's death as a broader pedagogical moment. The affectivity generated by the mutual decision to die and to let die is transfigured into an object of therapeutic value, e.g., the love and kinship bond between Jerika and Jen becomes an extractable resource, a commodity that can be leveraged as a rehabilitative salve to heal the world whose contemporary atmosphere Zhuang describes as "destructive and hateful." We cannot be sure exactly what Zhuang is referring to. It could refer to an atmosphere generated by the overwhelming political divisiveness leading up to the 2016 presidential election; or perhaps, it could refer more specifically to an atmosphere generated by the ongoing movements for racial justice and police accountability (e.g., Black Lives Matter). What is clear, though, is that Zhuang's comment functions as a metonym for the mainstream narrative, wherein Jerika's pain, suffering, and the event of her death are commodified and function as tools of rehabilitation for her audience. Within the space of the GoFundMe, we see more clearly how the affectivity Jerika incites (love, admiration, adulation) simultaneously engenders her value as an exceptional disabled girl subject, facilitating her ascendence into economies of disability visibility, as well as works to rationalize her death as tragic, aspirational, and necessary.

The Spectacle of Black Girlhood: Anti-Black Debilitation and the Docility of Jerika Bolen

"J's Last Dance" operated as a symbolic and moving end to Jerika's spectacular story.[19] On July 22, 2016, over a thousand people flocked to Appleton to witness Jerika's liveliness on the dance floor, many meeting her for the first and last time. Reportedly, one family from Napa, California drove 2,000 miles to attend. The patriarch of the family, John Current, told the *Post-Crescent* that he was "captivated" by Jerika's story. "It's inspiring, it's sad and emotional," he said, justifying the thirty-one-hour drive as his opportunity to see Jerika smile and "live life" out on the dance floor (Collar 2016d). For all those who could not attend, "J's Last Dance" was heavily documented: videos and images were circulated widely online post-event, showcasing the dance's grandeur (it was decked out in lime green and black—Jerika's favorite colors) and vivacity. The most circulated visual artifacts from the event were images and videos of Jerika juxtaposed with police officers. Multiple news articles mention that Jerika was escorted by 17 squad cars to the dance, with lights and sirens flashing. In "Last Dance: Huge Outpouring for Dying Appleton Teen," Collar (2016d) writes that Jerika and her friends and family "were given an escort fit for presidents." One photograph shows two police officers, Lt. Jeff Miller and Chief Todd Thomas, greeting Jerika prior to escorting her to the dance. Both police officers are crouched around Jerika, one has his hand up waving and the other has a wide smile, gazing directly at Jerika. Jerika appears to be getting the finishing touches of glitter sprinkled on her blue hair and the final strokes of henna on her arm prior to leaving for the dance. She is also smiling widely. In multiple articles one of the officers from the photograph, Chief

Todd Thomas, is quoted offering his best wishes to Jerika: "We're just blessed to be able to help out. It's an honor for us, and what an amazing young lady. She makes you appreciate what you have. She makes you think about using your time wisely. She's making an impact."

Haunting the image of the police officers and Jerika—the juxtaposition of Jerika's smiling countenance and the white police officers' calm demeanors—is the photographic inverse, the specter of the contemporaneous Black girls whose encounters with the police are less affable. Existing in stark contrast are the images and videos of Black girls being obstinate, violently protesting the terms of their death or debilitation, such as the viral images and videos of Ma'Khia Bryant (whom I discussed previously), Dajerria Becton, and Shakara Murphy (both of whom I will discuss later in this chapter). Again, I return to Christina Sharpe (2016), and ask, "what happens when we look at and listen to these other Black girls across time" and space (51)? Although other representations of Black girls brutalized at the hands of the police might seem worlds apart from Jerika Bolen's encounter, specifically her smiling face and dance escort "fit for a president," they all circulate in what Herman Gray (2015) calls a "new media ecology" that profits off the suffering, pain, and death of Black people.

In June of 2015, one year prior to Jerika's spectacular story, the images of Officer David Eric Casebolt assaulting fifteen-year-old Dajerria Becton circulated widely on the internet. In a viral video that was recorded at the incident in McKinney, Texas and immediately posted to YouTube, the viewer witnesses Dajerria violently wrestled to the ground by a white police officer, who drew his gun as he "tried to break up a pool party." She was dragged by her hair, pinned to the ground in her bathing suit, and handcuffed. In the video she cries out in pain. In an official statement, police reported that the "large crowd refused to comply with police commands," and Officer Casebolt's lawyer specifically stated that "[Casebolt] let his emotions get the better of him" (Cleary 2015). Dajerria clarifies in an interview that she believes Officer Casebolt justified his use of excessive force because he believed she was being "rude" to him.[20]

The same year that the images and video of Dajerria went viral, another video of a police officer brutalizing a Black girl went viral. In this video, a white police officer, later identified as school resource officer Ben Fields, wraps his forearms around Shakara Murphy's neck, flips her and her desk backward onto the floor, and then tosses and handcuffs her (Associated Press 2016). He then drags her across a classroom (Stelloh and Connor 2015). Sixteen-year-old Shakara was "arrested on a charge called 'disturbing schools,'" as she allegedly refused to give up her cellphone after she was asked (Yan 2015).[21] Another Black girl, Niya Kenny, who recorded the incident was also arrested on the disturbing schools charge. She reportedly "verbally challenged" the school resource officer, speaking against the use of force that left Shakara with "a carpet burn over her right eye, a hairline fracture on her wrist and trauma that she will carry for years" (Associated Press 2016; Simonpillai 2021).

Like the image and video footage of Jerika and the police officers, the images and video footage from both these cases became "titillating objects of persistent media spectacle" (Noble 2018, 148). However, unlike Jerika, in these two examples the Black girl is figured as improperly affective, and her bodymind is imagined as disorderly and in need of discipline. In the first example, the police's reference to a "refusal of compliance" is the very language of unruly Blackness, or of the pathologization of the Black bodymind. Whereas Officer Casebolt's lawyer defended his actions using the supposed natural volatility of emotion as an excuse for his violence, Dajerria and the other Black youths' affectivity was positioned as dangerous and in need of containment, as they are figured as part of "uncultivatable poor and racialized populations who are reduced to their base instincts and impulses" (Haritaworn 2015, 89). In the second example, the violence enacted on both Shakara and Niya by school resource officer Fields (and the teacher who called for him) was justified based on perceived indocility. Niya, speaking out against the racialized and gendered violence enacted on Shakara, refused the deference of "burdened individuality" (Hartman 1997, 121) and instead used her voice as a "practice of Black ungovernability" (Shange 2019, 6). And she, too, was punished.

Black girls are disproportionately surveilled and punished, especially when they are perceived as "too much" or "too loud," as they are measured against "standards of normative white femininity" (Annamma 2018, 15; Ritchie 2017; Shange 2019; Smith 2019; Battle 2020).[22] Dajerria Becton, Shakara Murphy, and Niya Kenny serve as reminders of the violence that is born out of the enduring incompatibility of Blackness and normative conceptualizations of girlhood.[23] Indeed, in these instances we see the debilitating effects of the hypercriminalization of Black girlhood, as the police officers violently assault and traumatize Black girls who question the false authority and power of white supremacy.

We could theorize that like the figure of Jerika, the figures of Dajerria, Shakara, and Niya, too, function pedagogically as they circulate in perpetuity online, serving as a reminder that the Black girl subject is "the noncitizen always available to and for death" (Sharpe 2016, 84). The trafficking in of these images of encounters between Black girls and the police are not only incredibly profitable for the digital media platforms that house and circulate them, but more insidiously the images perform work in the service of the enduring domination of Black people in the United States (Noble 2018).[24] These visual records are means of power and control, a "powerful reminder that one must be ever-vigilant and ever in fear for one's life" (Sutherland 2017, 35). As such, these images attest to the fact that the production of the spectacular Black disabled girl subject is contingent upon the spectacle of Black girl debilitation. Jerika's "welcoming home" into the national imaginary not only functions to uphold and valorize ableist and neoliberal norms, but also functions to shore up white supremacy as it is tethered to the project of US ablenationalism. As a precondition for Jerika's entrance into the national imaginary as an exceptional disabled girl subject, her Blackness must be contained and commodified by the docile exceptionalism of disabled girlhood. Again, as Chief Todd Thomas articulates, "She makes you appreciate what you have. She makes you think about using your time wisely. She's making an impact." Her inevitable death is resignified and she comes to symbolize what a properly affective and affecting bodymind can and should be like: respectability's[25] exemplar. Like other exceptional disabled girls that populate *Cripping Girlhood*, her positive affectivity—happiness, bravery, confidence—engenders her value as she is able to orient her able-bodied audience toward an apolitical promise of a better future. But, this is only a better future for some, as the affective attachment to Jerika's spectacular story obscures the racialized debilitation, the bodily exclusion, injury, and slow death that is endemic to the contemporary United States.

Unlike Jerika, the Black girls who are not intelligible as disabled, those whose disability is non-apparent or intermittently apparent, those whose bodyminds fall away from the normative, neurotypical standard and are interpellated as disruptive or unruly, or those whose debilitation is not recognized as producing a disabled subjecthood, remain outside of the available paradigms for inclusion that a post-ADA disability rights imaginary proffers. Jerika, however, within the mainstream narrative is held up and recognized as an exceptional disabled girl subject and is offered inclusion into our national imaginary, but it is always, already in anticipation of her death. The politics of visibility and social recognition for disabled people, here, only go so far. The affective attachments to Jerika's decision cloud the porous boundary between letting die and making die, and the Black girl subject remains tethered to death.

Not only does the celebration of Jerika's decision re-secure the long-held, but perhaps more recently well-hidden eugenicist impulse that suggests death as the preferable option over a life of chronic pain and disability, but Jerika's case also highlights how anti-Black racism and ablenationalism must be considered as projects that co-constitute each other. Jerika's Blackness, as I argued, is contained by the docile exceptionalism of disabled girlhood—her value exemplified by the images and words of the police officers that witnessed her final public engagement. Compliantly wheeling toward her inevitable death, Jerika teaches her able-bodied audience what good dying looks like: it is resignified as an act of love and bodily self-sovereignty in precarious times. The affective attachments to her case insidiously work to depoliticize disability by de-linking her death from ableism and racism as systems of power, instead offering a tragic yet aspirational story of a disabled girl whose life ended too soon. It is important to emphasize again that in this reading, Jerika's spectacular ascendence to visibility and her value are contingent upon her death. Ultimately, her inclusion into the national imaginary as an exceptional disabled girl—an "able-disabled" subject—is purely symbolic.

Tending to the Crip Afterlife of Jerika Bolen

"My name and legacy will be, my memory will carry on, I hope."
—Jerika Bolen (2016)

"We ask one last question: What might have happened if Jerika's request for a 'last dance' had been met with overwhelming public and media encouragement to live instead of a massive thumb on the scale in support of her death?"
—Not Dead Yet (2016)

I end this chapter with these two quotes above. The first, one of Jerika's that was circulated in multiple *Post-Crescent* articles. The second, an excerpt from Not Dead Yet's "Statement on Mourning the Death of Jerika Bolen." I remain haunted[26] by the story of Jerika Bolen. I have been sitting with and working through Jerika's story since it broke news headlines in 2016, when I wrote about it for the final chapter of my dissertation. Over the course of the six years that have since passed, I have asked myself repeatedly: What does it mean to tend to Jerika's memory? To handle it with care? What would it mean to respect Jerika's voice? The last question, especially, speaks to the core intention of *Cripping Girlhood*. And you, reader, you are well aware now that historically, disabled girls have not had their voices respected, they have not been entrusted to make decisions about their own bodies and minds. At the whim of parents and other institutional figures (medical professionals, researchers, teachers), disabled girls have been deemed incompetent, vulnerable, and unable to understand and comprehend their own bodymind—and the pleasure and pain that comes with living in a bodymind. So, how can we hold Not Dead Yet's question in productive tension with Jerika's voice? How can we come to understand the co-option of Black disabled girl death for a post-ADA, neoliberal capitalist vision of America, its symbolic and affective leveraging of the ghost of Jerika, while at the same time come to honor her ghost, as she implores us to ponder the radical potentiality of desiring and enacting death on one's own terms? I am not suggesting here that Jerika's "choice" to die was not a constrained choice, as I have made clear the structures that undergirded her life and death. But, what if, for one brief moment, we also considered Jerika's decision a radical refusal? A refusal to the call of cure, rehabilitation, of overcoming, of happy futures, of the promise that things will turn out alright. What would it mean for us to read Jerika's decision as an enactment of her desire and as an act of cripping girlhood? For me, tending to Jerika's memory means asking these questions, too.

Coda

Cripping Disability Visibility in Fascist Times

"The future is disabled."
—Alice Wong

On October 6, 2021, nineteen-year-old Grace Schara was admitted to St. Elizabeth hospital in Appleton, Wisconsin for low oxygen. Grace, a white girl with Down syndrome, had tested positive for COVID-19 five days prior to her hospital admission. According to news outlets, on October 13, Grace was given three medications—a combination of a sedative, an anxiety medication, and morphine (Ellefson 2022). Grace's sister, Jessica, reported that Grace felt cold after the morphine injection at 6:15 pm. One nurse claimed that this was a normal reaction, and another claimed that they could not intervene because Grace was coded as Do Not Resuscitate (DNR) (Zimmerman 2022). Grace's family alleges that they never signed a DNR order, nor was Grace wearing a DNR bracelet. Despite Grace's parents' and Jessica's pleads, Grace was not resuscitated. Grace died at 7:27 later that evening (Ellefson 2022). Articles note that Grace was unvaccinated, but her parents do not believe that her death was caused by COVID, although that is what appears on her death certificate. They allege her death was due to the medication that she was given and the DNR order that they claim no one ever signed. "All we would like to have happen is the death certificate changed to the truth," Grace's father notes in an interview, demanding justice (Zimmerman 2022).

Grace's father, Scott Schara, went on to create "Our Amazing Grace's Light Shines On, Inc.," a website that memorializes Grace and details the decisions leading up to her death. The website lists Grace's top ten jokes, documents her love of Elvis Presley, and includes several notes of remembrance from family and friends. Grace is described as a "shining light" by her mother. Her sister notes that she was adventurous. Grace's father writes that Grace always "gave [him] more love than she received." The website also serves as a propaganda hub for anti-vax theories about COVID hospitals, government dictates, and the "truth" behind COVID as a "worldwide genocide plan to reduce population" (Our Amazing Grace 2022). The website claims that there is a "spiritual battle going on right now," and that, "as a nation, we are getting what we deserve because we have rejected God and the beliefs this nation was founded on" (Our Amazing Grace 2022). In a press release posted on the website, July 19, 2022, in alleged collaboration with a Holocaust survivor, Scott writes that hospitals are being used as tools during this worldwide genocide, likening it to the Nazi's T-4 Euthanasia Program, the program that targeted disabled people.

I end this book with the spectacular story of another disabled girl's death. This is not because I want to emphasize the extraordinary nature of Grace's story, but, rather, quite the opposite. I began this book as a graduate student, in 2014, when I first wrote a paper about *Miss You Can Do It* for my biopolitics seminar. In some ways this feels like a lifetime ago. Not only personally—as my life looks very different now than it did then—but it feels like we are living in a very different time than the time we were living in when I first watched and wrote about *Miss You Can Do It*, about six months after it premiered on HBO. The world has since experienced profound technological, political, social, and economic shifts. And we are now living through what many have termed the most extensive mass disabling event in recent history, the COVID-19 pandemic. In the United States alone, over one-hundred million cases of COVID-19 have been reported, and over one million people have died (and that is estimated to be a massive undercount). And although it is very unclear exactly how many people go on to experience long haul symptoms, it is estimated that up to one in four people are affected, regardless of the severity of their initial infection.

The pandemic has thrown into sharp relief the uneven dynamics of disposability under late-stage capitalism. As mask mandates and mandatory sick leave end, and as people are forced back into the classroom and into the workplace, many more people will get sick and die. Disabled people, Black, brown, Indigenous, queer, and trans people have already disproportionately experienced the burden of sickness and death, and this will only intensify in the name of "getting back to normal." Many disability justice activists had valid fears early in the pandemic about medical discrimination, healthcare rationing, and DNR orders. Anti-vaxxer conspiracy theories, the sole focus on the vaccine as a silver bullet to end the pandemic, and the general inaccessibility of medical care for many has also led to disproportionate death, disability, and debilitation in the United States. It seems that the circumstances that led to Grace's death are not extraordinary or exceptional in these times.

Grace's story continues to trouble me. I want to know what she thought about her life, her future, her day-to-day experience of living as a disabled girl. Her father's narrative, how he mobilizes her death as a symbol of spiritual warfare to prop up anti-vaxxer conspiracy theories and discourses of Christian nationalism and white supremacy, is something that troubles me. The hospital's actions and her unclear cause of death, these are all things that trouble me too. I fear that there will be more disabled girls who meet the same fate as Grace as the pandemic rages on, and as Christian nationalism continues to gain a stronger foothold in the United States.

At first glance, this story about Grace might seem worlds away from the bus bench billboard image that I opened this book with. The young girl with Down syndrome with the painted American flag face in the "Love Has No Labels" campaign is wielded to tell a remarkably different narrative about the United States than the narrative that Grace and her death are mobilized to tell for "Our Amazing Grace's Light Shines On, Inc." One might write off a critical examination of both—as the first appears to be worth celebrating, gesturing toward a new era of inclusion for disabled girls, and the second appears to be so extreme that one might perceive it as a limit case. *Cripping Girlhood*, both the book and as a heuristic, however, humbly suggests one last time, that disabled girls are not only worthy of critical examination, but it is of vital importance that scholars look and listen to them. What does cripping representations of Grace's death and her afterlife tell us about contemporary disability politics? I suggest that Grace's story implores feminist disability studies scholars and scholars of girlhood to urgently wrestle with Christian nationalism, defined as a form of nascent or proto-fascism by religious studies scholars Andrew L. Whitehead and Samuel L. Perry (2020), to critically consider how, as an ideology, it often recruits disability and girlhood. Cripping girlhood also provokes us to think about the insidious connections *between* the symbolic mobilization of the disabled girl on the bus bench billboard and Grace. What similar discourses and affects collide to facilitate the spectacularization and exceptionalism of both disabled girl figures? Despite the celebratory veneer of inclusion that attaches itself to many of the representations of disabled girls and girlhoods that this text explores—including the bus bench billboard—I uncovered throughout that the figure of the disabled girl is still very much mired in and reproduces medicalized understandings of disability and chrononormative and cis-heteronormative understandings of girlhood. She is often wielded to re-secure the white, nuclear family as the ideal locus of care. How are these throughlines also present in Grace's story? As I hope to have emphasized, especially in the previous chapter, the spectacularization and exceptionalism of certain disabled girls works to cover over the disposability and debilitation of other girls—those who are not intelligible as disabled girls or those who cannot assimilate into the new norms of disabled girlhood. The material stakes for disabled and crip girls can be deadly, as exceptionalism and symbolic value does not guarantee the recognition of one's full humanity. Symbolic value is not a guarantee of life itself. Lastly, cripping girlhood forwards the unwavering political demand to listen to disabled girls. What can only Grace tell us?

• • •

Throughout *Cripping Girlhood* I have explored how the figure of the disabled girl in contemporary, post-ADA times is a "dense site of meaning" (Dyer 2017, 291). I have tracked how she is mobilized as a spectacular representational symbol. As a disabled "future girl," an object of happiness, an online disability educator-cum-social media influencer, a sentimentalized testament to the rehabilitative properties of the service dog, and as a pedagogue of death, she emerges in media culture at this moment to serve as a resource to work through anxieties about the family, healthcare, labor, US citizenship, and the precarity of the bodymind. Ultimately, the exceptional disabled girl figures that populate *Cripping Girlhood*, the disabled girls who ascend into spectacular visibility in contemporary media culture, all grease the wheels of the US project of ablenationalism and unwittingly participate in a depoliticization of disability. They become tethered to narratives that secure the idea of US disability exceptionalism and the hegemony of the nuclear family as the ideal locus of care. They are used to shore up harmful rehabilitative logics and neoliberal ideals of productivity, autonomy, and self-management. They become tools of white supremacy and heteronormativity under the guise of disability inclusion. In essence, they are welcomed home into the national imaginary as valuable subjects, but only under the condition that they reinforce the normative power structure.

Cripping Girlhood, however, has also tracked how disabled girls themselves have much to say about contemporary disabled girlhood and the day-to-day experience of living as a disabled girl in the twenty-first century. What they have to say is so much more radical than the narratives that tether disabled girlhood to the future of the nation or to heteronormative ideas about what it means to be a girl. Disabled girls are writing their own narratives, deftly theorizing their experiences of ableism, sexism, and ageism. They are cultivating communities online, creating archives of disability knowledge and politicizing other disabled people in the process. They are affirming the value of care labor against the neoliberal and ableist expectation that growing up necessarily means autonomy that is solely defined by independence. And they are enacting their desires, making decisions about their bodyminds and carving out futures that might not look like what we expect them to look like.

I want to end *Cripping Girlhood* with how I began the coda, with disability justice activist Alice Wong's statement that she turned into a hashtag for the Disability Visibility Project in 2016, "the future is disabled." There are many ways to interpret this. One could interpret it as a simple visceral truth, especially in the wake of the pandemic. But one could also interpret it as a crip axiom, one that positions disabled people at the forefront of visions of a more liberatory and just future for all. Disabled girls are some of the people at the helm, steering this new future into existence.

Notes

Introduction

1. For example, see Berman et al. (1999); Bauer (2001); Jewell (2007); Shandra and Chowdhury (2012).

2. Abrams (2018) argues the proliferation of disabled voices online is a productive backlash from the 2016 election of Donald Trump, which "inadvertently" sparked a "new disability rights movement," as the attempt to repeal the Affordable Care Act activated new conversations around healthcare, disability, and rights, mobilizing a new generation of disability activists.

3. Among the campaign's official partners are Bank of America, Walmart, State Farm, and Prudential. The Human Rights Campaign, GLAAD, AARP, Story Corps, and the National Women's Law Center are among the nonprofit partners.

4. As of 2022, the commercial has over 60 million views on YouTube.

5. My use of cripping girlhood as a heuristic is indebted to Julie Avril Minich's (2016) proposal that critical disability studies, itself, is a methodology. It is one that involves the "scrutinizing of social norms that define particular attributes as impairments, as well as the social conditions that concentrate stigmatized attributes in particular populations" (Minich 2016, para. 6).

6. For example, see Bailey's (2020) discussion on "moving at the speed of trust" in the writing of her co-authored book *#Hashtag Activism*. The authors worked closely with the hashtag activists, paying them to write short contributions for the book. Bailey (2020) wanted to "give the users whose tweets [the authors] referenced a more transparent experience with academics using their tweets in scholarship" (240). I look to this collaborative work as a model for future directions in my work on disabled girlhood and social media.

7. I heed James Overboe (1999) who argues that "the term 'person with a disability' demonstrates and is underscored by a 'normative' resemblance that we can attain if we achieve the status of being deemed 'people first' (with the term's emphasis on independence and extreme liberal individualism) in the eyes of an ableist centered society" (24).

Chapter 1

1. The Peabody Awards, named after American philanthropist and businessman, George Peabody, were created in 1938 by the National Association of Broadcasters as the radio equivalent of the Pulitzer Prize. In 1948, television was introduced, and in the 1990s other categories were introduced, including media such as documentary films, distributed through the internet. Awards are not given based on commercial success or popularity, but rather, according to the Peabody Awards website, based on excellence in storytelling that "powerfully reflect the pressing social issues and the vibrant emerging voices of our day."

2. The euphemistic phrase "special needs" is one that many disability activists and scholars take issue with because it "reinforces the idea that disabled people should be, or are somehow inherently, set apart from nondisabled or neurotypical peers" (Apgar 2023, 3; Linton 1998).

3. Leading up to the DSM-5 change, debates in autism research proliferated between two distinct streams of thought about the serious discrepancy in diagnosis between boys and girls. On one side, researchers affirmed the discrepancy, suggesting a theory that "females" are inherently more "protected" from developing autism (Gilman et al. 2011; Levy et al. 2011; Robinson et al. 2013; Jacquemont et al. 2014). Named the "female protective effect" (FPE), according to Hull et al. (2020), it contends that "females require greater environmental and/or genetic risk than males to express the same degree of autistic characteristics, and, hence, that females are 'protected' from autistic characteristics relative to males with a comparable level of risk factors" (307). However, on the other side of the debate were autism researchers who believed the discrepancy was due to gender biases, arguing that girls are routinely underdiagnosed because "their presentation of autism is qualitatively different to the typical male presentation" (Hull et al. 2020, 308). The "gender bias" theory recognizes that gender plays a role in the construction of diagnostic criteria, in the routine evaluation of autistic behaviors, and in the expression of autistic behaviors. It also proposes that practitioners likely project their own gender stereotypes onto their clients, thus leading to under or misdiagnoses of girls (Haney 2016). One could posit that the "gender bias theory" is, in some ways, a feminist intervention, as it makes visible the harm caused by the universalization of autistic traits and behaviors, the concomitant elision of gender "difference," and it simultaneously pushes back against the biological essentialism implied in the FPE theory.

Chapter 2

1. Vlogger is a portmanteau of "video" and "blogger."

2. At the time of revising this chapter in 2021, *Q&A: Deaf Awareness Week* has been retitled to *What is Being Deaf?*

3. Here I use d/Deaf to signify both Deaf people, those who identify with Deaf culture, as well as deaf people, or people who are hard-of-hearing. Throughout the chapter I use "deaf" as an umbrella term to describe all types of deaf people unless the specific person I am discussing has self-identified as Deaf. Because Rikki

identifies as both deaf and disabled and uses the language of ableism and audism to describe her experience, I do so too throughout this chapter. For more about deaf identity see Brenda Jo Brueggemann, *Deaf Subjects: Between Identities and Places* and Susan Burch and Alison Kafer, eds. *Deaf and Disability Studies: Interdisciplinary Perspectives*. For more about recent debates in Deaf studies see Annelies Kusters, Maartje De Meulder, and Dai O'Brien, eds. *Innovations in Deaf Studies: The Role of Deaf Scholars*.

4. In several videos Charisse explains low tone cerebral palsy affects her movement—her muscle tone is low, which makes it difficult to control her movements. Her body also is subject to uncontrollable jerks because of her ataxia.

5. Micro-influencers, as opposed to a "mid-tier influencer" like Rikki, or "macro-influencers" with 500,000 to 1,000,000 subscribers, are characterized by proportionally higher levels of engagement to total subscribers. In the past few years, the micro-influencer has become much buzzed about as an exploitable, underutilized niche segment for corporate brands. On the surface, it would make sense that brands desire to exclusively partner with "elite-influencers" or creators on YouTube—those with hundreds of thousands or millions of subscribers—because of their expansive reach and cultural capital, which translates into advertising power. However, elite creator's high cost of sponsorship as well as perceived "inauthenticity" has driven brands to consider the benefits of working with smaller channels.

6. According to Statista, a market and consumer data company, Google is the only website as of 2022 that received more traffic than YouTube. In terms of social media platforms, specifically, Facebook has more active users than YouTube, followed by WhatsApp and Instagram.

7. Alice Marwick's (2013) insightful chapter on the cultural history of Web 2.0 also notes that the celebratory discourse of Web 2.0 "shone a spotlight back on the young entrepreneurs and thought leaders of Silicon Valley," post-2001 dot com crash, and "in the process, it brought utopianism back to the front lines and created new investments and personal fortunes" (24). It positioned "social technology" rather than political participation and activism as solutions to political problems and created a strain of "idealistic techno-determinism" that further entrenches capitalist logics (Marwick 2013, 24).

8. It has become common for vloggers to say some variation of "sorry—are you okay?" when they drop the camera, for example. The implication being that the camera has become the viewer, and the viewer has become the camera.

9. Indeed, deaf and disabled people's parental fitness is often questioned. Take the case of Shannon Duchesneau and Candace McCullough, a deaf lesbian couple who became a national sensation and were publicly condemned for "failing" to protect their child from deafness (and queerness), as they choose to use their deaf friend's sperm. In "selecting for" disability, as Kafer (2013) would put it, the couple was demonized for imposing the burden of disability on their child and thus failing to properly reproduce the family.

10. As of 2020, to join the YouTube partner program (YPP), the creator must have at least 4,000 watch hours in the past 12 months as well as at least 1,000

subscribers. The creator must also follow the monetization policies, which include YouTube's community guidelines, terms of service, Google's AdSense program guidelines, and copyright guidelines. Videos that are not eligible for monetization or that are potentially demonetized are vaguely defined as videos that are not "advertiser-friendly" such as videos that contain "shocking content," "controversial issues," "sensitive events," "inappropriate language," and "adult content."

11. Take, for example, Rikki's most recent brand partnership with Grinding Coffee Co., a small, Black, LGBTQ+, woman-led coffee company. Announcing the partnership June 25, 2020, she wrote on the YouTube community tab:

"I'm very happy to announce that I am now affiliated with Grinding Coffee Co, a Black and LGBT+ coffee company. If you would like to order some coffee and get a discount, use "RIKKI" for 15% off and use this referral link if you would like. I receive commission if you buy through this link: https://grindingcoffee.co/?ref=rikki."

Brand deals and partnerships can take shape in various ways. Here we see that Rikki has access to an affiliate code and link, where her audience can directly order product for a discounted price. Every time someone uses her link, she receives commission. In a sponsorship arrangement, brands require that the content creator use the brand's product or service in a video, or simply mention the product or service somewhere on their socials. Usually sponsorship rates are dependent on the content creator's audience size and engagement. The bigger the audience and the higher the engagement—variously gauged with comments, likes, and clicks—the more influencers can demand for their partnership.

12. According to the U.S. Department of Labor's disability employment statistics, in 2021 only 36.7% of disabled people ages 16–64 were actively participating in the labor force. This is in stark contrast to the 76.6% of non-disabled people who were actively participating in the labor force during this time.

13. In 2021, influencer marketing and research firm Izea found that although female creators make up 83% of influencer marketing deals, across platforms men made about 30% more per post (Rubio-Licht 2022).

Chapter 3

1. It is important to note that there are debates about the utility of "speciesism" as a category of analysis. It can easily erase ontological debates about racialized populations, white supremacy, and the status of human. Speciesism was popularized by philosopher Peter Singer, who is widely critiqued for his ableism.

2. Other notable films and television series about service dogs: *Through a Dog's Eyes* (2010); *Max* (2015); *SEAL Dog* (2015); *The Buddy System* (2016); *Adele and Everything After* (2017); *Megan Leavy* (2017); *Rescue Dog to Super Dog* (2017); *Pick of the Litter* (2018); *To Be of Service* (2019); *The Greatest Bond* (2020); *A Dog's Service* (2020).

3. For example, in their systematic review of literature assessing the impact of service dogs on disabled children, specifically, Sally Lindsay and Kavitha Thi-

yagarajah (2021) conclude that service dogs have been proven to increase mobility, have a positive impact on blood glucose/hypoglycemia alerts, improve "quality of life," enhance safety particularly for autistic children, reduce anxiety, help to calm disabled children down, and increase self-confidence and independence.

4. In 1944, US congress approved a million-dollar bill to authorize the Veterans Administration to provide seeing-eye dogs for blind veterans (see: "Providing Seeing-Eye Dogs for Blind Veterans," Senate Committee on Finance, Congress Session 78–2, April 12, 1944). In the report they state, "It is entirely consistent with the obligation to which the Nation owes to disabled veterans that every reasonable means of assisting blind veterans should be utilized."

5. The distinction between a service animal and an emotional support animal (ESA), for example, hinges on this definition of task. As opposed to a service animal, an ESA "helps an individual by simply being present during social interactions or situations" (Campbell 2016, 74).

6. In a person diagnosed with Morquio syndrome, the body does not produce enough of an enzyme that breaks down sugar chains called glycosaminoglycans that help to build cartilage, bone, skin, and connective tissue. As a result, glycosaminoglycans build up in the connective tissue, cells, and blood. This can affect organ function and mobility, leading to a pronounced spine curvature, or a heart murmur, for example.

7. VACTERL is an acronym for vertebral abnormalities, anal atresia, cardiac defects, tracheal-esophageal abnormalities, renal and radial abnormalities, limb abnormalities, and single umbilical artery.

8. More precisely, in 2017 ByteDance bought app Musical.ly, a platform where users created and shared short lip-synching videos. In 2018, ByteDance merged Musical.ly and TikTok (the sister app of Douyin) and retained the name TikTok for the app.

9. It's reported that over half of TikTok's global audience (57%) is "female" (Aslam 2022). 43% of the global audience is between eighteen to twenty-four years old, and it is reported that as of 2021, the largest age group on the app is ten- to nineteen-year-olds (25%) (Aslam 2022).

10. Unlike YouTube's partner program that is advertiser funded, the TikTok creator fund is an in-house partnership program for eligible users to monetize their content (through accumulating and cashing out earnings based on video views). As of 2021, eligible users must be 18 years old, have over 100,000 video views in the past 30 days, and have a baseline of 10,000 followers. Their content also must be within TikTok community guidelines. At the start of the program in 2020, the fund started with two hundred million dollars earmarked for the United States, with the intention of growing the fund to two billion dollars globally (O'Brien 2021).

11. In my research, I did not find any evidence that supports Claire's contention that service dogs are especially at risk of being stolen by dog thieves. Most lists online that document the "top types" of dogs that are stolen are breed based. However, the National Service Animal Registry has a blog post that explains that disabled people are at particular risk by "dog scammers." They explain: "Disabled

people with service animals might be particularly at risk from [scammers], as a thief might target someone with a special bond and dependence on their pet and are most likely to pay a reward" (NSAR 2022).

Chapter 4

1. One article from *The Washington Post* explicitly notes that Jerika was gay and had a girlfriend (Premack 2016). I am not sure if that is how she personally identified or if the fact that she had a girlfriend denoted that identity to the journalist.

2. Spinal Muscular Atrophy type 2 (SMA type 2) is a genetic, neuromuscular disability. People who are diagnosed with SMA type 2 lose motor neurons in the spinal cord that control muscle movement. Without motor neurons, muscles do not receive the nerve signals to make them move, thus certain muscles can become smaller without use, or atrophy.

3. The four organizations—Not Dead Yet, Disabled Parents Rights, the Autistic Self Advocacy Network, and NMD United—filed for a child protection referral and Disability Rights Wisconsin filed for a separate referral. According to the *Post-Crescent*, the child protection referrals cited Wisconsin's child neglect statute (which defines neglect as a "caregiver's failure, refusal or inability to provide medical or dental care or shelter so as to seriously endanger the physical health of the child") (Collar 2016g).

4. Here I am alluding to abolitionist and prison scholar Ruth Wilson Gilmore's (2007) definition of racism as "the state-sanctioned and/or extra-legal production and exploitation of group-differentiated vulnerability to premature death" (28).

5. Anti-carceral, abolitionist, and Black feminists have long critiqued the child welfare system as its historic function has been in the service of white supremacy, operating through surveilling, punishing, and maiming Black, Indigenous, disabled mothers and children of color (Roberts 2002, 2014; Lee 2016). Perhaps seemingly well intentioned, this move by disability rights organizations upholds the very structures we would assume they desire to eradicate.

6. Here I evoke both sociologist Evelyn Nakano Glenn's (2000) definition of care as "a practice that encompasses an ethic (caring about) and an activity (caring for)" (86) as well as disability justice activist and poet Leah Lakshmi Piepzna-Samarasinha's (2018) specific operationalization of care work in a crip context as it emphasizes collective responsibility, revolutionary love without charity, and interdependency.

7. For more on the ethics of representing violence, specifically, representing Black death and pain with care, see Katherine McKittrick's 2014 article, "Mathematics Black Life" in *The Black Scholar*.

8. For critiques of Scarry, see Ommen et. al (2016), "The Contemporary Making and Unmaking of Elaine Scarry's *The Body in Pain*" and their special issue of *Subjectivity* 9 (4). Bourke (2017) contends that Scarry does not quite parse out the historical and sociocultural nature of pain, as the way people talk about pain has

indeed shifted over time, reflecting the historic, social, and cultural contexts in which they lived. She goes on to argue further for a recognition that specific rhetorics of pain have been historically utilized to maintain racist and sexist hierarchies of personhood, with white men on one end of the "great chain of feeling" and enslaved people on the other.

9. Interestingly, bell hooks (1992) elaborates on Scarry's assertion to argue that there is no language for Black male pain (both material pain caused by racist violence and psychic pain caused by dehumanizing structures) and because of the lack of available public discourse, Black men are unable to articulate and acknowledge their pain.

10. Jerika's pain, for example, is also described as "persistent" and leading up to her death, tough days were becoming more "frequent" (Collar 2016a). Her SMA type 2 is described as "terminal" and her muscles are described as "wasting" away (Collar 2016b; Collar 2016c).

11. Part of the funds raised for "J's Last Dance" were also earmarked for ferrying Jerika to Avery's Race to visit with her SMA friends "one last time." Avery's Race to Cure SMA is an annual event in Lancaster, Wisconsin that raises money for SMA. The event, named after Avery Lynn, a disabled girl who was diagnosed with SMA type 1, was first held in 2010.

12. Referencing Jean-Paul Sartre, Ahmed (2004) argues that pain is contingent in that it is linked to the "sociality of being 'with' others" (28).

13. Much work in Black, postcolonial, and critical race theory has taken up the pathologized space of melancholia to theorize racialization, subjectivity, loss, and depression, complicating Freud's "privileged theory" of unresolved grief (see Eng and Han's [2019] *Racial Melancholia, Racial Dissociation: On the Social and Psychic Lives of Asian Americans*). Other scholars such as Christina Sharpe refuse "diagnostic categories of normative grief altogether" in discussing the ongoing history of anti-Blackness and the normativity of premature Black death (Wool 2020, n.p.).

14. Moreover, digital media scholars have argued that GoFundMe's business model itself is "sustained by the labor of intimacy" (Dobson, Carah, and Robards 2018, 10).

15. According to digital media scholars, these sites where the production of public grief occurs facilitate the spatial and social expansion of "the social processes around death and bereavement" (Brubaker, Hayes and Dourish 2013, 160). The temporal persistence of "virtual crypts" as archives of the dead provoke a redefining of memorialization itself, as they now depend less on the "implied eternity of a built physical environment than on the entirely different eternity of circulating information" (Grider qtd. in Brubaker, Hayes and Dourish 2013, 162).

16. Specifically, 30.4 million Americans are uninsured as of 2020. This data comes out of the National Center for Health Statistics' "National Health Survey Early Release Program" authored by Robin A. Cohen et. al. The report also notes that poor (21.8%) and near poor (23.9%) people were more likely to be uninsured than not poor people (8.8%). Latinx adults were also found more likely to be uninsured (26.5%) than non-Latinx Black adults (13.2%), non-Latinx white adults (9.7%)

and non-Latinx Asian adults (9.3%). Further, adults (18–64) living in non-Medicaid expansion states are twice as likely to be uninsured than those adults (18–64) who live in a state that opted in for Medicaid expansion.

17. NPR's Bill of the Month is a series that solicits ridiculous medical bills to learn more about the healthcare system in the United States. Recent headlines include, "The ER charged him $6,589.77 for six stiches, a cost that led his wife to avoid the ER"; "Same hospital and insurer, but the bill for his second jaw procedure was $24,000 more,"; and "Her doctor's office moved 1 floor up. Why did her treatment cost 10 times more?".

18. A 2020 report from AARP and the National Alliance for Caregiving has found that 1 in 5 American adults are now unpaid caregivers (Schoch 2020).

19. It is telling that Jerika's final summer culminated in a dance, as prom holds cultural significance in the U.S. as a gendered ritual. More than just a sexual rite of passage, it is an event that facilitates the becoming or transformation of a subject (Best 2004; Zlatunich 2009).

20. No criminal charges were brought against Officer Casebolt, but two years after the incident in 2017, Dajerria and her guardian sued Casebolt, the McKinney Police department and the city of McKinney. After being awarded a $184,850 settlement, Dajerria's lawyer reported that she was going to throw her a pool party. Reportedly, Dajerria had not been swimming since the incident, the lingering trauma prevented her from feeling safe to go to a pool (Moye 2018).

21. Three years after this incident, in 2018, then Governor Henry McMaster signed an amendment to repeal the crime of "disturbing schools" as it disproportionately targeted Black youth for subjective and vague offenses—ranging from talking back to a teacher, being loud in the lunchroom, to speaking out about police misconduct (Hinger 2018).

22. Further, as scholar of Black girlhood, Nazera Wright (2016) succinctly contends, "Black girls are not viewed as children and young people who need protection and care" (181). In other words, Black girls are not afforded a Black *girlhood*, or at least one that is distinct from a Black womanhood (Halliday 2019).

23. As Andrea J. Ritchie (2017) points out in *Invisible No More: Police Violence Against Black Women and Women of Color*, Black girls made up "approximately 33 percent of girls referred to law enforcement or arrested on school grounds but only 16 percent of the female student population" (77).

24. Noble (2018) recognizes that historically, images of Black death and dying have also been used to galvanize civil rights organizing. For example, of note is Ida B. Wells and the NAACP's work reframing lynching photographs to organize abolitionist movements against Jim Crow segregation (Noble 2018). However, Noble (2018) argues that we must think critically about virality and the speed at which contemporary images and videos travel on the Internet, and whether anti-racist organizations are able to just as quickly reframe these images.

25. Here I draw on Saidiya Hartman's concept of a "pedagogy of respectability." She explains: "In freedman's handbooks, the displacement of the whip can be discerned in the emphasis on self-discipline and policing. The whip was not to

be abandoned; rather, it was to be internalized. The emphasis on correct training, proper spirit, and bent backs illuminated the invasive forms of discipline idealized as the self-fashioning of the moral and rational subject" (Hartman 1997, 140). Shange (2019) too discusses respectability in relation to the legacy of the Moynihan report in the United States and argues that "respectability has been used as a tool to manage Black people across the hemispheres in the wake of emancipation and decolonization" (6).

26. To be haunted, "is to be in a heightened state of awareness; the hairs on our neck stand up: being affected by haunting, our bodies become alert, sensitive. The challenge may simply be to sit with this state of awareness, not to flee into action" (Ferreday and Kuntsman 2011, 9). To explain, it might be helpful to consider Jerika, briefly, in the context of Avery Gordon's theorization of haunting in relation to the ghost. Gordon argues that "haunting is linked to the project of peaceful reconciliation which transforms a 'shadow of a life into an undiminished life'" (Ferreday and Kuntsman 2011, 5). Haunting is the "sociality of living with ghosts," or people (communities, generations) that are no longer physically here, but are nonetheless "demanding attention, looking for justice, challenging the way we know, act and feel" (Ferreday and Kuntsman 2011, 1). The "socio-political-psychological," or affective, state of haunting prompts "something-to-be-done" (Ferreday and Kuntsman 2011, 2). Gordon emphasizes that the ghost needs to be treated with respect "rather than simply speaking for them, or, worse, making them 'abandoned and disappeared again' through the very process of dealing with haunting" (Ferreday and Kuntsman 2011, 2).

Bibliography

ABC 13 Eyewitness News. 2015. "Young Girl with Rare Genetic Disorder Forms Special Bond with Service Dog." *ABC 13 Eyewitness News.* November 5. https://abc13.com/service-dog-great-dane-special-bond-morquio-syndrome/1069711/

Abidin, Crystal. 2015. "Communicative Intimacies: Influencers and Perceived Interconnectedness." *ADA: A Journal of Gender, New Media, and Technology* (8): 1–16. https://scholarsbank.uoregon.edu/xmlui/handle/1794/26365

Abidin, Crystal. 2016. "Visibility Labour: Engaging with Influencers' Fashion Brands and #OOTD Advertorial Campaigns on Instagram." *Media International Australia* 161 (1): 86–100. https://doi.org/10.1177/1329878X16665177

Abidin, Crystal. 2021. "From 'Networked Publics' to 'Refracted Publics': A Companion Framework for Researching 'Below the Radar' Studies." *Social Media + Society* 7 (1). https://doi.org/10.1177/2056305120984458

Abrams, Abigail. 2018. "'Our Lives Are at Stake.' How Donald Trump Inadvertently Sparked a New Disability Rights Movement." *Time*, February 26. https://time.com/5168472/disability-activism-trump/

Ad Council. 2022. "Love Has No Labels." https://lovehasnolabels.com/about

Adams, Rachel. 2020. "The Art of Interspecies Care." *New Literary History* 51 (4): 695–716.

Ahmed, Sara. 2004. *The Cultural Politics of Emotion.* Edinburgh: Edinburgh University Press.

Ahmed, Sara. 2010. *The Promise of Happiness.* Durham: Duke University Press.

Ahmed, Sara. 2017. *Living a Feminist Life.* Durham: Duke University Press.

Akyel, Esma. 2014. "#Direnkahkaha (Resist Laughter): 'Laughter Is a Revolutionary Action.'" *Feminist Media Studies* 14 (6): 1093–94. https://doi.org/10.1080/14680777.2014.975437

Albrecht, Gary L. 1999. "Disability Humor: What's in a Joke?" *Body & Society* 5 (4): 67–74. https://doi.org/10.1177/1357034X99005004007

Alper, Meryl. 2014. *Digital Youth with Disabilities.* Cambridge, MA: MIT Press.

Andrejevic, Mark. 2011. "Social Network Exploitation." In *A Networked Self: Iden-*

tity, Community, and Culture on Social Network Sites, edited by Zizi Papacharissi, 82–101. New York: Routledge.

Annamma, Subini A. 2018. *The Pedagogy of Pathologization: Dis/abled Girls of Color in the School-prison Nexus*. New York: Routledge.

Anzaldúa, Gloria. 1987. *Borderlands / La Frontera: The New Mestiza*. San Francisco: Aunt Lute Books.

Apgar, Amanda. 2023. *The Disabled Child: Memoirs of a Normal Future*. Ann Arbor: University of Michigan Press.

Armbruster, Karla. 2002. "'Good Dog': The Stories We Tell About Our Canine Companions and What They Mean for Humans and Other Animals." *Papers on Language and Literature* 38 (4): 351–76.

Ascarelli, Miriam. 2010. *Independent Vision: Dorothy Harrison Eustis and the Story of the Seeing Eye*. West Layfette, IN: Purdue University Press.

Aslam, Salman. 2022. "TikTok by the Numbers: Stats, Demographics & Fun Facts." *Omnicore*, March 13. https://www.omnicoreagency.com/tiktok-statistics/

Associated Press. 2016. "Deputy Who Tossed a S.C. High School Student Won't Be Charged." *New York Times*, September 2. https://www.nytimes.com/2016/09/03/afternoonupdate/deputy-who-tossed-a-sc-high-school-student-wont-be-charged.html

Bailey, Moya. 2021. "The Ethics of Pace." *South Atlantic Quarterly* 120 (2): 285–99. https://doi.org/10.1215/00382876-8916032

Banet-Weiser, Sarah. 2012. *AuthenticTM: The Politics of Ambivalence in a Brand Culture*. New York: New York University Press.

Banet-Weiser, Sarah. 2018. *Empowered: Popular Feminism and Popular Misogyny*. Durham: Duke University Press.

Barad, Karen. 2007. *Meeting the Universe Halfway: Quantum Physics and the Entanglement of Matter and Meaning*. Durham: Duke University Press.

Barcelos, Chris A. 2019. "'Bye-Bye Boobies': Normativity, Deservingness and Medicalisation in Transgender Medical Crowdfunding." *Culture, Health & Sexuality* 21 (12): 1394–1408. https://doi.org/10.1080/13691058.2019.1566971

Battle, Nishaun T. 2020. *Black Girlhood, Punishment, and Resistance: Reimagining Justice for Black Girls in Virginia*. New York: Routledge.

Bauer, Anne. 2001. "'Tell Them We're Girls': The Invisibility of Girls with Disabilities." In *Educating Young Adolescent Girls*, edited by Patricia O'Reilly, Elizabeth M. Penn, and Kathleen deMarrais, 29–47. Mahwah, NJ: Lawrence Erlbaum Associates.

Ben Ayoun, Emma. 2021. "Toward a Theory of Disability Documentary: Alison O'Daniel's *The Tuba Thieves* (2013–Present)." *The Velvet Light Trap* 88 (September): 4–24. https://doi.org/10.7560/VLT8802

Berlant, Lauren. 1997. *The Queen of America Goes to Washington City: Essays on Sex and Citizenship*. Durham: Duke University Press.

Berlant, Lauren. 2008. *The Female Complaint: The Unfinished Business of Sentimentality in American Culture*. Durham: Duke University Press.

Berlant, Lauren. 2011. *Cruel Optimism*. Durham: Duke University Press.

Berlant, Lauren, and Sianne Ngai. 2017. "Comedy Has Issues." *Critical Inquiry* 43 (2): 233–49. https://doi.org/10.1086/689666

Berman, Helene, Dorothy Harris, Rick Enright, Michelle Gilpin, Tamzin Cathers, and Gloria Bukovy. 1999. "Sexuality and the Adolescent with a Physical Disability: Understandings and Misunderstandings." *Issues in Comprehensive Pediatric Nursing* 22 (4): 183–96. https://doi.org/10.1080/014608699265275

Berryman, Rachel, and Misha Kavka. 2017. "'I Guess A Lot of People See Me as a Big Sister or a Friend': The Role of Intimacy in the Celebrification of Beauty Vloggers." *Journal of Gender Studies* 26 (3): 307–20. https://doi.org/10.1080/09589236.2017.1288611

Bertsche, Rachel. 2015. "11-Year-Old Learns How to Walk with Great Dane's Help." *Yahoo! Sports*, November 9. https://sports.yahoo.com/news/11-year-old-learns-how-to-walk-with-great-danes-191102676.html?guccounter=1&guce_referrer=aHR0cHM6Ly93d3cuZ29vZ2xlLmNvbS8&guce_referrer_sig=AQAAAH4Mh5anAlU5-j3Bnze-2YUTt9vBPqpxQy1LCJ4Jjvnqjdu9gKcPSxVl YgXoAb8VK7Q7aYTe5SFZdfE1xwYFIbIOG8k1e0EUlMD5FKVUcLiYg DEYf_nd2wrJEXS6Mh3mYql5Kdf91WKh9uzLoNN5aIsr7VMtnP4RXJn5z ztzjvDg

Best, Amy L. 2004. "Girls, Schooling, and the Discourse of Self-Change: Negotiating Meanings of the High School Prom." In *All About the Girl: Culture, Power, and Identity*, edited by Anita Harris with a foreword by Michelle Fine, 195–203. New York: Routledge.

Boffone, Trevor, ed. 2022. *TikTok Cultures in the United States*. New York: Routledge.

Bogel-Burroughs, Nicholas. 2022. "Officer Who Killed Ma'Khia Bryant Will Not Face Charges." *New York Times*, March 11. https://www.nytimes.com/2022/03/11/us/makhia-bryant-police-charges.html

Bogel-Burroughs, Nicholas, Ellen Barry, and Will Wright. 2021. "Ma'Khia Bryant's Journey Through Foster Care Ended with an Officer's Bullet." *New York Times*, May 8. https://www.nytimes.com/2021/05/08/us/columbus-makhia-bryant-foster-care.html

Boggs, Colleen Glenney. 2013. *Animalia Americana: Animal Representations and Biopolitical Subjectivity*. New York: Columbia University Press.

Boisseron, Bénédicte. 2018. *Afro-Dog: Blackness and the Animal Question*. New York: Columbia University Press.

Bourke, Joanna. 2017. *The Story of Pain: From Prayer to Painkillers*. New York: Oxford University Press.

boyd, danah. 2007. "Why Youth (Heart) Social Network Sites: The Role of Networked Publics in Teenage Social Life." In *Youth, Identity, and Digital Media*, edited by David Buckingham, 119–42. Cambridge, MA: MIT Press.

Brown, Wendy. 2008. *Regulating Aversion: Tolerance in the Age of Identity and Empire*. Princeton, NJ: Princeton University Press.

Brubaker, Jed R., Gillian R. Hayes, and Paul Dourish. 2013. "Beyond the Grave: Facebook as a Site for the Expansion of Death and Mourning." *The Information Society* 29 (3): 152–63. https://doi.org/10.1080/01972243.2013.777300

Brueggemann, Brenda Jo. 2009. *Deaf Subjects: Between Identities and Places.* New York: New York University Press.
Brylla, Catalin, and Helen Hughes, eds. 2017. *Documentary and Disability.* London: Palgrave Macmillan.
Burch, Susan, and Alison Kafer, eds. 2010. *Deaf and Disability Studies: Interdisciplinary Perspectives.* Washington, DC: Gallaudet University Press.
Burgess, Jean, and Joshua Green. 2009. *YouTube: Online Video and Participatory Culture.* Cambridge; Malden, MA: Polity.
Butler, Judith. 2009. *Frames of War: When Is Life Grievable?* London; New York: Verso.
Butler, Judith. 2020. "Companion Thinking: A Response." *New Literary History* 51 (4): 687–94. https://doi.org/10.1353/nlh.2020.0042
Cammaerts, Bart. 2008. "Critiques on the Participatory Potentials of Web 2.0." *Communication, Culture & Critique* 1 (4): 358–77. https://doi.org/10.1111/j.1753-9137.2008.00028.x
Campbell, Fiona Kumari. 2009. *Contours of Ableism: The Production of Disability and Abledness.* London: Palgrave Macmillan UK.
Campbell, Kayla. 2016. "Supporting Adoption of Legislation Criminalizing Fake Service and Emotional Support Animals." *Journal of Animal & Environmental Law* 8 (1): 73–93.
Carlson, Licia. 2010. *The Faces of Intellectual Disability.* Bloomington: Indiana University Press.
Cartwright, Lisa. 1995. *Screening the Body: Tracing Medicine's Visual Culture.* Minneapolis: University of Minnesota Press.
Casey, Caroline. 2020. "Is The Social Media Generation Transforming Disability Representation?" *Forbes,* September 14. https://www.forbes.com/sites/carolinecasey/2020/09/14/is-the-social-media-generation-transforming-disability-representation/?sh=5ec979966084
Castañeda, Claudia. 2002. *Figurations: Child, Bodies, Worlds.* Durham: Duke University Press.
Chaney, Jen. 2018. "Must Love Dogs." *Vulture,* November 13. https://www.vulture.com/2018/11/dogs-netflix-review.html
Chau, Clement. 2010. "YouTube as a Participatory Culture." *New Directions for Youth Development* 128 (winter): 65–74. https://doi.org/10.1002/yd.376
Chen, Mel Y. 2012. *Animacies: Biopolitics, Racial Mattering, and Queer Affect.* Durham: Duke University Press.
Cheney, Kristen. 2014. "'Giving Children a Better Life?' Reconsidering Social Reproduction, Humanitarianism and Development in Intercountry Adoption." *The European Journal of Development Research* 26 (2): 247–63. https://doi.org/10.1057/ejdr.2013.64
Cineas, Fabiola. 2021. "Why They're Not Saying Ma'Khia Bryant's Name." *Vox,* May 1. https://www.vox.com/22406055/makhia-bryant-police-shooting-columbus-ohio
Clare, Eli. 1999. *Exile and Pride: Disability, Queerness, and Liberation.* Boston: South End Press.

Clare, Eli. 2010. "Resisting Shame: Making Our Bodies Home." *Seattle Journal for Social Justice* 8 (2): 455–65. https://digitalcommons.law.seattleu.edu/sjsj/vol8/iss2/2

Clare, Eli. 2017. *Brilliant Imperfection: Grappling with Cure.* Durham: Duke University Press.

Clark, Rosemary. 2016. "'Hope in a Hashtag': The Discursive Activism of #WhyIStayed." *Feminist Media Studies* 16 (5): 788–804. https://doi.org/10.1080/14680777.2016.1138235

Cleary, Tom. 2015. "Eric Casebolt: 5 Fast Facts You Need to Know." *Heavy*. Updated April 8, 2021. https://heavy.com/news/2015/06/eric-casebolt-mckinney-texas-police-officer-cop-suspended-black-teens-pool-party-arrest-video-leave-investigation-photo-gun-background-name/

Cohen, Robin A., Emily P. Terlizzi, Amy E. Cha, and Michael E. Martinez. 2021. "Health Insurance Coverage: Early Release of Estimates from the National Health Interview Survey, January-June 2020." *National Center for Health Statistics*. Released February 2021. https://www.cdc.gov/nchs/data/nhis/earlyrelease/insur202102-508.pdf

Collar, Jim. 2016a. "Appleton Teen Makes Heartbreaking Decision to Die." *Post-Crescent Appleton Part of the USA Today Network*, July 14. https://www.postcrescent.com/story/news/2016/07/14/appleton-teen-makes-heartbreaking-decision-die/86510526/

Collar, Jim. 2016b. "Lessons Plentiful as Teen Prepares to Die." *Post-Crescent Appleton Part of the USA Today Network*, July 18. https://www.postcrescent.com/story/news/local/2016/07/18/lessons-plentiful-teen-prepares-die/86868036/

Collar, Jim. 2016c. "Jerika, Family Prepare for Last Dance." *Post-Crescent Appleton Part of the USA Today Network*, July 21. https://www.postcrescent.com/story/news/2016/07/21/jerika-family-prepare-her-last-dance/87393370/

Collar, Jim. 2016d. "Last Dance: Huge Outpouring for Dying Appleton Teen." *Post-Crescent Appleton Part of the USA Today Network*, July 24. http://www.postcrescent.com/story/news/2016/07/23/last-dance-huge-outpouring-dying-appleton-teen/87471814/

Collar, Jim. 2016e. "Jerika's Plan to Die Draws Disability Groups' Interest." *Post-Crescent Appleton Part of the USA Today Network*, September 6. https://www.postcrescent.com/story/news/2016/09/06/jerikas-plan-die-draws-disability-groups/89926762/

Collar, Jim. 2016f. "Child Neglect Claimed in Jerika's Hospice Battle." *Post-Crescent Appleton Part of the USA Today Network*, September 7. https://www.postcrescent.com/story/news/2016/09/07/child-neglect-claimed-jerikas-hospice-battle/89976496/

Collar, Jim. 2016g. "Friends Say Jerika Taught Life Lessons." *Post-Crescent Appleton Part of the USA Today Network*, September 23. https://www.postcrescent.com/story/news/local/2016/09/23/friends-say-jerika-taught-life-lessons/90956036/

Collar, Jim. 2016h. "Farewell, Jerika: 'She Was Absolutely Beautiful.'" *Post-Crescent Appleton Part of the USA Today Network*, October 5. https://www.postcrescent

.com/story/news/2016/10/05/farewell-jerika-she-absolutely-beautiful/91609434/

Cooper, Harriet. 2020. *Critical Disability Studies and the Disabled Child: Unsettling Distinctions*. New York: Routledge.

Corker, Mairian. 1999. "'Disability'—The Unwelcome Ghost at the Banquet... and the Conspiracy of 'Normality.'" *Body & Society* 5 (4): 75–83. https://doi.org/10.1177/1357034X99005004008

Corker, Mairian, and Sally French, eds. 1999. *Disability Discourse*. Philadelphia: Open University Press.

Coté, Mark, and Jennifer Pybus. 2007. "Learning to Immaterial Labour 2.0: MySpace and Social Networks." *Ephemera* 7(1): 88–106. http://www.ephemerajournal.org/contribution/learning-immaterial-labour-20

Cvetkovich, Ann. 2003. *An Archive of Feelings*. Durham: Duke University Press.

Cyphers, Luke. 2015. "Meet the Little Girl Who Wiped out Government Use of the R-Word." *ESPN*, July 20. https://www.espn.com/espnw/news-commentary/story/_/id/13287823/meet-little-girl-wiped-government-use-r-word

Desjardins, Michael. 2012. "The Sexualized Body of the Child: Parents and the Politics of 'Voluntary' Sterilization of People Labeled Intellectually Disabled." In *Sex and Disability*, edited by Robert McRuer and Anna Mollow, 69–88. Durham: Duke University Press.

Diamond-Lenow, Chloe. 2020. "US Military Nationalism and the Intimate Public Sphere: The Role of the Dog in US Militarism." *Journal of Intercultural Studies* 41 (1): 8–23. https://doi.org/10.1080/07256868.2019.1617255

DiBlasio, Natalie. 2014. "10-year-old petitions for Disabled American Girl Doll." *USA Today News*, January 2. https://www.usatoday.com/story/news/nation/2014/01/02/american-girl-disabled-doll/4287897/

Dobson, Amy Shields, Nicholas Carah, and Brady Robards. 2018. "Digital Intimate Publics and Social Media: Towards Theorising Public Lives on Private Platforms." In *Digital Intimate Publics and Social Media*, edited by Amy Shields Dobson, Brady Robards, and Nicholas Carah, 3–27. Cham: Springer International Publishing.

Donaldson, Elizabeth, and Catherine Prendergast. 2011. "Introduction: Disability and Emotion 'There's No Crying in Disability Studies!'" *Journal of Literary & Cultural Disability Studies* 5 (2): 129–35. https://doi.org/10.3828/jlcds.2011.11

Doyle, Nancy. 2021. "Don't Do Us Any Favors, Inclusion Is Profitable: Broadcaster Samantha Renke On The Power Of Disability Representation." *Forbes*, October 8. https://www.forbes.com/sites/drnancydoyle/2021/10/08/dont-do-us-any-favors-inclusion-is-profitable-broadcaster-samantha-renke-on-the-power-of-disability-representation/?sh=458c565f5259

Driel, Loes van, and Delia Dumitrica. 2021. "Selling Brands While Staying 'Authentic': The Professionalization of Instagram Influencers." *Convergence: The International Journal of Research into New Media Technologies* 27 (1): 66–84. https://doi.org/10.1177/1354856520902136

Driscoll, Catherine. 2008. "Girls Today—Girls, Girl Culture and Girl Studies." *Girlhood Studies* 1 (1): 13–32. https://doi.org/10.3167/ghs.2008.010103

Duffy, Brooke Erin. 2017. *(Not) Getting Paid to Do What You Love: Gender, Social Media, and Aspirational Work*. New Haven; London: Yale University Press.

Duggan, Lisa. 2004. *The Twilight of Equality? Neoliberalism, Cultural Politics, and the Attack on Democracy*. Boston: Beacon Press.

Dunlap, Tiare. 2015. "'How To Dance in Ohio': Inside the Documentary that Follows Three Girls with Autism as They Prepare for Prom." *People.com*, October 26. https://people.com/celebrity/how-to-dance-in-ohio-three-girls-with-autism-prepare-for-prom/

Duque, Camille, and Bonnie Lashewicz. 2018. "Reframing Less Conventional Speech to Disrupt Conventions of 'Compulsory Fluency': A Conversation Analysis Approach." *Disability Studies Quarterly* 38 (2). https://doi.org/10.18061/dsq.v38i2.5821

Dyer, Hannah. 2017. "Queer Futurity and Childhood Innocence: Beyond the Injury of Development." *Global Studies of Childhood* 7 (3): 290–302. https://doi.org/10.1177/2043610616671056

Ebben, Hannah. 2018. "The Desire to Recognize the Undesirable: De/Constructing the Autism Epidemic Metaphor and Contagion in Autism as a Discourse." *Feminist Formations* 30 (1): 141–63. https://doi.org/10.1353/ff.2018.0007

Edelman, Lee. 2004. *No Future: Queer Theory and the Death Drive*. Durham: Duke University Press.

Ellefson, Meg. 2022. "Wisconsin Hospital Kills Down Syndrome Teenager." *WSAU*, April 7. https://wsau.com/2022/04/07/wisconsin-hospital-protocols-kill-19-year-old-downs-syndrome-girl/

Ellis, Katie. 2015. *Disability and Popular Culture: Focusing Passion, Creating Community and Expressing Defiance*. Burlington: Ashgate.

Elman, Julie Passanante. 2010. "After School Special Education: Rehabilitative Television, Teen Citizenship, and Compulsory Able-bodiedness." *Television & New Media* 11 (4): 260–92. https://doi.org/10.1177/1527476409357762

Elman, Julie Passanante. 2014. *Chronic Youth: Disability, Sexuality, and U.S. Media Cultures of Rehabilitation*. New York: New York University Press.

Elman, Julie Passanante, and Robert McRuer. 2020. "'The Gift of Mobility': Disability, Queerness, and the Cultural Politics of Rehabilitation." *Feminist Formations* 32 (2): 52–78. https://doi.org/10.1353/ff.2020.0025

Eng, David L. 2003. "Transnational Adoption and Queer Diasporas." *Social Text* 21 (3): 1–37. https://doi.org/10.1215/01642472-21-3_76-1

Eng, David. L. 2006. "Political Economics of Passion: Transnational Adoption and *Global Woman*: Roundtable on *Global Woman*." *Studies in Gender and Sexuality* 7 (1): 49–59.

Eng, David L., and Shinhee Han. 2019. *Racial Melancholia, Racial Dissociation: On the Social and Psychic Lives of Asian Americans*. Durham: Duke University Press.

Erevelles, Nirmala. 2011. *Disability and Difference in Global Contexts*. New York: Palgrave Macmillan US.

Erevelles, Nirmala, and Kagendo Mutua. 2005. "'I am a Woman Now!': Rewriting Cartographies of Girlhood from the Critical Standpoint of Disability!"

In *Geographies of Girlhood: Identities In-Between*, edited by Pamela Bettis and Natalie G. Adams, 253–69. New York: Routledge.

Eustis, Dorothy Harrison. 1927. "The Seeing Eye." *The Saturday Evening Post*.

Felperin, Leslie. 2015. "'How to Dance in Ohio' Sundance Review." *Hollywood Reporter*, January 30. https://www.hollywoodreporter.com/movies/movie-news/how-dance-ohio-sundance-review-768569/

Ferreday, Debra, and Adi Kuntsman. 2011. "Introduction: Haunted Futurities." *borderlands e-journal* 10 (2): 1-14.

Fishman, Gerald A. 2003. "When Your Eyes Have a Wet Nose: The Evolution of the Use of Guide Dogs and Establishing the Seeing Eye." *Survey of Ophthalmology* 48 (4): 452–58. https://doi.org/10.1016/S0039-6257(03)00052-3

Freeman, Elizabeth. 2010. *Time Binds: Queer Temporalities, Queer Histories*. Durham: Duke University Press.

Freud, Sigmund. 1918. *Reflections on War and Death*. New York: Moffat, Yard.

Freud, Sigmund. 1922. "Mourning and Melancholia." *The Journal of Nervous and Mental Disease* 56 (5): 543–45. https://doi.org/10.1097/00005053-192211000-00066

Fritsch, Kelly. 2013. "The Neoliberal Circulation of Affects: Happiness, Accessibility and the Capacitation of Disability as Wheelchair." *Health, Culture and Society* 5 (1): 135–49. https://doi.org/10.5195/HCS.2013.136

Garland-Thomson, Rosemarie. 1997. *Extraordinary Bodies: Figuring Physical Disability in American Culture and Literature*. New York: Columbia University Press.

Garland-Thomson, Rosemarie. 2002a. "The Politics of Staring: Visual Rhetorics of Disability in Popular Photography." In *Disability Studies: Enabling the Humanities*, edited by Sharon L. Snyder, Brenda Jo Brueggemann, and Rosemarie Garland-Thomson, 56–75. New York: Modern Language Association of America.

Garland-Thomson, Rosemarie. 2002b. "Integrating Disability, Transforming Feminist Theory." *NWSA Journal* 14 (3): 1–32. https://www.jstor.org/stable/4316922

Garland-Thomson, Rosemarie. 2005. "Staring at the Other." *Disability Studies Quarterly* 25 (4). https://dsq-sds.org/article/view/610/787

Garland-Thomson, Rosemarie. 2011. "Misfits: A Feminist Materialist Disability Concept." *Hypatia* 26 (3): 591–609. https://www.jstor.org/stable/23016570

Genzlinger, Neil. 2013. "Challenged, but Determined to Compete for the Tiara." *New York Times*, June 23. https://www.nytimes.com/2013/06/24/arts/television/miss-you-can-do-it-showcases-challenged-girls.html

Genzlinger, Neil. 2015. "Review: 'How to Dance in Ohio,' A Documentary on HBO: Follows Three Women on the Autism Spectrum." *New York Times*, October 25. https://www.nytimes.com/2015/10/26/arts/television/review-how-to-dance-in-ohio-a-documentary-on-hbo-follows-three-women-on-the-autism-spectrum.html

Gerber, David A. 2003. "Disabled Veterans, the State, and the Experience of Disability in Western Societies, 1914–1950." *Journal of Social History* 36 (4): 899–916. https://doi.org/10.1353/jsh.2003.0095

Giddens, Anthony. 1991. *Modernity and Self-Identity: Self and Society in the Late Modern Age*. Stanford: Stanford University Press.

Gill, Rosalind. 2007. "Postfeminist Media Culture: Elements of a Sensibility." *European Journal of Cultural Studies* 10 (2): 147–66. https://doi.org/10.1177/1367549407075898

Gilman, Sarah R., Ivan Iossifov, Dan Levy, Michael Ronemus, Michael Wigler, and Dennis Vitkup. 2011. "Rare De Novo Variants Associated with Autism Implicate a Large Functional Network of Genes Involved in Formation and Function of Synapses." *Neuron* 70 (5): 898–907. https://doi.org/10.1016/j.neuron.2011.05.021

Gilmore, Ruth Wilson. 2007. *Golden Gulag: Prisons, Surplus, Crisis, and Opposition in Globalizing California*. Berkeley: University of California Press.

Glenn, Evelyn Nakano. 2000. "Creating a Caring Society." *Contemporary Sociology* 29 (1): 84. https://doi.org/10.2307/2654934

Gonick, Marnina. 2006. "Between 'Girl Power' and 'Reviving Ophelia': Constituting the Neoliberal Girl Subject." *NWSA Journal* 18 (2): 1–23. https://www.jstor.org/stable/4317205

Goodley, Dan, Kirsty Liddiard, and Katherine Runswick-Cole. 2018. "Feeling Disability: Theories of Affect and Critical Disability Studies." *Disability & Society* 33 (2): 197–217. https://doi.org/10.1080/09687599.2017.1402752

Gordon, James. 2015. "Lean on Me: Girl, 11, with Genetic Condition which Left Her Unable to Walk Takes Her First Steps in Nine Years with the Help of Her Pet Great Dane George." *Daily Mail*, Updated on November 11, 2015. https://www.dailymail.co.uk/femail/article-3312348/Lean-Girl-11-genetic-condition-left-unable-walk-takes-steps-nine-years-help-pet-Great-Dane-George.html

Gray, Herman. 2013. "Subject(ed) to Recognition." *American Quarterly* 65 (4): 771–98. https://www.jstor.org/stable/43822990

Gray, Herman. 2015. "The Feel of Life: Race, Resonance, and Representation." *International Journal of Communication* 9: 1108–19. https://ijoc.org/index.php/ijoc/article/view/2238

Groner, Rachael. 2012. "Sex as 'Spock': Autism, Sexuality, and Autobiographical Narrative." In *Sex and Disability*, edited by Robert McRuer and Anna Mollow, 263–84. Durham: Duke University Press.

Haigney, Sophie. 2020. "TikTok is the Perfect Medium for the Splintered Attention Spans of Lockdown." *The Guardian*, May 16. https://www.theguardian.com/commentisfree/2020/may/16/tiktok-perfect-medium-splintered-attention-spans-coronavirus-lockdown

Halliday, Aria, ed. 2019. *The Black Girlhood Studies Collection*. Toronto: Women's Press.

Haney, Jolynn L. 2016. "Autism, Females, and the DSM-5: Gender Bias in Autism Diagnosis." *Social Work in Mental Health* 14 (4): 396–407. https://doi.org/10.1080/15332985.2015.1031858

Haraway, Donna. 1997. "enlightenment@science_wars.com: A Personal Reflection on Love and War." *Social Text*, no. 50: 123. https://doi.org/10.2307/466820

Haraway, Donna. 2008. *When Species Meet*. Minneapolis: University of Minnesota Press.
Haritaworn, Jin. 2015. *Queer Lovers and Hateful Others: Regenerating Violent Times and Places*. London: Pluto Press.
Harris, Anita. 2004. *Future Girl: Young Women in the Twenty-First Century*. New York: Routledge.
Harris, Anita, and Amy Shields Dobson. 2015. "Theorizing Agency in Post-Girlpower Times." *Continuum* 29 (2): 145–56. https://doi.org/10.1080/10304312.2015.1022955
Harris, Kathleen I., and Stephanie D. Sholtis. 2016. "Companion Angels on a Leash: Welcoming Service Dogs Into Classroom Communities for Children With Autism." *Childhood Education* 92 (4): 263–75. https://doi.org/10.1080/00094056.2016.1208003
Hartman, Saidiya V. 1997. *Scenes of Subjection: Terror, Slavery, and Self-Making in Nineteenth-Century America*. New York: Oxford University Press.
Harvey, David. 2011. *A Brief History of Neoliberalism*. New York: Oxford University Press.
Helton, William S., ed. 2009. *Canine Ergonomics: The Science of Working Dogs*. Boca Raton: CRC Press/Taylor & Francis.
Hemmings, Clare. 2005. "Invoking Affect: Cultural Theory and the Ontological Turn." *Cultural Studies* 19 (5): 548–567. https://doi.org/10.1080/09502380500365473
Hevey, David. 2013. "The Enfreakment of Photography." In *The Disability Studies Reader*, edited by Lennard J. Davis, 432–46. New York: Routledge.
Hill, Sarah. 2017. "Exploring Disabled Girls' Self-representational Practices Online." *Girlhood Studies* 10 (2): 114–30. https://doi.org/10.3167/ghs.2017.100209
Hill, Sarah. 2022. "Locating Disability within Online Body Positivity Discourses: An Analysis of #DisabledAndCute." *Feminist Media Studies*, February, 1–16. https://doi.org/10.1080/14680777.2022.2032254
Hilyard, Scott. 2009. "Adoption Completes Family Touched by Down Syndrome." *The State Journal-Register*, Updated November 30. https://www.sj-r.com/story/news/2009/11/30/adoption-completes-family-touched-by/47082257007/
Hinger, Sarah. 2018. "South Carolina Legislature Repeals Racist 'Disturbing School' Law for Students." National Juvenile Justice Network, June 28. https://www.njjn.org/article/south-carolina-legislature-repeals-racist-disturbing-school-law-for-students
Hochschild, Arlie. 1983. *The Managed Heart: Commercialization of Human Feeling*. Berkeley: University of California Press.
Hoffmann, Diane E., and Anita J. Tarzian. 2001. "The Girl Who Cried Pain: A Bias against Women in the Treatment of Pain." *Journal of Law, Medicine & Ethics* 29 (1): 13–27. https://doi.org/10.1111/j.1748-720X.2001.tb00037.x
hooks, bell. 1992. *Black Looks: Race and Representation*. Boston: South End Press.
Hughes, Bill. 2012. "Fear, Pity and Disgust: Emotions and the Non-disabled Imaginary." In *Routledge Handbook of Disability Studies*, edited by Nick Watson, Alan Roulstone, and Carol Thomas, 67–78. New York: Routledge.

Hull, Laura, K. V. Petrides, and William Mandy. 2020. "The Female Autism Phenotype and Camouflaging: A Narrative Review." *Review Journal of Autism and Developmental Disorders* 7 (4): 306–17. https://doi.org/10.1007/s40489-020-00197-9

Inside Edition Staff. 2021. "How This Great Dane Has Helped His 13-Year-Old Owner Learn to Walk Without Crutches." *Inside Edition*, July 6. https://www.insideedition.com/how-this-great-dane-has-helped-his-13-year-old-owner-learn-to-walk-without-crutches-68165

Irvin, Sally. 2014. "The Healing Role of Assistance Dogs: What These Partnerships Tell Us about the Human–Animal Bond." *Animal Frontiers* 4 (3): 66–71. https://doi.org/10.2527/af.2014-0024

Jackson, Sarah J., Moya Bailey, and Brooke Foucault Welles. 2020. *#Hashtag Activism: Networks of Race and Gender Justice*. Cambridge, MA: MIT Press.

Jackson, Zakiyyah Iman. 2020. *Becoming Human: Matter and Meaning in an Anti-Black World*. New York: New York University Press.

Jacquemont, Sébastien, Bradley P. Coe, Micha Hersch, Michael H. Duyzend, Niklas Krumm, Sven Bergmann, Jacques S. Beckmann, Jill A. Rosenfeld, and Evan E. Eichler. 2014. "A Higher Mutational Burden in Females Supports a 'Female Protective Model' in Neurodevelopmental Disorders." *American Journal of Human Genetics* 94 (3): 415–25. https://doi.org/10.1016/j.ajhg.2014.02.001

Jain, Sarah Lochlann. 2007. "Living in Prognosis: Toward an Elegiac Politics." *Representations* 98 (1): 77–92. https://doi.org/10.1525/rep.2007.98.1.77

James, Jennifer C. 2011. "Gwendolyn Brooks, World War II, and the Politics of Rehabilitation." In *Feminist Disability Studies*, edited by Kim Q. Hall, 136–58. Bloomington: Indiana University Press.

Jenkins, Henry. 2006. *Convergence Culture: Where Old and New Media Collide*. New York: New York University Press.

Jewell, Paul. 2007. "Policy as Ethics: Sterilisation of Girls with Intellectual Disability." *Policy and Society* 26 (3): 49–64. https://doi.org/10.1016/S1449-4035(07)70115-7

Johnson, Merri Lisa. 2021. "Neuroqueer Feminism: Turning with Tenderness toward Borderline Personality Disorder." *Signs: Journal of Women in Culture and Society* 46 (3): 635–62. https://doi.org/10.1086/712081

Johnson, Merri Lisa, and Robert McRuer. 2014. "Cripistemologies: Introduction." *Journal of Literary & Cultural Disability Studies* 8 (2): 127–47. https://doi.org/10.3828/jlcds.2014.12

Johnson, Taylor. 2021. "Please Don't Pet: Reflections on Life with My Diabetes Alert Dog." In *(Un)doing Diabetes: Representation, Disability, Culture*, edited by Bianca C. Frazer and Heather R. Walker, 195–201. London: Palgrave Macmillan.

Kafai, Shayda. 2021. *Crip Kinship: The Disability Justice & Art Activism of Sins Invalid*. Vancouver: Arsenal Pulp Press.

Kafer, Alison. 2013. *Feminist, Queer, Crip*. Bloomington: Indiana University Press.

Kafer, Alison. 2019. "Crip Kin, Manifesting." *Catalyst: Feminism, Theory, Technoscience* 5 (1): 1–37. https://doi.org/10.28968/cftt.v5i1.29618

Kafer, Alison. 2021. "After Crip, Crip Afters." *South Atlantic Quarterly* 120 (2): 415–34. https://doi.org/10.1215/00382876-8916158
Kelly, Peter. 2001. "Youth at Risk: Processes of Individualisation and Responsibilisation in Risk Society." *Discourse: Studies in the Cultural Politics of Education* 22 (1): 23–33.
Kennedy, Melanie. 2020. "'If the Rise of the TikTok Dance and E-girl Aesthetic Has Taught Us Anything, It's That Teenage Girls Rule the Internet Right Now': TikTok Celebrity, Girls and the Coronavirus Crisis." *European Journal of Cultural Studies* 23 (6): 1069–76.
Kete, Kathleen. 1994. *The Beast in the Boudoir: Petkeeping in Nineteenth-Century Paris*. Berkeley: University of California Press.
Khamis, Susie, Lawrence Ang, and Raymond Welling. 2016. "Self-Branding, 'Micro-Celebrity' and the Rise of Social Media Influencers." *Celebrity Studies* 8 (2): 191–208. https://doi.org/10.1080/19392397.2016.1218292
Kim, Claire Jean. 2015. *Dangerous Crossings: Race, Species, and Nature in a Multicultural Age*. Cambridge: Cambridge University Press.
Kim, Eunjung. 2017. *Curative Violence: Rehabilitating Disability, Gender, and Sexuality in Modern Korea*. Durham: Duke University Press.
King, Wilma. 2005. *African American Childhoods: Historical Perspectives from Slavery to Civil Rights*. New York: Palgrave Macmillan.
Kittay, Eva Feder. 2009. "The Personal is Philosophical is Political: A Philosopher and Mother of a Cognitively Disabled Person Sends Notes from the Battlefield." *Metaphilosophy* 40 (3–4): 606–27. https://doi.org/10.1111/j.1467-9973.2009.01600.x
Kolářová, Kateřina. 2015. "Death by Choice, Life by Privilege: Biopolitical Circuits of Vitality and Debility in the Times of Empire." In *Foucault and the Government of Disability*, edited by Shelley Tremain, 396–424. Ann Arbor: University of Michigan Press.
Kuntsman, Adi. 2012. "Introduction: Affective Fabrics of Digital Cultures." In *Digital Cultures and the Politics of Emotion: Feelings, Affect and Technological Change*, edited by Athina Karatzogianni and Adi Kuntsman, 1–18. New York: Palgrave Macmillan.
Kusters, Annelies, Maartje De Meulder, and Dai O'Brien, eds. 2017. *Innovations in Deaf Studies: The Role of Deaf Scholars*. New York: Oxford University Press.
Kuusisto, Stephen. 2018. *Have Dog, Will Travel. A Poet's Journey*. New York: Simon & Schuster.
Labrecque, Lauren I., Ereni Markos, and George R. Milne. 2011. "Online Personal Branding: Processes, Challenges, and Implications." *Journal of Interactive Marketing* 25 (1): 37–50. https://doi.org/10.1016/j.intmar.2010.09.002
Lamm, Nomy. 2015. "This Is Disability Justice." *The Body Is Not an Apology*, September 2. https://thebodyisnotanapology.com/magazine/this-is-disability-justice/
Lazzarato, Maurizio. 1996. "Immaterial Labor." Generation Online. https://www.generation-online.org/c/fcimmateriallabour3.htm
Lee, Tina. 2016. *Catching a Case: Inequality and Fear in New York City's Child Welfare System*. New Brunswick: Rutgers University Press.

Lesko, Nancy. 2012. *Act Your Age! A Cultural Construction of Adolescence*. Second edition. New York: Routledge.

Levy, Dan, Michael Ronemus, Boris Yamrom, Yoon-ha Lee, Anthony Leotta, Jude Kendall, Steven Marks, et al. 2011. "Rare De Novo and Transmitted Copy-Number Variation in Autistic Spectrum Disorders." *Neuron* 70 (5): 886–97. https://doi.org/10.1016/j.neuron.2011.05.015

Liebman, Lydia. 2016. "HBO Documentary President Sheila Nevins at Barnard College, Athena Film Festival." *Education Update Online*, March/April. http://www.educationupdate.com/archives/2016/MAR/HTML/cov-nevins.html

Liddiard, Kirsty, and Jenny Slater. 2018. "'Like, Pissing Yourself is Not a Particularly Attractive Quality, Let's Be Honest': Learning to Contain Through Youth, Adulthood, Disability, and Sexuality." *Sexualities* 21 (3): 319–33. https://doi.org/10.1177/1363460716688674

Lindsay, Sally, and Kavitha Thiyagarajah. 2021. "The Impact of Service Dogs on Children, Youth and Their Families: A Systematic Review." *Disability and Health Journal* 14 (3): 101012. https://doi.org/10.1016/j.dhjo.2020.101012

Linton, Simi. 1998. *Claiming Disability*. New York: New York University Press.

Livingston, Julie. 2005. *Debility and the Moral Imagination in Botswana*. Bloomington: Indiana University Press.

Longmore, Paul K. 2016. *Telethons: Spectacle, Disability, and the Business of Charity*. Edited by Catherine Jean Kudlick. New York: Oxford University Press.

Lopez Cardenas, Leah. 2020. "Pets are the Best Medicine: How Service & Therapy Dogs Heal Those in Need." *Daily Paws*, September 1. https://www.dailypaws.com/living-with-pets/pet-owner-relationship/how-service-and-therapy-dogs-heal-those-in-need

Lorde, Audre. 1978. *Uses of the Erotic*. New York: Out & Out Books.

Lorde, Audre. 1981. "The Uses of Anger: Women Responding to Racism." *Women's Studies Quarterly* 9 (3): 7–10.

Lundblad, Michael. 2020. "Animality/ Posthumanism/ Disability: An Introduction." *New Literary History* 51 (4): v–xxi. https://doi.org/10.1353/nlh.2020.0040

Lunsford, Erica. 2021. "Disabled Army Veteran Receives Mobility Assistance Service Dog." *WKYT*, Updated June 14. https://www.wkyt.com/2021/06/14/disabled-army-veteran-receives-mobility-assistance-service-dog/

MacPherson-Mayor, Devon, and Cheryl van Daalen-Smith. 2020. "At Both Ends of the Leash: Preventing Service-Dog Oppression Through the Practice of Dyadic-Belonging." *Canadian Journal of Disability Studies* 9 (2): 73–102. https://doi.org/10.15353/cjds.v9i2.626

Mairs, Nancy. 1992. *Plaintext: Essays*. Tucson: University of Arizona Press.

Malatino, Hil. 2020. *Trans Care*. Minneapolis: University of Minnesota Press.

Mandavilli, Apoorva. 2015. "The Lost Girls." *Spectrum News*, October 19. https://www.spectrumnews.org/features/deep-dive/the-lost-girls/

Mandy, William. 2018. "In DSM-5 Guidance on Girls with Autism is Short but Savvy." *Spectrum News*, May 9. https://www.spectrumnews.org/opinion/dsm-5-guidance-girls-autism-short-savvy/

Marre, Diana, and Laura Briggs, eds. 2009. *International Adoption: Global Inequali-*

ties and the Circulation of Children. New York University Press. https://doi.org/10.18574/nyu/9780814791011.001.0001

Marwick, Alice Emily. 2013. *Status Update: Celebrity, Publicity, and Branding in the Social Media Age*. New Haven: Yale University Press.

Mascaro, Thomas A. 2008. "Overview: Form and Function." In *The Essential HBO Reader*, edited by Gary R. Edgerton and Jeffrey P. Jones, 239–61. Lexington: University Press of Kentucky.

Matthews, Cate. 2014. "This Beauty Vlogger is Hard of Hearing, and She's Stepping Up Her Game." *Huffington Post*, October 6. https://www.huffpost.com/entry/rikki-poynter-deaf-hoh-beauty-vlogger_n_5941160

Mauldin, Laura. 2018. "'Coming out' Rhetoric in Disability Studies: Exploring the Limits of Analogy by Looking at Its Fit with the Deaf Experience." *Disability Studies Quarterly* 38 (2). https://dsq-sds.org/index.php/dsq/article/view/5863/4900

McGlotten, Shaka. 2013. *Virtual Intimacies: Media, Affect, and Queer Sociality*. Albany: State University of New York Press.

McGuire, Anne. 2016. *War on Autism: On the Cultural Logic of Normative Violence*. Ann Arbor: University of Michigan Press.

McKittrick, Katherine. 2011. "On Plantations, Prisons, and a Black Sense of Place." *Social & Cultural Geography* 12 (8): 947–63. https://doi.org/10.1080/14649365.2011.624280

McKittrick, Katherine. 2014. "Mathematics Black Life." The Black Scholar: Journal of Black Studies and Research 44 (2): 16–28. https://doi.org/10.1080/00064246.2014.11413684

McRobbie, Angela. 2004. "Post-feminism and Popular Culture." *Feminist Media Studies* 4 (3): 255–64. https://doi.org/10.1080/1468077042000309937

McRobbie, Angela. 2009. *The Aftermath of Feminism: Gender, Culture and Social Change*. London: SAGE.

McRuer, Robert. 2006. *Crip Theory: Cultural Signs of Queerness and Disability*. New York: New York University Press.

McRuer, Robert. 2018. *Crip Times: Disability, Globalization, and Resistance*. New York: New York University Press.

McRuer, Robert, and Anna Mollow, eds. 2012. *Sex and Disability*. Durham: Duke University Press.

Melamed, Jodi. 2011. *Represent and Destroy: Rationalizing Violence in the New Racial Capitalism*. Minneapolis: University of Minnesota Press.

Michalko, Rod. 1999. *The Two-in-One: Walking with Smokie, Walking with Blindness*. Animals, Culture, and Society. Philadelphia: Temple University Press.

Milbrodt, Teresa. 2018. "'Today I Had an Eye Appointment, and I'm Still Blind': Crip Humor, Storytelling, and Narrative Positioning of the Disabled Self." *Disability Studies Quarterly* 38 (2). https://doi.org/10.18061/dsq.v38i2.6163

Mingus, Mia. 2017. "Access Intimacy, Interdependence and Disability Justice." *Leaving Evidence (blog)*, 12 April. https://leavingevidence.wordpress.com/2017/04/12/access-intimacy-interdependence-and-disability-justice/

Minich, Julie Avril. 2016. "Enabling Whom? Critical Disability Studies Now." *Lateral: Journal of the Cultural Studies Association* 5 (1). https://csalateral.org/issue/5-1/forum-alt-humanities-critical-disability-studies-now-minich/

Mitchell, David T., and Sharon L. Snyder. 2000. *Narrative Prosthesis: Disability and the Dependencies of Discourse*. Ann Arbor: University of Michigan Press.

Mitchell, David T., and Sharon L. Snyder. 2015. *The Biopolitics of Disability: Neoliberalism, Ablenationalism, and Peripheral Embodiment*. Ann Arbor: University of Michigan Press.

Mitchell, David, Susan Antebi, and Sharon Snyder, eds. 2019. *The Matter of Disability: Materiality, Biopolitics, Crip Affect*. Ann Arbor: University of Michigan Press.

Mollow, Anna. 2015. "Disability Studies Gets Fat." *Hypatia* 30 (1): 199–216. https://doi.org/10.1111/hypa.12126

Moye, David. 2018. "Black Texas Teenager Brutalized in 2015 Finally Gets Her Pool Party." *HuffPost*, June 20. https://www.huffpost.com/entry/dajerria-becton-pool-party-viral-video_n_5b2a751be4b0a4dc99233e9d

Mykhalovskiy, Eric, Rita Kanarek, Colin Hastings, Jenna Doig, and Melanie Rock. 2020. "Normative Tensions in the Popular Representation of Children with Disabilities and Animal-Assisted Therapy." *Canadian Journal of Disability Studies* 9 (2): 10–38. https://doi.org/10.15353/cjds.v9i2.624

Nakamura, Lisa. 2008. *Digitizing Race: Visual Cultures of the Internet*. Minneapolis: University of Minnesota Press.

National Service Animal Registry (NSAR). 2022. "Dognapping: Protecting Your Service Dog or ESA." https://www.nsarco.com/dognapping-protect-your-service-dog-or-esa/

Ndopu, Eddie. 2013. "Able Normative Supremacy and the Zero Mentality." *The Feminist Wire*, February 5. https://thefeministwire.com/2013/02/able-normative-supremacy-and-the-zero-mentality/

Neustatter, Angela. 2015. "Autism is Seen as a Male Thing—but Girls Just Implode Emotionally." *The Guardian*, July 14. https://www.theguardian.com/education/2015/jul/14/autism-girls-emotion-self-harm-school

Ngai, Sianne. 2012. *Our Aesthetic Categories: Zany, Cute, Interesting*. Cambridge, MA: Harvard University Press.

Nguyen, Xuan Thuy. 2020. "Whose Research Is It? Reflection on Participatory Research with Women and Girls with Disabilities in the Global South." *Jeunesse: Young People, Texts, Cultures* 12 (2): 129–53. https://doi.org/10.3138/jeunesse.12.2.129

Nicole, Shelli. 2021. "'Hey Mamas' Lesbians, Explained." *Autostraddle*, April 12. https://www.autostraddle.com/hey-mamas-lesbian/

Nielsen. 2022. "Visibility of Disability: Answering the Call for Disability Inclusion in Media." *Nielsen*, July 28, 2021. https://www.nielsen.com/us/en/insights/article/2021/visibility-of-disability-answering-the-call-for-disability-inclusion-in-media/

Noble, Safiya Umoja. 2018. "Critical Surveillance Literacy in Social Media: Interrogating Black Death and Dying Online." *Black Camera* 9 (2): 147–60. https://doi.org/10.2979/blackcamera.9.2.10

Not Dead Yet. 2016. "Statement on Mourning the Death of Jerika Bolen." Not Dead Yet. https://notdeadyet.org/statement-on-mourning-the-death-of-jerika-bolen

O'Brien, Clodagh. 2021. "How Much Money Does TikTok Pay Creators?" *Digital Marketing Institute*, October 25. https://digitalmarketinginstitute.com/blog/how-much-does-tiktok-pay-creators

Odem, Mary E. 1995. *Delinquent Daughters: Protecting and Policing Adolescent Female Sexuality in the United States, 1885–1920*. Gender and American Culture. Chapel Hill: University of North Carolina Press.

Oliver, Kelly. 2016. "Service Dogs: Between Animal Studies and Disability Studies." *PhiloSOPHIA* 6 (2): 241–58. https://doi.org/10.1353/phi.2016.0021

Oliver, Michael. 1990. *The Politics of Disablement*. Basingstoke: Palgrave Macmillan.

Ommen, Clifford van, John Cromby, and Jeffery Yen. 2016. "The Contemporary Making and Unmaking of Elaine Scarry's *The Body in Pain*." *Subjectivity* 9 (4): 333–42. https://doi.org/10.1057/s41286-016-0012-8

Ostermeier, Mark. 2010. "History of Guide Dog Use by Veterans." *Military Medicine* 175 (8): 587–93.

"Our Amazing Grace." 2022. *Our Amazing Grace's Light Shines On*. http://www.ouramazinggrace.net/Foundation

Overboe, James. 1999. "Difference in Itself: Validating Disabled People's Lived Experience." *Body & Society* 5 (4): 17–29. https://doi.org/10.1177/1357034X99005004002

Paasonen, Susanna. 2005. *Figures of Fantasy: Internet, Women, and Cyberdiscourse*. New York: Peter Lang.

Patsavas, Alyson. 2014. "Recovering a Cripistemology of Pain: Leaky Bodies, Connective Tissue, and Feeling Discourse." *Journal of Literary & Cultural Disability Studies* 8 (2): 203–18. https://doi.org/10.3828/jlcds.2014.16

Pawlowski, A. 2015. "'Amazing': Service Dog Helps 11-Year-Old Girl With Rare Disorder Walk." *Today*, November 10. https://www.today.com/health/amazing-service-dog-helps-11-year-old-girl-rare-disorder-t55101

Peabody Awards. 2015. "How to Dance in Ohio." Peabody Awards. https://peabodyawards.com/award-profile/how-to-dance-in-ohio/

Peers, Danielle, and Lindsay Eales. 2017. "Moving Materiality: People, Tools, and This Thing Called Disability." *Art/Research International: A Transdisciplinary Journal* 2 (2): 101. https://doi.org/10.18432/R2JS8W

Piepzna-Samarasinha, Leah Lakshmi. 2018. *Care Work: Dreaming Disability Justice*. Vancouver: Arsenal Pulp Press.

Premack, Rachel. 2016. "'I'm going to be free': Terminally Ill Wisconsin Teen Schedules Her Death and One 'Last Dance.'" *Washington Post*, July 21. https://www.washingtonpost.com/news/morning-mix/wp/2016/07/21/one-last-dance-for-this-wisconsin-teen-who-has-scheduled-her-own-death/

Price, Margaret. 2015. "The Bodymind Problem and the Possibilities of Pain." *Hypatia* 30 (1): 268–84. https://doi.org/10.1111/hypa.12127

Price, Margaret. 2017. "What is a Service Animal? A Careful Rethinking." *Review of Disability Studies: An International Journal* 13 (4): 1–18. https://rdsjournal.org/index.php/journal/article/view/757

Projansky, Sarah. 2014. *Spectacular Girls: Media Fascination and Celebrity Culture*. New York: New York University Press.

"Providing Seeing-Eye Dogs for Blind Veterans," Senate Committee on Finance, Congress Session 78–2, April 12, 1944.

Przybylo, Ela, and Breanne Fahs. 2018. "Feels and Flows: On the Realness of Menstrual Pain and Cripping Menstrual Chronicity." *Feminist Formations* 30 (1): 206–29. https://doi.org/10.1353/ff.2018.0010

Puar, Jasbir. 2007. *Terrorist Assemblages: Homonationalism in Queer Times*. Durham: Duke University Press.

Puar, Jasbir. 2013. "Rethinking Homonationalism." *International Journal of Middle East Studies* 45 (2): 336–39. https://doi.org/10.1017/S002074381300007X

Puar, Jasbir. 2017. *The Right to Maim: Debility, Capacity, Disability*. Durham: Duke University Press.

Raffety, Erin. 2019. "Chinese Special Needs Adoption, Demand, and the Global Politics of Disability." *Disability Studies Quarterly* 39 (2). https://doi.org/10.18061/dsq.v39i2.6662

Raun, Tobias. 2012. "DIY Therapy: Exploring Affective Self-Representations in Trans Video Blogs on YouTube." In *Digital Cultures and the Politics of Emotion*, edited by Athina Karatzogianni and Adi Kuntsman, 165–80. London: Palgrave Macmillan UK.

Raun, Tobias. 2018. "Capitalizing Intimacy: New Subcultural Forms of Micro-Celebrity Strategies and Affective Labour on YouTube." *Convergence: The International Journal of Research into New Media Technologies* 24 (1): 99–113. https://doi.org/10.1177/1354856517736983

Reddy, Chandan. 1998. "Home, Houses, Nonidentity: *Paris is Burning*." In *Burning Down the House: Recycling Domesticity*, edited by Rosemary Marangoly George. New York: Routledge.

Reid, D. Kim, Edy Hammond Stoughton, and Robin M. Smith. 2006. "The Humorous Construction of Disability: 'Stand-up' Comedians in the United States." *Disability & Society* 21 (6): 629–43. https://doi.org/10.1080/09687590600918354

Rembis, Michael. 2011. *Defining Deviance: Sex, Science, and Delinquent Girls: 1890–1960*. Urbana: University of Illinois Press.

Ringrose, Jessica. 2007. "Successful Girls? Complicating Post-feminist, Neoliberal Discourses of Educational Achievement and Gender." *Gender and Education* 19 (4): 471–89. https://doi.org/10.1080/09540250701442666

Ritchie, Andrea J. 2017. *Invisible No More: Police Violence Against Black Women and Women of Color*. Boston: Beacon Press.

Roberts, Dorothy E. 2002. *Shattered Bonds: The Color of Child Welfare*. New York: Basic Books.

Roberts, Dorothy E. 2014. "Child Protection as Surveillance of African American

Families." *Journal of Social Welfare and Family Law* 36 (4): 426–37. https://doi.org/10.1080/09649069.2014.967991

Robins, Mary. 2021. "Service Dogs Provide a New Future for Children with Autism." *American Kennel Club*, April 28. https://www.akc.org/expert-advice/news/therapy-dogs-help-children-with-autism/

Robinson, Elise B., Paul Lichtenstein, Henrik Anckarsäter, Francesca Happé, and Angelica Ronald. 2013. "Examining and Interpreting the Female Protective Effect against Autistic Behavior." *Proceedings of the National Academy of Sciences* 110 (13): 5258–62. https://doi.org/10.1073/pnas.1211070110

Rubio-Licht, Nat. 2022. "Women Dominate the Creator Economy. They Still Don't Make as Much as Men." *Protocol*, March 9. https://www.protocol.com/bulletins/creator-economy-pay-gap

Sacks, Harvey. 1984. "On Doing 'Being Ordinary.'" In *Structures of Social Action: Studies in Conversation Analysis*, edited by J. Maxwell Atkinson and John Heritage, 413–29. Cambridge: Cambridge University Press.

Samuels, Ellen. 2017. "Six Ways of Looking at Crip Time." *Disability Studies Quarterly* 37 (3). https://doi.org/10.18061/dsq.v37i3.5824

Samuels, Ellen, and Elizabeth Freeman. 2021. "Introduction: Crip Temporalities." *South Atlantic Quarterly* 120 (2): 245–54. https://doi.org/10.1215/00382876-8915937

Sandahl, Carrie. 2003. "Queering the Crip or Cripping the Queer?: Intersections of Queer and Crip Identities in Solo Autobiographical Performance." *GLQ: A Journal of Lesbian and Gay Studies* 9 (1): 25–56. https://doi.org/10.1215/10642684-9-1-2-25

Scarry, Elaine. 1985. *The Body in Pain: The Making and Unmaking of the World*. New York: Oxford University Press.

Schalk, Sami. 2018. *Bodyminds Reimagined: (Dis)Ability, Race, and Gender in Black Women's Speculative Fiction*. Durham: Duke University Press.

Schalk, Sami, and Jina B. Kim. 2020. "Integrating Race, Transforming Feminist Disability Studies." *Signs: Journal of Women in Culture and Society* 46 (1): 31–55. https://doi.org/10.1086/709213

Schoch, Deborah. 2020. "1 in 5 Americans Now Provide Unpaid Family Care." AARP, June 18. https://www.aarp.org/caregiving/basics/info-2020/unpaid-family-caregivers-report.html

Senft, Theresa M. 2008. *Camgirls: Celebrity and Community in the Age of Social Networks*. New York: Peter Lang.

Shakespeare, Tom. 1999. "Joking a Part." *Body & Society* 5 (4): 47–52. https://doi.org/10.1177/1357034X99005004004

Shandra, Carrie, and Afra Chowdhury. 2012. "The First Sexual Experience Among Adolescent Girls With and Without Disabilities." *Journal of Youth and Adolescence* 41 (4): 515–32. https://doi.org/10.1007/s10964-011-9668-0

Shange, Savannah. 2019. "Black Girl Ordinary: Flesh, Carcerality, and the Refusal of Ethnography." *Transforming Anthropology* 27 (1): 3–21. https://doi.org/10.1111/traa.12143

Sharon, Keith. 2016. "Navy SEAL's fight to reconnect with dog he served with in war leads to new mission." *Orange County Register*. Last modified October 26, 2016. https://www.ocregister.com/2016/10/26/navy-seals-fight-to-reconnect-with-dog-he-served-with-in-war-leads-to-new-mission/

Sharpe, Christina. 2016. *In the Wake: On Blackness and Being*. Durham: Duke University Press.

Sheppard, Emma. 2018. "Using Pain, Living with Pain." *Feminist Review* 120 (1): 54–69. https://doi.org/10.1057/s41305-018-0142-7

Sheppard, Emma. 2020. "Chronic Pain as Emotion." *Journal of Literary & Cultural Disability Studies* 14 (1): 5–20. https://doi.org/10.3828/jlcds.2019.17

Shildrick, Margrit. 2015. "Death, Debility and Disability" *Feminism & Psychology* 25 (1): 155–60. http://dx.doi.org/10.1177/0959353514562816

Shildrick, Margrit, and Janet Price, eds. 1998. *Vital Signs: Feminist Reconfigurations of the Bio/logical Body*. Edinburgh: Edinburgh University Press.

Siebers, Tobin. 2001. "Disability in Theory: From Social Constructionism to the New Realism of the Body." *American Literary History* 13 (4): 737–54. https://www.muse.jhu.edu/article/1951

Siebers, Tobin. 2008. *Disability Theory*. Ann Arbor: University of Michigan Press.

Siebers, Tobin. 2012. "A Sexual Culture for Disabled People." In *Sex and Disability*, edited by Robert McRuer and Anna Mollow, 37–53. Durham: Duke University Press.

Simonpillai, Radheyan. 2021. "On These Grounds: A Shocking Film About Police Brutality Within US Schools." *The Guardian*, September 21. https://www.theguardian.com/film/2021/sep/21/on-these-grounds-documentary-police-brutality-us-schools

Singer, Peter. 2009. "Speciesism and Moral Status." *Metaphilosophy* 40 (3–4): 567–81. https://doi.org/10.1111/j.1467-9973.2009.01608.x

Slater, Jenny. 2012. "Youth for Sale: Using Critical Disability Perspectives to Examine the Embodiment of 'Youth.'" *Societies* 2: 195–209. https://doi.org/10.3390/soc2030195

Smith, Ashley. 2019. "Theorizing Black Girlhood." In the *Black Girlhood Studies Collection*, edited by Aria Halliday, 21–44. Toronto: Women's Press.

Snyder, Sharon, and David Mitchell. 2010. "Introduction: Ablenationalism and the Geo-Politics of Disability." *Journal of Literary & Cultural Disability Studies* 4 (2): 113–25. https://doi.org/10.3828/jlcds.2010.10

Sothern, Matthew. 2007. "You Could Truly Be Yourself if You Just Weren't You: Sexuality, Disabled Body Space, and the (Neo)liberal Politics of Self-Help." *Environment and Planning D: Society and Space* 25 (1): 144–59. https://doi.org/10.1068/d1704

Stelloh, Tim, and Tracy Connor. 2015. "Video Shows Cop Body-Slamming High School Girl in S.C. Classroom." *NBC News*, Updated October 27. https://www.nbcnews.com/news/us-news/video-appears-show-cop-bodyslamming-student-s-c-classroom-n451896

Stienstra, Deborah. 2015. "Trumping All? Disability and Girlhood Studies." *Girlhood Studies* 8 (2): 54–70. https://doi.org/10.3167/ghs.2015.080205

Stiker, Henri-Jacques. 1999. *A History of Disability*. Ann Arbor: University of Michigan Press.

Stockon, Kathryn Bond. 2009. *The Queer Child, or Growing Sideways in the Twentieth Century*. Durham: Duke University Press.

Sutherland, Tonia. 2017. "Making a Killing: On Race, Ritual, and (Re)Membering in Digital Culture." *Preservation, Digital Technology & Culture* 46 (1): 32–40. https://doi.org/10.1515/pdtc-2017-0025

Szalavitz, Maia. 2016. "Autism—It's Different in Girls." *Scientific American*, 1 March. https://www.scientificamerican.com/article/autism-it-s-different-in-girls/

Taylor, Chloë, Kelly Struthers Montford, and Stephanie Jenkins, eds. 2021. *Disability and Animality: Crip Perspectives in Critical Animal Studies*. New York: Routledge.

Taylor, Sunaura. 2017. *Beasts of Burden: Animal and Disability Liberation*. New York: New Press.

Terranova, Tiziana. 2000. "Free Labor." *Social Text* 18 (2): 33–58. https://doi.org/10.1215/01642472-18-2_63-33

Thompson, Vilissa. 2016. "Letters for Jerika: Showing Up for Jerika Bolen." Ramp Your Voice Blog, August 17. https://web.archive.org/web/20201128103859/http://www.rampyourvoice.com/letters-jerika-showing-jerika-bolen/

Thompson, Vilissa. 2019. "How Technology Is Forcing the Disability Rights Movement into the 21st Century." *Catalyst: Feminism, Theory, Technoscience* 5 (1): 1–5. https://doi.org/10.28968/cftt.v5i1.30420

"TikTok's Rapid Growth Shows the Potency of Video." 2021. *The Economist*, October 7. https://www.economist.com/graphic-detail/2021/10/07/tiktoks-rapid-growth-shows-the-potency-of-video

Titchkosky, Tanya. 2003. "Governing Embodiment: Technologies of Constituting Citizens with Disabilities." *Canadian Journal of Sociology / Cahiers Canadiens de Sociologie* 28. https://www.jstor.org/stable/pdf/3341840.pdf

Tremain, Shelley. 2001. "On the Government of Disability." *Social Theory and Practice* 27 (4): 617–36. https://doi.org/10.5840/soctheorpract200127432

Turchiano, Danielle. 2018. "'Dogs' Docuseries Gets Netflix Premiere Date, First Trailer (EXCLUSIVE)." *Variety*, October 29. https://variety.com/2018/tv/news/netflix-dogs-docuseries-premiere-date-trailer-1203004139/

Vänskä, Annamari. 2016. "'Cause I wuv You!' Pet Dog Fashion and Emotional Consumption." *Ephemera: Theory & Politics in Organization* 16 (4): 75–97. https://ephemerajournal.org/contribution/%25E2%2580%2598cause-i-wuv-you%25E2%2580%2599-pet-dog-fashion-and-emotional-consumption

Wall, Tyler. 2016. "'For the Very Existence of Civilization': The Police Dog and Racial Terror." *American Quarterly* 68 (4): 861–82. https://doi.org/10.1353/aq.2016.0070

Weaver, Harlan. 2021. *Bad Dog: Pit Bull Politics and Multispecies Justice*. Seattle: University of Washington Press.

Wendell, Susan. 1996. *The Rejected Body: Feminist Philosophical Reflections on Disability*. New York: Routledge.
Wendell, Susan. 2001. "Unhealthy Disabled: Treating Chronic Illnesses as Disabilities." *Hypatia* 16 (4): 17–33. https://www.jstor.org/stable/3810781
Whitehead, Andrew L., and Samuel L. Perry. 2020. *Taking America Back for God: Christian Nationalism in the United States*. New York: Oxford University Press.
Wool, Zoë. 2020. "Mourning, Affect, Sociality: On the Possibilities of Open Grief." *Cultural Anthropology* 35 (1): 40–47. https://doi.org/10.14506/ca35.1.06
Wright, Nazera Sadiq. 2016. *Black Girlhood in the Nineteenth Century*. Urbana: University of Illinois Press.
Wynter, Sylvia. 2003. "Unsettling the Coloniality of Being/Power/Truth/Freedom: Towards the Human, After Man, Its Overrepresentation—An Argument." *CR: The New Centennial Review* 3 (3), 257–337. https://www.jstor.org/stable/41949874
Yan, Holly. 2015. "South Carolina School Officer Fired, But More Fallout Possible." *CNN*, Updated April 29. https://www.cnn.com/2015/10/29/us/south-carolina-school-arrest-videos/index.html
Yergeau, Melanie. 2018. *Authoring Autism: On Rhetoric and Neurological Queerness*. Durham: Duke University Press.
Zeng, Jing, Crystal Abidin, and Mike S. Schäfer. 2021. "Research Perspectives on TikTok and Its Legacy Apps." *International Journal of Communication* 15: 3161–72.
Zimmerman, Jason. 2022. "Family's Fight with Hospital Leads to Rally Outside St. Elizabeth Hospital." *WBAY*, Updated April 8. https://www.wbay.com/2022/04/08/familys-fight-with-hospital-leads-rally-outside-st-elizabeth-hospital/
Zlatunich, Nichole. 2009. "Prom Dreams and Prom Reality: Girls Negotiating 'Perfection' at the High School Prom." *Sociological Inquiry* 79 (3): 351–75. https://doi.org/10.1111/j.1475-682X.2009.00294.x

Filmography

"10 Years of Becoming Beautifully Different—Bullied Then Becoming an Inspiration." 2020. YouTube video, 18:26, posted by Charisse Living with Cerebral Palsy, March 27, 2020. https://www.youtube.com/watch?v=uuR6xu1zzHI
"Charisse's Story—My Life Journey with Cerebral Palsy." 2012. YouTube video, 17:35, posted by Charisse Living with Cerebral Palsy, June 13, 2012. https://www.youtube.com/watch?v=0nnuHj5M5FE
"Deaf Awareness: I'm on the Huffington Post! | Closed Captioned." 2014. YouTube video, 3:51, posted by Rikki Poynter. Oct. 8, 2014. https://www.youtube.com/watch?v=Dmd2xUFcKDk
"George (Great Dane)—2015 Humane Fund Awards for Canine Excellence." 2016. YouTube video, 4:03, posted by American Kennel Club, February 10, 2016. https://www.youtube.com/watch?v=KhUA2dLzho0
How to Dance in Ohio. 2015. Directed by Alexandra Shiva. USA: HBO Documentary Films, 2015, Television.

"John Cena Love Has No Labels 'We are America'" 2016. YouTube video, 3:37, posted by WWE, July 4, 2016. https://www.youtube.com/watch?v=IApvU6S Mq-8&t=5s

"Learning Sign Language As A Deaf Adult." 2016. YouTube video, 13:17, posted by Rikki Poynter, September 12, 2016. https://www.youtube.com/watch?v=SHpK mR61GBA

Lexy [@muslimsevicedogmom28]. "#greenscreen #greenscreenvideo yes I know they make mistakes but because of her breed the first she slips up in a large public place she gets verbally attacked #28XTREMES #queermuslim #servicedoglife #serivcedog #diabeticalertdog #lesbian #pitbull #queens." TikTok, January 13, 2021.

Lexy [@muslimsevicedogmom28]. "Pretty sure she's lesbian also #28XTREMES #queermuslim #servicedoglife #serivcedog #diabeticalertdog #lesbian #pitbull #queens." TikTok, June 15, 2021.

Lexy [@muslimsevicedogmom28]. "we had to put my other one down because she got really bad cancer and was suffering #28XTREMES #servicedog #real #diabetes #pitt #fyp." TikTok, January 13, 2021.

"Love Has No Labels | Diversity & Inclusion | Ad Council." 2015. YouTube video, 3:19, posted by Ad Council, March 3, 2015. https://www.youtube.com/watch?v=PnDgZuGIhHs

Miss You Can Do It. 2013. Directed by Ron Davis. USA: HBO Documentary Films, 2013, Television.

"My Body Doesn't Oppress Me, Society Does." 2017. YouTube video, 5:08, posted by Barnard Center for Research on Women, May 9, 2017. https://www.youtube.com/watch?v=7r0MiGWQY2g

"#NoMoreCraptions: How To Properly Caption Your Videos." 2016. YouTube video, 10:44, posted by Rikki Poynter, September 25, 2016. https://www.youtube.com/watch?v=-O4YcVQt5NM

"Q&A: Deaf Awareness Week | Close Captioned." 2014. YouTube video, 22:22, posted by Rikki Poynter, Oct. 1, 2014. https://www.youtube.com/watch?v=5PApS9aKH58

Rosie [@rosie.the.sd]. "She's my yellow #servicedog #servicedogintraining #sdit #servicedogsoftiktok #servicedogteam #servicedogtraining #goldenretriever." TikTok, August 24, 2021.

Rosie [@rosie.the.sd]. "Why Rosie's tail is dyed! #dyeddog #rainbowtail #servicedog #servicedogoffduty #servicedogintraining #sdit #servicedoglife #goldenretriever #golden." TikTok, October 1, 2021.

"Service Dog Changed Bella's Life." 2016. YouTube video, 3:27, posted by The Doctors, May 5, 2016. https://www.youtube.com/watch?v=hmBVKFPEsV8

"Shit Hearing People Say (Things You Don't Say to Deaf & Hard of Hearing)." 2014. YouTube video, 2:54, posted by Rikki Poynter, November 5, 2014. https://www.youtube.com/watch?v=wCGko6m_WZQ

"Special Guests R2-D2 & Mark Hamill Surprise Bella." 2016. YouTube video, 5:01, posted by The Doctors, May 5, 2016. https://www.youtube.com/watch?v=KaCE8ozKdmw

"The Kid with a Dog." 2018. *Dogs*. Produced by Amy Berg and Glen Zipper. USA: Netflix, November 16, 2018, Streaming.

"The Rescuers." 2019. *Dogs with Extraordinary Jobs*. Produced by Caroline Hawkins and Victoria Stilwell. USA: Smithsonian Channel, May 4, 2019, Streaming.

"Walking & running with Cerebral Palsy." 2010. YouTube video, 1:43, posted by Charisse Living with Cerebral Palsy, June 10, 2010. https://www.youtube.com/watch?v=gdiMNPOclnU

"What I Want the World to Know." 2012. YouTube video, 4:09, posted by Charisse Living with Cerebral Palsy, September 11, 2012. https://www.youtube.com/watch?v=n_VADDvHxCY

Index

able-bodiedness/mindedness, 4, 5, 13, 40; compulsory, 5, 28, 30, 37, 57, 78, 87, 122, 127; and gender, 32, 105, 113; and heterosexuality, 40, 60, 129; logic of, 47, 97, 152; striving toward, 115
"able-disabled," 39, 167
ableism, 15, 28, 41–42, 50, 61, 63, 80, 91, 93, 140; anti-, 31, 68, 85–88; and audism, 95–96, 177n3; as common sense, 24; discourses of, 121; and the family, 52; individualized, 31, 68, 90; intersections of, 17–19, 25, 136, 142–145, 154, 167, 173; and love, 23; and speciesism, 107; theorization of, 64, 83
ablenationalism, 13, 37, 52, 62–63, 104, 112, 172; and anti–Black racism, 143, 148, 166–167; and the disabled girl, 11–14, 29, 37, 62, 105, 140, 156; emotional habitus of, 91; logics of, 3; and the love machine, 118–123 narratives, 48, 63; and state violence, 19; subject of, 32
accessibility, 18, 71; barriers to, 43, 150; captions, 94–96; and care, 122–123, 147, 156; in-, 46, 93, 94, 147; monetized, 67; and the social model, 15; uneven, 20
Adams, Rachel, 128
aesthetics, 75, 93, 96; affectivity, 50, 120; channel, 71; and cuteness, 121; judgment, 120; lo-fi, 70, 81, 98

affect, 21–25, 32, 39, 43–44, 75, 112, 159, 171; labor, 30, 46; negative, 31, 44, 80, 85, 120; normative, 3; pedagogue, 47; positive, 35, 45–46, 59, 62; proper, 61; readers, 26
affective: attachment, 32, 33, 141, 162, 166–167; economy, 112; encounter, 80; grammar, 121; relations, 31, 75–76, 110–111, 121; resignification, 162
affectivity, 61, 162, 165–166; of disability rights, 96; of service dogs, 110–111, 119, 123; and gender, 37; positive, 166; sentimental, 104, 110, 127, 152–153
Affordable Care Act, 175n2
Ahmed, Sara, 16, 45, 162
Akyel, Esma, 95
ambivalence, 18, 25–26, 144–145, 154, 160
American dream, 97, 152
American Girl Doll, 2, 6–7
American Kennel Club, 103, 118
American Psychiatric Association (APA), 54
American Sign Language (ASL), 76–77, 90
American with Disabilities Act (ADA) 2, 20, 96, 111–112; twenty-fifth anniversary, 97
Amigo, Emilio 54, 57, 58–59
Amigo Family Counseling, 54
animality: paradigm of, 106

Annamma, Subini, 4
Antebi, Susan, 24
anti-ableist solidarity, 31, 68
Antoine, 38
anxiety, 36–37, 44, 46, 60, 125, 162; of autistic girl futures, 29, 37, 53–57, 62; of disabled girls futures, 14, 35, 115; and eugenics, 153; about heterosexuality, 60; medication, 169; national, 143; reduction, 179n3
Anzaldúa, Gloria, 23
Apgar, Amanda, 40, 46, 59, 117
Apple, 71, 97
Appleton, Wisconsin, 33, 139, 148, 149, 163, 169
archives, 25–29, 143; of disability knowledge, 173; of feeling, 76, 80
Asperger, Hans; 55
Asperger's, 57
assisted dying ethics of, 139
audism, 86–88, 95
authenticity, 81, 115–116
autism, 7, 27, 28, 34–35, 47, 56; and the DSM, 176n3; as gendered epidemic, 27, 30, 37, 54–55; industrial-complex, 61; narratives of, 35, 38, 55, 60; as queer, 58; research and advocacy, 56–57
Autism: The Musical, 38
Autistic Self-Advocacy Network, the, 141, 180n3

Bailey, Moya, 175n6
banality, 86–87, 154; of ableism, 88
Banet-Weiser, Sarah, 100
Barad, Karen, 24
beauty pageant, 25, 34, 37–42; contestants, 10, 29, 62
#BeBeautifullyDifferent, 94, 98–100
becoming disabled, 24, 32, 106, 123, 147
Becton, Dajerria, 164, 165, 182n20
behavioralism, 56
belonging, 81, 83–84, 88, 95, 101; assimilationist, 100

benevolence, 4, 40, 50
Berg, Amy, 103
Berlant, Lauren, 24, 55, 80, 85
Berne, Patty, 15
Bill and Melinda Gates Foundation, The, 73
bipedal ambulation, 114
blackness, 140, 154; and girlhood, 165; systemic devaluation of, 141
Body and Soul (De Corpo e Alma), 38
bodymind, 2–4, 23, 28, 148, 168, 172–173; autistic, 54–57, 58; capacitating, 8, 52, 93; disabled, 12–15, 19–20, 24, 37, 79, 83–84, 116, 150; expectations, 18; gendered, 10, 20, 22, 30, 41, 57; as lacking, 64; non-disabled, 158; non-normative, 15, 33, 42, 143, 166; "out-of-time," 37, 56–57; pained, 146–147, 151, 155; perceptions of, 78, 83; racialized, 20, 143, 154, 165; return to, 77; temporalization of, 41, 47, 57, 151–152
Boggs, Colleen, 110–111
Bolen, Jen, 140, 143, 146, 155–156, 160; narrative of, 156–158
Bolen, Jerika, 18–19, 25, 27, 32–33, 64, 139, 143, 163–169; and care labor, 160; childhood, 153; commodified, 162, 166; death, 141, 155–156, 167–168; depoliticization of, 160, 167; and JuJuBee, 156; local coverage, 149–154, 155–156; memory of, 167–168; pain narratives, 145–146, 154, 156, 158, 162, 181n10; public mourning of, 143, 154; and radical refusal, 168; representations of, 144–145; spectacularization of, 140, 142–143, 158, 163–164, 166–167
A Boogie Wit Da Hoodie, 132
borderline personality disorder, 125, 148
Bryant, Ma'Khia, 144, 164
Burke, Molly, 73
Burton, Bella, 112, 117

Canadian Department of Veteran Affairs, 110

capacitation, 10, 39, 117, 124; of body-minds, 8; frame, 97; re-, 20, 29, 44, 51, 53, 91, 142; tools of, 32, 118
capacity, 32, 39, 50, 59, 154; and affect, 24, 61, 68, 111, 120; and ageism, 155; change in, 151–152; commodified, 75; and debility, 8; healing, 104; and homonationalism, 12; in- 88, 161; individual, 42, 143; to influence, 92–93; to make decisions, 141, 145; to teach, 153, 161; to work, 45
care, 4, 18, 51, 112, 180n6; burden of, 143, 160; cost of, 161; ethics of, 128, 148; inaccessible, 147; mutual acts of, 127; object of, 120; privatized, 32, 122–123; standard of, 150; work, 129, 142
Cartwright, Lisa, 36
Castañeda, Claudia, 7
Cawley, Meghan, 117
Cena, John, 11–12
Centers for Disease Control and Prevention, 54
cerebral palsy, 39, 42–43, 44, 47, 64, 66, 79, 101; difficulties living with, 84
Chaney, Jen, 103
Charisse living with cerebral palsy, 27, 30, 66, 70. *See also* Hogan, Charisse
Chen, Mel, 21, 136
child, the, 35; disabled, 35–36
Christian nationalism, 171
chrononormativity, 13, 32, 41, 47, 62–63, 113, 152; of development, 41, 47, 57, 114; and girlhood, 105, 122
Cineas, Fabiol, 144
citational practice, 17, 40
citizenship, 2, 4, 8, 9, 12, 29, 32; assimilationist, 100; and good dying, 143, 156; neoliberal, 31, 89; post-ADA, 52, 89; proto-, 29, 35, 44, 117
Clare, Eli, 3, 21
Clark, Rosemary, 95
Collar, Jim, 148–149, 151–153, 163
Columbus, Ohio, 29, 35
commodification, 22; of cripistemology, 95–96; of disability identity, 94

common sense, 24, 32, 53, 59, 63, 143
community, 4, 10, 95, 124; Deaf, 77; healing power of, 85; of misfits, 84; online, 80
confessional culture. *See* therapeutic culture
consumption, 13; media, 74; as productive, 75
Cooper, Harriet, 26
Corker, Mairian, 87
Coté, Mark, 75
County Board of Developmental Disabilities, 56
COVID-19 pandemic, 33, 72, 104, 124, 147, 169–173; anti-vax theories, 170–171
crip, 2, 20–22, 28, 136; afterlife, 33, 139, 144, 146, 167, 171; axioms, 173; claiming, 29, 81, 84, 124; consciousness-raising, 88; humor, 81, 85–89; solidarity, 142; theory, 22; time, 127; joy, 63
crip-fluencer, 22, 31, 65, 73, 92–94, 125; post-ADA, 97; spectacularization of, 95
cripistemology, 4, 95, 161; Black disabled girl, 155; of pain, 147
cripping girlhood (heuristic), 3, 17–18, 22, 24, 26, 30, 64, 68, 168, 171–172
Crow, Liz, 148
cultural production, 21, 66; monetization of, 92
cure, 18, 146, 150–151, 168
Curran, Abbey, 29–30, 37, 38, 54, 117
cuteness, 121
Cvetkovich, Anne, 24
cyberbullying, 98

d/Deaf people, 66, 176n3
Daily Mail, The, 112
dancing, 58
Davis, Ron, 34, 36
deaf: Awareness Week, 65; community, 76; culture, 65; identity, 77
#DeafTalent, 67

death, 14, 170; facilitating, 150; good, 161–162; over disability, 160; pedagogue of, 32, 143, 153–154, 156, 162; premature, 141, 143, 180n4; rationalized, 163; uneven chances of, 170
debilitation, 171; anti-black, 163–166
debility, 8, 14, 20, 33
deep pressure therapy (DPT), 128
dependence, 41, 120; independence dichotomy, 56, 129; perpetual, 114; on technology, 119
dependency, 56, 119, 129, 152; discourses of, 154; intimacy of, 125; temporality of, 129
depoliticization, 5, 19, 32, 105, 161, 167; of the "problem" of disability, 46; via film, 64; via inclusion, 14, 92
desire, 5, 160, 168, 173; for autonomy, 106; to die, 18, 140, 143, 146; theorizations of, 142; the turn to, 148
development, 41, 45, 47, 149; and autism 54–56, 62; child, 8, 57; and cure, 151; failures, 10; heterosexual, 59–60; "lagging," 58; self-, 161; telos of, 53, 117
diagnosis, 28, 43–44, 48, 54–55
Diagnostic and Statistical Manuel of Mental Disorders (DSM-5), 54, 55, 176n3
digital media studies, 26
disability, 111; activism, 2, 5, 14, 21, 68, 92, 106, 170; as affinity, 28; community, 66, 68, 80, 140; as cultural system, 16; desire for, 91; documentary, 36–38; educators, 90, 172; entrepreneur, 92; feelings about 36; fetishized, 91; identity, 22, 71, 83; intellectual, 47; intimacies, 89–91, 93; invisible, 124, 134, 136; justice, 142, 170; knowledge, 40; objectivity of, 115; politics, 50; production of, 44; rights organizations, 140–141, 145, 146, 180n5; and sex, 86–88; subjectivity, 65–69, 76–77, 93, 100–101; technology, 71, 121; tolerance, 51–52; value of, 37, 40, 51, 64; vlogging, 19, 21, 30, 68, 73, 74–80, 158
Disability Rights Wisconsin, 141, 180n3
disability studies, and the "animal question," 106; feminist 4, 14, 15–18, 20, 22, 146–148, 171; as methodology, 175n5
disability visibility, 5, 13, 19, 21–22, 32, 76, 163; affective power of, 101–102; economy of, 97, 101, 104, 107, 123; monetization, 68; politics of, 166; Project, 173; revolution, 6, 30, 66, 69–71, 73
disabled girl handler, 103–104, 123–124, 128, 134
Disabled Parents Rights, 141, 180n3
disappointment, 14, 41
Disney, 73
disposability, 170
diversity, 11
docility, 163, 165–167
Doctors, The, 112, 119, 120
dogs, 31, 103, 114
Dogs with Extraordinary Jobs, 114
domesticity, 110, 111
Donaldson, Elizabeth, 23
dove, 73
Down Syndrome, 1, 6, 48–52, 169, 171
Doyle, Nancy, 97
dread, 28
Duffy, Brooke Erin, 93
dysfunction, 9

Eales, Lindsey, 114
Economist, The, 124
Edelman, Lee, 35
Elman, Julie, 8
Elmwood, Illinois, 48
emotion. *See* affect
emotional support animal, 179n5
empire, 20, 23
empowerment, 5
Eng, David, 49, 51
epilepsy, 103, 114–116
Erevelles, Nirmala, 4, 19, 57

ethics: research, 26–27
eugenics, 8, 12, 55, 142, 167
Eustis, Dorothy Harrison, 109, 111
exceptionalism, 12–13, 42, 101, 171, 172; disability, 2, 94, 97; docile, 166, 167; and the disabled girl, 156, 161, 163, 166–167; national, 4; post-ADA, 29, 36, 94, 97; rehabilitative, 107, 111, 119, 127, 129, 136
exclusion, 5, 14, 43

Facebook, 6, 70, 74, 97
family, 2, 4, 19, 34, 48–51, 55; and animals, 103, 107, 111, 122–123; healing, 104; as locus of care, 112, 118, 122, 161, 172; nuclear, 29, 51, 106, 110–111, 160, 172; post-ADA formation, 19; reproduction, 177n9; securing the, 111, 118; whiteness of, 122, 172
fear, 34, 56
female protective effect (FPE) theory, 176n3
feminism, 8; Black, 23, 180n5; of color, 23; popular, 100; post-, 9, 31, 42
flags: American, 1, 11, 38, 40, 171; rainbow, 132
flexibility, 51–52, 93, 95; of "crip," 2; and subjectivity, 9–10, 52
4 Paws for Ability, 114, 115, 122
Fritsch, Kelly, 45
future girl, 9–10, 13, 29, 40; autistic, 37, 53–55, 60; disabled, 30, 37, 38–39, 43, 46–47, 54, 62, 117, 172
futurity, 10, 34, 53–54, 63; lack of, 62, 63; reproductive, 101, 152

Garland-Thomson, Rosemarie, 16–17, 28, 78, 84
Gaze, 7, 55; able-bodied, 80, 82; medicalized, 36
gender, 16, 40–41, 54–55
generalizability, 26
George/Bella dyad, 105, 111, 112–114, 118–121

Gerber, 10
Germany, 109
girls' studies, 4
Glee, 7
Glenn, Evelyn Nakano, 180n6
GoFundMe; 27, 146, 155–156, 158–159, 181n14; and affect, 159, 162; "J's Last Dance" campaign, 32–33, 139, 143, 155–160, 163
Gogolewski, Corrine; 103–104, 114, 116
Good Food for Thought, 60–61
Google, 71, 92, 97, 177n6
Gordon, Avery, 182n26
governance, 45, 161
Gray, Herman 73, 164
grief, 14, 44–45, 63, 148, 157–158, 160, 181n13; mother's, 156–157; normative 181n13; public, 181n15
Groner, Rachel, 58
Guardian, The, 124

happiness, 14, 34, 44; duty, 162; happy future, 168; happy object, 37, 43–48, 50–52, 172
Haraway, Donna, 127
Harris, Anita, 8, 39
Hartman, Saidiya, 182n25
hashtag, 95; campaigns, 94–96, 175n6
hate crime, 52
HBO, 2, 29, 34, 53, 170
healthcare, 2, 29, 156; dysfunction, 159; universal, 159
heteronormativity, 3, 13, 37, 40, 58, 100, 152
Hill, Sarah, 4
Hochschild, Arlie, 61
Hogan, Charisse, 30–31, 66, 67–68, 73, 89, 177n4; channel content, 74, 76, 79–80, 81–85, 98–102; commodified, 75–76; crafting intimacy, 80–81; as educator, 89–90
Hollywood Reporter, The, 35
homonationalism, 12–13
hooks, bell, 181n9

hope, 42, 57, 158
Houang, Antoine, 38
How to Dance in Ohio, 29, 34–37, 53–58, 62
human: as exclusionary category, 106–107
Hutchison-Gilford progeria, 73
hygiene, 56, 58, 59–60
hyper-able, 121

identity first language, 28
imaginaries: ableist, 143, 150–151; cultural, 2, 9, 39–40, 68, 155; curative, 63; heteronormative, 134; medicalized, 15; national, 2, 10, 13, 30–32, 39, 54, 92, 161, 166–167, 172; neoliberal, 63, 158, 160; post–ADA disability rights, 33, 143, 166; public, 145
impairment, 15, 20, 23, 28, 45, 77–78, 102, 115; and crip time, 127; and disability, 17, 21; and gender, 41; negativity of, 148; and staring, 36, 42, 78–79
inclusion, 19–20, 31, 39, 57, 91, 94, 171–172; ablenationalist model, 42–43, 112; fantasy of, 97, 101; and the human, 106–107; post–ADA, 30–33, 68, 97, 101, 143; and social capital, 61, 76; symbolic, 167; uneven, 12, 14, 37
independence, 56, 62, 114, 117, 173; desire for, 32, 106; idealization of, 129; loss of, 152; promise of, 62; of womanhood, 41
infantilization, 41, 47
influencer, 2, 10, 92, 172; economy, 93, 124; marketing, 92; self-narrative, 95; tiers, 177n5. *See also* crip-fluencer
inspiration, 34–35, 45, 72, 89, 113, 140, 145, 159–160, 163
In the Dark, 107
Instagram, 30, 70
institutionalization, 64
Inter-Country Adoption (ICA), 49, 51
interdependency, 32, 56, 106, 108, 129, 180n6; ethical obligation of, 136

International Day of the Girl Child, 6
International Symbol of Access (ISA), 45
intersectionality, 16, 21, 64, 136; in disability justice framework, 142
intervention, 51, 54–55, 58, 60, 62, 104; biomedical, 56, 146; discursive, 95; feminist, 176n3; necessity of, 10, 115
intimacy, 4, 68, 75, 81, 87, 125; of dependency, 124; desire for, 83; disability, 89–90; as a force, 80; interspecies, 118; monetization of, 92; technology of, 158
intimate publics, 31, 80–81, 124; digital disability, 68, 78–81, 85, 87, 91
Ipswich, Massachusetts, 112
isolation, 81, 98, 128

Jackson, Zakiyya Iman, 106
Jenkins, Henry, 74
Jenkins, Stephanie, 106
Johnson, Merri Lisa, 148
Johnson, Taylor, 136

Kafer, Alison, 10, 17, 28, 35, 39, 150, 177n9
Kanner, Leo, 55
Keelan-Chaffins, Jennifer, 7
Kennedy, Melanie, 124
Kenny, Niya, 165
Kewanee, Illinois, 39
Kim, Eunjung, 150–151
Kim, Jina, 16–17, 19
kinship, 23, 85, 123, 162; interspecies, 19, 106
Kolářová, Kateřina, 20, 161
Kuusisto, Stephen: and Corky, 124

labor, 2, 4, 8, 13, 27, 30, 60, 68, 147; affective, 29, 46, 62, 95, 111, 118–120; autistic, 61; emotional, 61; immaterial, 31, 68, 74, 80, 83, 93; intimate, 128; and leisure, 93; market, 37; physical, 111, 120; political, 68; unpaid, 161
Lady/Lexy dyad, 132, 134

Lazzarato, Maurizio, 75
lesbian, 131–133; hey mama archetype, 132–133
LGBTQ, 128, 178n11; rights-based movement, 12; subjects, 13
Liddiard, Kirsty, 116
Life According to Sam, 38
liminality, 56–57, 77; queer/crip, 152
Linton, Simi, 7
Livingston, Julie, 20
Locke, John, 110–111
Lorde, Audre, 23
Los Angeles, California, 1
love, 4, 12, 23, 162; familial, 161; heteronormative, 100; machine, 32, 110, 118–120, 121, 123; non-innocent, 127; puppy, 105, 112, 121; toward animals, 110–111
"Love Has No Labels," 11, 13, 22, 35, 171
Lucas, Carrie Ann, 141
Lundblad, Michael, 106

Mairs, Nancy, 21
Marcellino, Rosa, 6, 10
Marwick, Alice, 177n7
McGlotten, Shaka, 80
McGuire, Anne, 55–56
McKinney, Texas, 164
McRobbie, Angela, 67
McRuer, Robert, 22, 28, 51
media culture: 5, 7, 10, 13, 14, 20, 31, 107, 111
medical professionals, 14, 155, 168
medical-industrial-complex, 147
Melamed, Jodi, 40
memorialization: virtual, 158
methods, 27
Michalko, Rod: and Smokie, 124
Milburn, Stacey, 15
Minich, Julie Avril, 175n5
misfitting, 84–85
Miss Iowa, 39, 41
Miss USA pageant, 39, 41
Miss You Can Do It, 25, 29–30, 35–37, 38

53–54, 58, 62, 91, 151, 170
Mitchell, David, 12, 24, 36, 42, 50
mobility, im-, 114; loss of, 152
models of disability, 15; medical, 14–15, 113, 150, 172; political/relational, 18; social, 15, 18, 21
Morquio syndrome, 112, 113, 179n6
mourning, 157–158; anticipatory, 154; and celebration, 162
multiculturalism, 40
Murphy, Shakara, 164–165
@muslimservicedogmom28, 106, 123, 129, 132; channel content, 132, 134–136
Mutua, Kagendo, 4, 57
myalgic encephalomyelitis (ME), 18

narrative prosthesis, 38
National Association of the Deaf (NAD), 96
Ndopu, Eddie, 64
neoliberalism, 8, 9, 13, 20, 29–30, 45, 62, 155; ideal subject of, 91
neomaterialism, 24
Netflix, 31, 73, 96, 103, 114
neuroscience, 56
neurotypicality: proper affectivity of, 54
Nevins, Sheila, 38
New York Times, The, 35
Ngai, Sianna, 87, 121
Nguyen, Xuan Thuy, 4
Nicole, Shelli, 132
"9 Months with Courteney Cox," 71, 98, 100, 101
#NoMoreCraptions, 67, 94–97
normalcy, 13, 43, 46, 55–57, 59, 122
normalization, 5, 15, 110
normate, 16
Not Dead Yet, 141, 154, 167–168, 180n3

Obama, Barak, 6
Oliver, Kelly, 106, 112
optimism, 24, 35, 37, 54, 82–83, 158–159; cruel, 101, 158; and Web 2.0, 74–75
Overboe, James, 175n7

overcoming: conceptualization of, 100; post–ADA narrative, 100; rhetoric of, 39–40, 42–44, 59, 68, 98

pain, 18, 32, 85, 143, 145–148, 180n8; anxiety about, 143–144; chronic, 139, 146, 149–154, 166; emotional, 146,147; exaggerated, 136; freedom from, 140; and gender, 154–155 management, 146, 150; medical paradigm of, 146, 150; psychic, 81, 146, 181n9; into pleasure, 87; representation of, 140, 146; and race, 154–55; sociality of, 157–158, 181n12; uneven distribution of, 147; and youngness, 155
participatory cultures, 74, 124
pathologization, 1, 13–14, 36, 42, 55–56, 88, 113, 115, 161; of Black women and girls, 142, 154, 164–165; rejection of, 77
pathology, 9, 55–56, 84, 115; speech, 90
patriotism, 11
Patsavas, Alyson, 146–147
Peabody Award, 34, 54, 176n1
pedagogy: in disability documentaries, 36–37; and pet dog keeping, 111; of proper affect, 111; respectability, 182n25
Peers, Danielle, 114
Perry, Samuel L., 171
Piepzna-Samarasinha, Leah Lakshmi, 180n6
pit bulls, 132–134
plasticity, 56
pleasure, 86–87
police, 90, 143; accountability, 163; dogs, 109, 111; -ing, 134; and Black girls, 163–167
politicization, 19, 83–84
Post-Crescent, 143, 146, 148, 150–154, 155, 157, 160
posthumanism, 24
Poynter, Rikki, 27, 30–31, 65–69, 73, 89, 176n3; channel content, 74, 76, 85–89; commodified, 75–76, 178n11; crafting intimacy, 80–81; deafness, 69, 76–77,

86; as educator, 89–90; influencer growth, 71–72; medium article, 96; as microcelebrity, 92
precarity, 2, 4, 93, 159, 161
Prendergast, Catherine, 23
Price, Margaret, 23, 112, 134, 148; and Ivy, 123
pride, 21
Prison Dogs, 107
productivity, 5, 9, 40, 46, 51, 61, 107, 114, 121, 172; loss of, 152
Puar, Jasbir, 8, 12, 20, 97
Pugh, Lisa, 141
Pybus, Jennifer, 75

queer, 21, 136; /crip, 21, 106, 120, 123–124, 129; -ness, 58, 134, 151, 177n9; phobia, 134; theory, 35

racial capitalism, 111, 154
racial justice, 163
Raffety, Erin, 49
RampYourVoice!, 5, 141
rationality, 13, 46
recognition, 84–85; institutional, 118; mis-, 83; mutual, 88; social, 166
recuperation, 4, 29, 40
Reddy, Chandan, 122
Reece's Rainbow, 49
rehabilitation, 5, 12, 14–15, 51, 60, 62, 151; able-bodied, 12, 31–32, 52, 68, 89–90, 143, 163; affective, 90; of autistic girls, 57–60; logics of, 8, 54–55, 105, 108–109, 111–113, 115, 172; refusal of, 168; spectacular tale, 100; tools of, 105, 109, 162–163, 172
representation, 2, 10, 12, 14, 20, 25–27, 44, 72–73, 97; affectivity of, 32, 105; cripping, 37, 171; politics, 29, 35; self, 2, 5, 19, 20, 25–27, 30, 105, 123; sentimental, 104–105, 108, 111, 113, 122, 123; symbol, 42
reproduction, 5
Respon.ability Social Therapy (RST), 29, 35, 37, 54–55, 57–60, 62

reworlding, 21–22
risk, 10; "at-risk," 9–10, 67; discourses of, 1, 3; of failure, 41, 114; genetic, 176n3; management 9; and youth, 114
Rory/Corrine dyad, 105, 111, 115, 116–118
Rosa's Law, 6
Rose, Adalia, 73
Rosie/Claire dyad, 127
@rosie.the.sd, 106, 123, 125, 136; channel content, 125–128

safety, 134
Sandahl, Carrie, 22
Scarry, Elaine, 145
Schalk, Sami, 16–17, 19
Schara, Grace, 33, 169–172
Schara, Scott, 169
Scott, Joan W., 28
Seeing Eye, The, 109
self-brand, 9, 22, 31, 67, 69, 97–98, 101; as disability activist and entrepreneur, 92, 94–97; -ing, 92, 93–94
self-disclosure, 78–80
sensory overstimulation, 59
service dog, 19, 23, 24, 27, 31, 32, 103, 121, 178n3n11; animacy of, 119; award, 118; companionship, 106, 111–112, 123; disabled girl handler dyad, 106–108, 112, 129, 136–138; and the "good dog" trope, 32, 105, 107, 112, 118, 123, 127, 136; history of, 108–111; and militarism, 108–110, 122; technology of rehabilitation, 103–106, 123, 128–129, 172; utility of, 108
Service Dog Project, the, 112
Sesame Street, 7
shame, 28, 68, 85, 87
Shang, Melissa, 2, 6, 10
Sharpe, Christina, 26, 145, 164
Shildrik, Margrit, 160
Shiva, Alexandra, 35, 36, 55
Sims, The, 144, 152
Singers, Peter, 106, 178n1
Sins Invalid, 15
Slater, Jenny, 114, 116

slow death, 33
small miracles trope, 113
Snyder, Sharon, 12, 24, 36, 42, 50
solidarity, 21, 87
"special needs," 176n2
Speciesism, 107, 178n1
Spinal Muscular Atrophy (SMA) Type II, 25, 62, 139, 146, 149–151, 153–154, 156, 180n2; fundraising, 181n11
sponsorship, 70–71, 73
Stampfli, Kari, 150, 153
Stare, 68, 78–79; able-bodied, 79
State-Journal Register, The, 49, 51
Stienstra, Deborah, 3, 4
Stockton, Kathryn Bond, 129
Strax/Meghan dyad, 105, 111, 115–117, 120, 122
Stroker, Ali, 7
Struthers Montford, Kelly, 106
Stuart, Melissa, 7
surveillance, 56; self-, 9

Taylor, Chloë, 106
Taylor, Sunaura, 106, 107, 128; and Bailey, 123
T-4 Euthanasia Program, 170
therapeutic culture, 76, 80
Thompson, Vilissa, 5; "Letters for Jerika" campaign, 141, 146, 154–155
TikTok, 2, 3, 25, 27, 30–31, 32, 179n10; pandemic growth, 124; service dog tok, 104–105, 123–124, 129
Titchkosky, Tanya, 20
Todd, Audrey, 60–61
tolerance, 4, 12–13, 68, 90–91
Tremain, Shelley, 17
Trump, Donald, 12, 175n2; era, 7
Twitter, 6, 30
Type 1 diabetes, 130, 136

Ukraine, 48, 50, 63
ungrievable subject, 144
United Kingdom, 7
United Nations, The, 6
uplift, 40

VACTERL, 115, 179n7
value, 75, 120, 150; to corporate brands, 93; surplus, 75; symbolic, 172; therapeutic, 162
Vänskä, Annamari, 110, 121
veterans: blind, 109; disabled, 109; paralyzed, 109
violence, 19, 106, 121, 141–142, 147; anti–Black, 144, 163–165; curative, 155; and domesticity, 23; extralegal, 154; and love, 127; physical, 116; sexual, 57; state, 19, 20, 144
virtual crypts, 158
vlogs, 30, 76–77, 89. *See also* disability: vlogging
vulnerability, 3, 83, 129, 134; affective, 161; radical, 80, 85

Weaver, Harlan, 104; and Haley, 133
Web 2.0, 30, 74, 177n7; post-, 26; revolution, 68, 74
Wendell, Susan, 18, 155
West Chester, Ohio, 103
wheelchair: negative association, 113, 120; self-propelled, 109

white supremacy, 4, 13, 19, 23, 97, 111, 166, 171
Whitehead, Andrew L., 171
whiteness, 91; and femininity, 165
will, 9, 43–45; free, 145, 154; to kill, 133, 149; mother's, 156, 162; societal, 107
Wisconsin Department of Children and Families, 141
womanhood, 9, 41, 57, 60; loss of, 152
Wong, Alice, 169, 173
World War I, 109; and disablement, 109–110
World War II, 109

Xenia, Ohio, 114

Yergeau, Remi, 58
youth, 114; border zone, 116; culture, 124
YouTube, 11, 25, 27, 30, 51, 65, 164; algorithm, 75; captions, 71; career, 98; channel membership, 71; early, 74; long form video, 124; partner program, 177n10